BROOKS LOCOMOTIVE
WORKS
DUNKIRK. N.Y.
U.S.A.

MADE IN THE COMPLETE ART-PRINTING WORKS OF
THE MATTHEWS-NORTHRUP CO.,
BUFFALO, N. Y.

BROOKS LOCOMOTIVE WORKS.

A CATALOGUE . . .

DESCRIPTIVE OF

SIMPLE AND COMPOUND

. . LOCOMOTIVES

BUILT BY

BROOKS LOCOMOTIVE WORKS,

DUNKIRK, N. Y.,

U. S. A.

ANNUAL CAPACITY, 400.

OFFICERS:

FREDERICK H. STEVENS, PRESIDENT.	ROBERT J. GROSS, VICE-PRESIDENT.
M. L. HINMAN, TREASURER.	T. M. HEQUEMBOURG, SECRETARY.
D. RUSSELL, GEN'L SUPERINTENDENT.	JAS. McNAUGHTON, SUPERINTENDENT.

1899.

CABLE ADDRESS, "BROOKS-DUNKIRK."

ISBN #978-1-935700-14-2
www.PeriscopeFilm.com

TO THE

RAILWAY OFFICIALS OF ALL COUNTRIES,

BY WHOSE COMMANDING GENIUS

THE DESERT HAS BEEN MADE TO BLOOM AND

WHOSE LABORS HAVE TRANSFORMED THE EARTH

INTO ONE BROAD HIGHWAY OF COMMERCE;

AND TO THE

MEN AT THE THROTTLE,

UPON WHOSE

COURAGE, FIDELITY AND INTELLIGENCE

DEPENDS THE SAFE AND SUCCESSFUL OPERATION

OF LOCOMOTIVES,

HOWEVER PERFECTLY CONSTRUCTED,

THIS BOOK

IS RESPECTFULLY DEDICATED.

INTRODUCTORY.

IN THE compilation of this new edition of our catalogue we have sought to bring together, in brief but comprehensive form, such illustrated and statistical information relating to the various types, construction and performance of "Brooks" locomotives as will render it deserving of the attention and consideration of all persons interested in the subject of motive power for railroads. It embodies much that is descriptive of the marked advance in locomotive construction and design which has obtained in the closing years of the century, and it aims to give such accurate data as will enable intending purchasers to arrive at an approximate understanding of their needs.

In the construction of our locomotives we employ only the highest grade of material and workmanship, and all the various details are accurately finished to standard gauges and templets, enabling us to guarantee their interchangeability on all locomotives of the same class.

We have special facilities for furnishing locomotive boilers, tanks and cylinders, and are prepared to furnish duplicate parts of any of our locomotives upon short notice.

Especial attention is invited to the "Brooks Improved Piston Valve," which is now in successful use on many of the engines of important trunk lines. The efficiency and economy which this form of valve has developed by reason of its simplicity and perfect balance bids fair to result in its superseding, to a great extent, the plain valve and the more complicated and expensive compound types. We submit it, with full confidence, to the thoughtful consideration of railway officials and engineers.

The increasing demand for heavier power has required the addition of adequate appliances and machinery for its construction. In this direction we have spared neither effort nor expense, and our shops are now equipped with the latest and most powerful machinery obtainable. Within the last two years there has been added to the plant a commodious erecting shop, and the boiler and hammer shops have been reconstructed and greatly enlarged. A large percentage of the machinery in the works is operated by electric power, and the shops are amply equipped with powerful electric cranes, pneumatic hoists and tools, hydraulic flanging press, etc.

In thus enlarging our capacity for the manufacture of locomotives we have not lost sight of the increasing service required of them. While pursuing a conservative policy we have designed our engines along bold lines and in keeping with modern ideas and practice, and are fully prepared to submit proposals for locomotives of the most recent and approved types, suitable for any required service, and constructed either from our own designs and specifications or in accordance with those of railway companies.

We have ample facilities for supplying locomotives based upon foreign specifications if within the limits of American practice. This applies to both single expansion and compound types, and contemplates the use of copper fireboxes, brass tubes, screw couplings, etc., as desired.

All material and workmanship entering into the construction of our locomotives is rigidly inspected by competent engineers. The engines are, in all cases, fully erected and tested in running order on our own tracks, and, if for transport to a foreign country, are taken apart and securely packed for sea shipment.

We invite the correspondence of railway officials and of others who may contemplate the purchase of locomotives, and request that, in writing for proposals, full particulars be furnished as to gauge of road, maximum curvature, grades, weight of rail, fuel to be used and the kind of service required.

A cipher code will be found on the last pages of the catalogue for convenience in telegraphing.

Other codes used by us include "Atlantic," "Western Union," "A. B. C., Fourth Edition," "Lieber's," and "Manufacturers' Export."

BROOKS LOCOMOTIVE WORKS.

DUNKIRK, N. Y., December 1, 1899.

A BRIEF HISTORY AND DESCRIPTION OF THE WORKS.

HORATIO G. BROOKS,

Founder of the Works.

A BRIEF HISTORY AND DESCRIPTION OF THE WORKS.

HORATIO G. BROOKS, founder of the BROOKS LOCOMOTIVE WORKS, was born on the 30th day of October, 1828, in the old historic city of Portsmouth, N. H. Sprung from that sturdy New England stock whose brain and brawn have left their deep impress upon the history of the century now closing, he, early in life, developed those marked traits which in later years made him a force in the affairs of his day and age. At 14 he passed his leisure hours on and about the engines of the Boston & Maine Railroad, and at 16, after much importunity, his parents yielded to his strong desire to learn the trade of a machinist, and placed him, as an apprentice, in the works of his cousins, Messrs. Isaac & Seth Adams, manufacturers of printing presses. Not finding this congenial, two years later he entered the shops of the Boston & Maine Railroad, at Andover, Mass. He became a close student of all that bore on the line of his work, and was tireless in acquiring all the knowledge then attainable concerning the construction and operation of locomotives. In order to extend his experience in this direction, he left the shops in 1848 and became a fireman on the Boston & Maine, and so valuable were the services he rendered in that capacity that a year later he was promoted to the position of engineer. Thus, at the early age of 21 he had made substantial progress along lines which later enabled him to put in successful play that organizing power which was the genius of his character. The course of railroading tended westward, and the young engineer, eager for pioneer work, enlisted his services with the New York & Erie Railroad, then extending its lines eastward from Dunkirk, its western terminus. The first duty assigned him was that of conveying from Boston, Mass., a locomotive for use on the new extreme western section of the road, and in November, 1850, by means of coaster, canal boats and other transports, he succeeded in discharging his ponderous freight upon the lines of the road for which it was intended, and to him belongs the honor of having blown the first locomotive whistle in the county of Chautauqua, among whose hills and valleys there now resounds and echoes the shrill screech of a thousand locomotives.

For six years Mr. Brooks continued at his post as engineer on the western section of the Erie Road, contributing largely, by an interested performance of his duty, to the road's rapid development. In 1856, he was tendered, and accepted, the position of Master Mechanic of the Ohio & Mississippi Railroad, where he remained four years, when he again returned to Dunkirk, and the Erie service, as Master Mechanic of the Dunkirk shops. Two years later, in recognition of the increasing value of his skill and judgment, he was made Superintendent of the western division of the road, and in 1865 was still further advanced, and became Superintendent of Motive Power and Machinery for the entire road extending from Dunkirk to New York. In 1869, under stress of financial difficulty and for purposes of retrenchment, the management of the Erie determined to close up the Dunkirk shops. Mr. Brooks, throughout his association with the road, held close his personal interest in the community in which his first Erie successes had been achieved, and which had grown, under his eye, to a large and busy town. In order to avert the calamity which now threatened it, he opened negotiations with the Erie Company, with a view of leasing the entire property and plant of the road in Dunkirk, for the purpose of manufacturing locomotives. His negotiations were successful, the lease was executed, and on the 13th of November the Brooks Locomotive Works was organized with a manufacturing capacity of one locomotive per month. Thus in the brief space of twenty years the progressive engineer of 1849 had become the proprietary head of a great manufacturing interest.

Among the most valuable of the assets of the new enterprise was the limitless faith and untiring energy which its founder brought into play in organizing and administering its affairs. So strong was his belief that the industrial growth of America was still in its infancy, and would advance rapidly and marvelously, that the new company at once adopted a policy of extension in line with that belief. As a result, the capacity of the works had increased to seventy-two engines per year in 1872, and to a manufacturing total of 100 engines per year in 1880. In two years more the output of the works doubled — 200 complete locomotives having been turned out in 1882. In July, 1883, the works purchased from the Erie Company the entire property which it had leased, and commenced at once the erection of extensive additions to the plant. Orders were placed for a large amount of new machinery of improved types, and so well was the work of extension carried on that, in 1885, the manufacturing capacity of the works had reached 250 per year. The success of the works had now become assured, the fine faith and foresight of its founder vindicated. Not only was the plant enlarged to meet the ever-increasing demand for locomotives, but the construction of the locomotives themselves was carried on with even greater attention to the needs and demands of the service required.

On the 20th of April, 1887, Mr. Brooks died. This was a severe blow to his associates, and his loss was felt throughout the entire railroad world. He had builded too well, however, to make himself necessary to the continued success of the works. The company, gathering force from his example, and pursuing his policy of extension, met with increasing prosperity.

Edward Nichols was elected to succeed him as President of the works in June, 1888. The death of Mr. Nichols occurred in January, 1892, and he was succeeded by M. L. Hinman as President, R. J. Gross being elected Vice-President.

At the Columbian Exposition, in 1893, the works exhibited nine locomotives of various types and designs, and were awarded a first medal for excellence of design and workmanship.

April 16, 1894, a Brooks 10-wheeled engine, coupled to a Lake Shore & Michigan Southern Railway train, known as the "Vanderbilt Special," made a speed record of 78 miles per hour. This was eclipsed, however, by the "Fastest of Fast Runs," which was made on the 24th of October, 1895, by a series of Brooks engines, in a run on the Lake Shore & Michigan Southern Railway, with a special train from Chicago to Buffalo, a distance of 540 miles. The average speed of this train, including all stops, was 63.6 miles. The maximum speed attained on the run was made on the Buffalo Division by a Brooks ten-wheeled engine with 17 x 24-inch simple cylinders, as follows:

1 mile at the rate of 92.3 miles per hour.
8 consecutive miles at the rate of 85.44 miles per hour.
21 consecutive miles at the rate of 82.44 miles per hour.
33 consecutive miles at the rate of 80 6 miles per hour.
86 consecutive miles at the rate of 72.92 miles per hour.

In 1896, Mr. Hinman's health became so seriously impaired, that he resigned his office, and Frederick H. Stevens was elected President of the works, and remains the active head of its management.

ERECTING SHOP.

From the foregoing it will be seen that the Brooks Locomotive Works, starting in 1869, with a capacity of one engine per month, and having a present capacity of 400 locomotives and upwards per annum, has kept pace with the remarkable industrial progress for which this century has become notable. The plant covers an area of about twenty (20) acres, and comprises some thirty-five buildings, equipped with all modern facilities for the rapid and perfect construction of locomotives. The machine shop proper is about 400 feet long by 100 feet wide, and contains a vast array of planers, lathes, milling machines, slotting machines, boring mills, many of which are electrically driven by motors placed on each machine. A number of the smaller tools, such as drills and hammers, are operated by pneumatic power. A separate machine shop is provided for taking care of the cylinders. This shop is over 200 feet long and about 58 feet wide, and is furnished with some of the largest and most powerful machinery made in this country.

The iron foundry is over 250 feet long by 100 feet wide, and has two thirty-ton cupolas, located near the center of the shop. This foundry is provided with two powerful electric overhead traveling cranes, which traverse the entire length of the building. In the south end are located three large core ovens. All the iron and coke for the cupolas are elevated to the charging floor by means of an electric elevator. Everything in this building is driven by electricity, no steam power being used.

Large and commodious boiler shops of steel construction have recently been constructed. One of these shops is about 450 feet long by 80 feet wide, and the other about 180 feet long by 90 feet wide, and have a total area of about 50,000 square feet. They are splendidly equipped with all the latest improved machinery including one of the most powerful hydraulic flanging presses in the world. This department is also provided with three powerful electric overhead traveling cranes, one of twenty-five tons lifting capacity, one of twenty tons and one of ten tons.

The carpenter shop is 269 feet long by 52 feet wide, and is a model of its kind.

The tank shop is a two-story building, 154 feet long by 65 feet wide.

In the steam-power house are located four batteries of the most modern type of water tube boilers, furnishing about 1,200 horse-power. Adjoining this building is the electric-power house, where all the electricity used in this extensive plant is generated by means of three large generators — one of 500 horse-power, another of 200 horse-power, and the third of 100 horse-power, all directly connected to automatic high-speed engines.

There has recently been added to the plant a new and commodious erecting shop. This new building is of approved and up-to-date design, and a description of its prominent features should prove of some interest to those who favor progressive and advanced methods of manufacture.

The building referred to covers an area of 17,595 square feet, is 255 feet long, 69 feet wide and 60 feet high to apex of roof. The frame of the building is composed wholly of structural steel. The walls above the upper crane runway are of brick, while below the runway the outside wall is wholly of glass, set in substantial frames, the lower tiers of which are arranged on balance weights, thus admitting of their being lifted for the convenient egress and admission of locomotives. The opposite side of the building opens directly into the old erecting shop, thereby more than doubling the floor space heretofore available for the erection of locomotives.

Within the floor space is included sixteen engine pits of brick masonry, four feet wide, and each extending forty feet in length between tracks.

IRON FOUNDRY.

The building is traversed its entire length by two Morgan Engineering Company's latest improved Electric Cranes. The larger of these cranes is of 120 tons capacity, and is equipped with two trolleys of sixty tons capacity each, one of the trolleys having in addition an auxiliary hoist of five tons capacity. This crane has a span of sixty-four feet, and runs upon a 100-lb. rail at a height of thirty-eight feet and one inch from floor, lifting and carrying with ease and rapidity the heaviest locomotives of modern construction. The smaller crane, equipped with two ten-ton trolleys, has a span of sixty-one feet, and runs upon a sixty-lb. rail twenty-seven feet three inches from floor. This crane is used in handling the lighter parts of engines during the process of their erection.

An indirect system of heating and ventilating has been installed, and may be described briefly as follows :

Exhaust steam is passed through a series of iron coils, thereby heating the air, which is passed over and among the coils by means of the suction produced by a large fan, which, in turn, distributes the heated air through two conduits running the full length of each side of the shop. These conduits admit the heated air into the building through openings at each one of the supporting columns of the building, by this means a continuous circulation of air is assured and the building amply heated and ventilated by an effective and economical process.

Not least among the improved processes in use in this new building is the means employed for disposing of the smoke and vapors formed in firing up and testing locomotives during their erection. For this purpose a smoke duct of brick, laid in cement, runs under the floor, and extends the entire length of the building close to and parallel with the end of the several engine pits. In firing, a workman connects the smoke stack of the locomotive with this smoke duct by means of a portable exhaust pipe and elbow, and the smoke and gases are drawn off through the duct and its outlet, by the suction of an exhaust fan operated by an electric motor.

The building is lighted with twenty-two arc lights of 2,000 candle-power, supplied by a Western Electric Generator.

In conclusion, the general extent and capacity of the works may be summed up approximately as follows :

Acreage comprised, ...	20
Number of buildings, ...	35
Number of employés, ...	2 000
Horse-power employed in operation of works, ...	2,500
Number of dynamos and motors employed in furnishing and transmitting power, ...	60
Number of electric traveling cranes, ...	10
Number of incandescent electric lamps in service, . . .	700
Number of arc electric lamps in service, ...	150
Consumption of coal per week, ...	400 tons.
Capacity of works per annum, ...	400 locomotives.

ELECTRICAL POWER HOUSE.

PISTON VALVES.

About two years ago, after proper experimenting, we concluded to introduce the use of valves of the piston type upon our heavier locomotives carrying high pressures, in place of slide valves, as we found with the latter, when made of sufficient size for the large cylinders and high pressures in use upon heavy power, that the wear not only of the valves and seats but also the entire link motion was excessive, and that such engines were hard to handle. We, therefore, adapted to our different types of locomotives our improved form of cylinders having the valve chests cast integral therewith and improved piston valves arranged with internal admission, enabling us to secure the shortest possible steam passage from the top of the cylinder saddle to the admission edges of the valve. This passage or chamber is of extremely large area with a very small surface exposed to external cooling influences, even this portion being jacketed over. The cylinder proper is practically free from the cooling influences which obtain in cylinders provided with slide valves and external steam chests. The steam ports from the valve chest to the cylinder are as short and direct as it is possible to make them, and, on account of this shortening in length, we are enabled to make them of much larger sectional area than is possible in a slide valve cylinder, thereby reducing the loss of pressure due to frictional resistance which is so noticeable in slide valve cylinder engines.

As the result of the foregoing improvements, indicator cards obtained from our locomotives equipped with improved piston valve cylinders show an admission line having a reduction in pressure not exceeding two per cent. of the boiler pressure itself.

Further, by the use of the improved piston valves, which are absolutely balanced under all conditions, we are enabled to use much larger steam ports than is possible or practicable with slide valves, at the same time putting no unnecessary strain and wear upon the link motion. This increase in the size of the ports permits the use of a longer lap on the valve than is possible with a slide valve, giving the same power at maximum cut-off as with the shorter lap on the slide valve. This combination gives a remarkably free opening on the exhaust side, consequently reducing the back pressure in the cylinder to as low a point as is desirable.

From the foregoing we obtain the following improvements and increase in efficiency :

First.—An increase of pressure on the admission line or positive side of the diagram.

Second.— A decrease of pressure on the exhaust line or negative side of the diagram.

Consequently, as the total efficiency of the engine is rated by the difference between the positive and negative side of the indicator card or diagram, it will readily be seen that the total efficiency or power developed by our piston valve cylinders is considerably higher than is obtainable from slide valve cylinders.

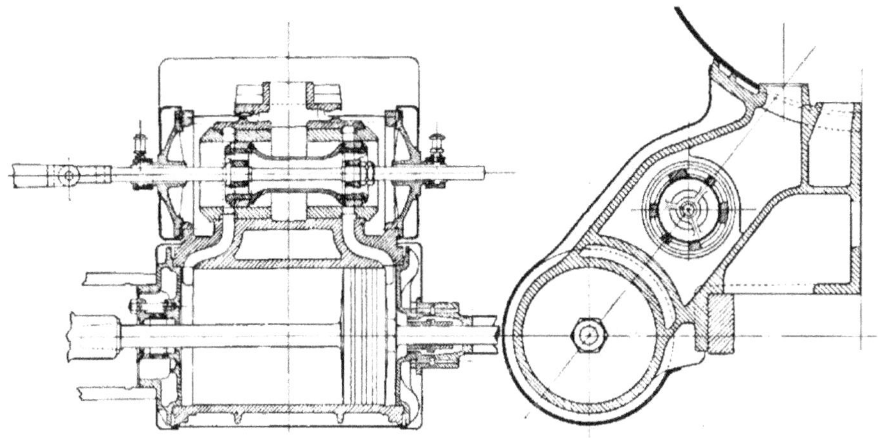

On account of the use of piston valve cylinders, the weights, not only of the cylinders themselves, but also their attachments and the forward end of the frames of locomotives so equipped, are materially reduced, the piston valve cylinders enabling us to secure a design throughout which is not only considerably lighter but also more efficient in every particular than on similar types of engines equipped with slide valve cylinders. This not only applies to the cylinders and allied parts themselves, but also to the frames and link motion. With piston valve cylinders we are enabled to use a very light and yet remarkably strong front end frame, in which the center line of strain, both from the cylinders and also from the draw bar or couplings, is centralized in the frame itself. The design of the piston valve cylinders themselves is such that a saving in weight of metal is effected and at the same time a considerable increase in the strength of the cylinder is obtained. There are also several other minor improvements in the construction of our locomotives equipped with piston valve cylinders which cannot be so readily applied to engines equipped with slide valve cylinders. We have a large number of engines equipped with piston valve cylinders in operation upon various large railroads in the United States and abroad, all of which are carrying from 180 to 210 pounds boiler pressure. The reports of the performance of these engines are most gratifying, both as regards power obtained, economy in fuel, speed, steady riding, easy handling, etc.

The general design of our cylinders, also the construction of the valve and packing, will be noted in the annexed cut.

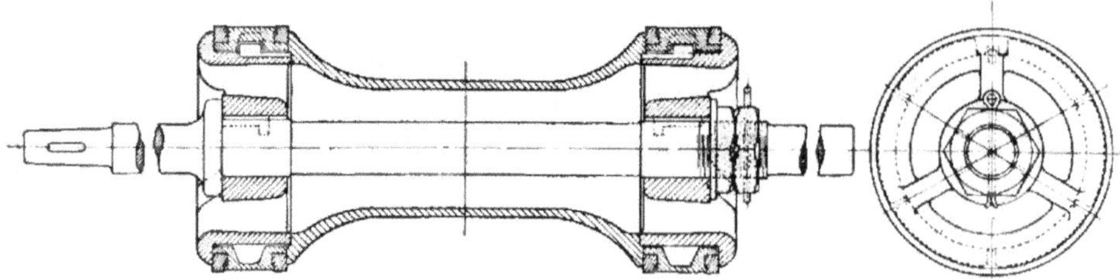

We have lately brought out an adaptation of the marine type of piston valve packing which so far has given us gratifying results. We are also engaged on other improvements in piston valves, which we expect to give even better results.

COMPOUND LOCOMOTIVES.

WE BUILD COMPOUND LOCOMOTIVES OF BOTH THE TWO AND FOUR CYLINDER TYPE.

TWO CYLINDER COMPOUNDS.

Our two cylinder engines are of the usual cross compound receiver type, fitted with a Player patent improved automatic com-

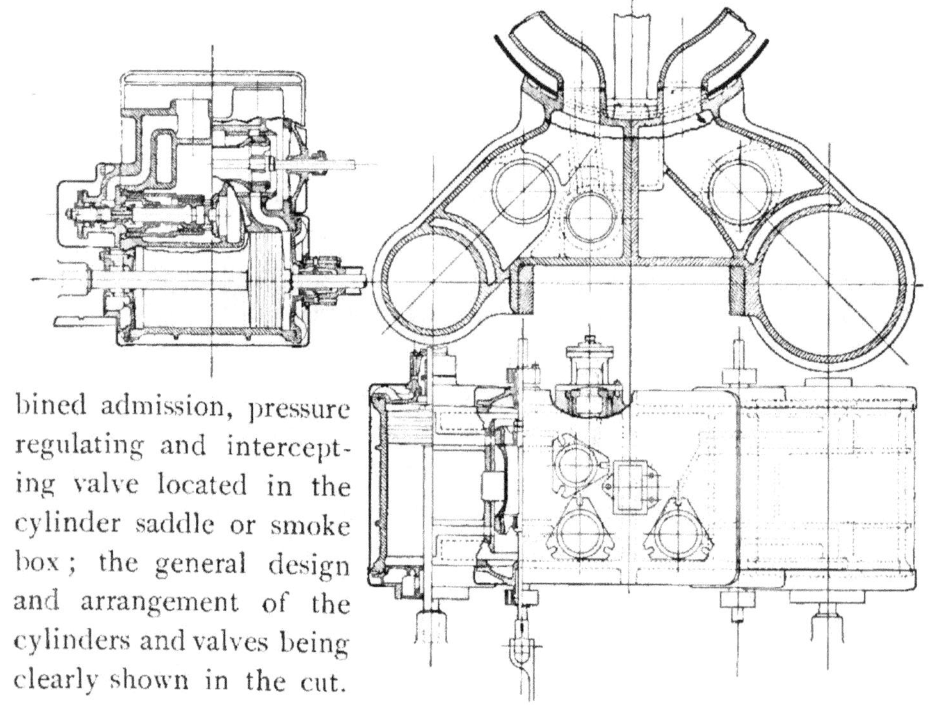

bined admission, pressure regulating and intercepting valve located in the cylinder saddle or smoke box; the general design and arrangement of the cylinders and valves being clearly shown in the cut.

The combined valve admits live steam at reduced pressure to the low pressure cylinder, this pressure being regulated in such ratio as desired, the intercepting valve at the same time automatically closing and preventing the live steam pressures from working against the high pressure piston, the reducing valve remaining open until such time as the pressure in the receiver pipe on the high pressure side of the intercepting valve becomes equal to or slightly in excess of that on the low pressure side, when the pressure regulating valve automatically closes and the intercepting valve opens simultaneously, the first cutting off the supply of live steam to the low pressure cylinder, the second opening connection between the two ends of the receiver and allowing the high pressure exhaust steam to act directly on the low pressure piston and at the same time locking the pressure regulating valve upon its seat and preventing the further admission of direct steam to the low pressure cylinder, these valves remaining in this position during the time the throttle valve is open. In order to give the engineman full command of the locomotive at all times, controlling valves are provided in the receiver, these are usually placed upon the bottom of the receiver, and are connected to the cab by suitable levers; they may, if desired, be of larger area and arranged in the upper portion of the receiver, connected with the exhaust pipe and arranged to work automatically in combination with the intercepting valve, so that the locomotive can be worked as a simple engine when required. However, on account of the arrangement of combined admission and pressure regulating valve, which at all times when necessary admits sufficient steam to the low pressure cylinder to give the locomotive its maximum power, the use of such a separate exhaust valve, whereby the engine can be worked simple for long periods, has been found in practice unnecessary, the arrangement of admission and pressure regulating valve previously referred to automatically performing all the requirements of a simple locomotive.

This valve operates as follows: Live steam operates upon the high pressure piston in the usual manner. At the same time steam is admitted to the high pressure end of the pressure regulating valve through the connecting pipe, causing the valve to open, passing thence through the hollow portion of the valve, causing the intercepting valve to automatically close against its seat. This steam flows through the passages of the intercepting valve into the low pressure end of the receiver and, acting upon the large end of the pressure regulating valve, causes it to partially close as soon as the requisite pressure is obtained, and thereafter regulates the amount of steam admitted by the pressure regulating valve, maintaining an even pressure in the receiver. The reduced pressure steam thus admitted to the receiver acts upon the low pressure piston in the usual manner. As soon, however, as the high pressure cylinder has exhausted sufficient steam into the high pressure end of the receiver to overbalance the intercepting valve, this valve opens automatically, at the same time locking the pressure regulating valve against its seat. The exhaust steam from the high pressure cylinder then flows through the receiver and acts directly upon the low pressure piston, the pressure of this exhaust steam, even when considerably reduced, being sufficient to keep the pressure regulating valve closed through the action of the combined valves at all times.

We build these engines, either with slide valves or improved piston valves as shown in cut, as desired.

This type of compound has been in successful operation for the past eight years.

FOUR CYLINDER COMPOUNDS.

Our four cylinder compounds are the Player patent tandem type, in which the low pressure cylinders and steam chests are attached to the smoke-box in the usual place and manner, and the high pressure cylinders and steam chests are attached preferably to the forward end of the low pressure cylinders, and having steam chests communicating with the steam chests of the low pressure cylinders. The steam is supplied to the high pressure valve chests through suitable connecting pipes, and the low pressure cylinder exhausts through the saddle in the usual way. The high pressure steam chests are fitted with hollow piston valves having internal admission, the low pressure

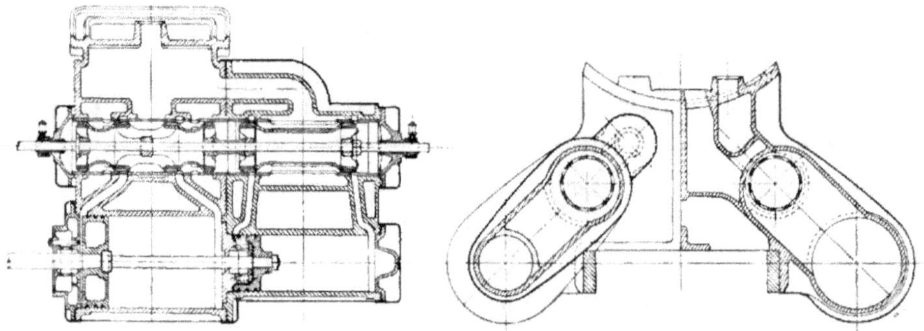

steam chests being also fitted with internal admission piston valves as shown in annexed cut.

One of the chief advantages of this type of compound is that the castings for the tandem compound cylinders are and can always be made absolutely interchangeable with those of a simple engine, this arrangement necessitating no change whatsoever back of the crosshead and valve rod keys or in the steam and exhaust pipes in the smoke-box, the compound cylinders thus giving no more cost for application than would be the case in applying a new pair of simple cylinders to an engine.

The high pressure cylinder is generally located ahead of the low pressure. This, however, is not necessary, and in some types of locomotives having four-wheel trucks it is preferable to place the high pressure cylinder back of the low pressure, thus materially reducing the weight and rendering the parts more accessible. The pistons of the high and low pressure cylinders are arranged upon the same rod, and the intermediate head between the high and low pressure cylinders is fitted with suitable metallic packing. The low pressure steam chest is provided with a reducing and starting valve connecting with the high pressure steam pipe. This valve is permitted to operate automatically when the reverse lever is in full forward or full back gear. In the intermediate positions of the lever, this reducing valve is locked to its seat so that it is rendered inoperative, and the engine must necessarily work compound at all times under all conditions of steam pressure when the reverse lever is in any other position except full gear. The use of this combined starting and reducing valve permits the introduction of steam into the low pressure cylinder at an equivalent to the maximum pressure obtained in this cylinder when the engine is working compound. Of course, as soon as the engine has made one revolution and the receiver is charged with exhaust steam from the high pressure cylinder, the starting valve becomes inoperative, thereby necessitating the engine to work compound.

The reducing and starting valve being automatic, responds absolutely to all variations of pressure and allows the engine to start without jerking or slipping, as is the case when high pressure steam is wire drawn into the low pressure cylinder.

We also have other types of valve gear for this engine, one with external admission valves, and another in which the high pressure valve has internal admission and the low pressure valve external.

This type of compound has been in successful operation for the past seven years.

TABLES.

We append three tables relating to compound locomotives.

Table A giving the relative diameters of cylinders for simple and compound locomotives, assuming the same boiler pressures. The ratio between high pressure and low pressure cylinder volumes for two cylinder compounds being 1—2.25, and for four cylinder compounds 1—3.5, these being the most desirable ratios at the prevailing pressures.

Table B gives the relative diameters of cylinders of simple engines and two cylinder compounds for various boiler pressures.

Table C gives the same information for four cylinder compounds.

TABLE A.

COMPOUND CYLINDERS.

Relative Diameters of Cylinders for Simple and Compound Locomotives.

SIMPLE ENGINES	TWO CYLINDER COMPOUNDS		FOUR CYLINDER COMPOUNDS	
DIAMETER OF CYLINDERS	DIAMETER OF HIGH PRESSURE CYLINDERS	DIAMETER OF LOW PRESSURE CYLINDERS	DIAMETER OF HIGH PRESSURE CYLINDERS	DIAMETER OF LOW PRESSURE CYLINDERS
10	11	16½	7	13
11	12	18	8	15
12	13	19½	9	17
13	14½	22	9½	18
14	15½	23½	10	18½
15	16½	25	11	20½
16	17½	26½	12	22½
17	19	28½	12½	23½
18	20	30	13	24½
19	21	31½	14	26
20	22	33	14½	27
21	23	34½	15½	29
22	24	36	16	30
23	25	37½	17	32
24	26	39	17½	33

Table B.

Relative Diameters of Cylinders.

For Two Cylinder Compound.

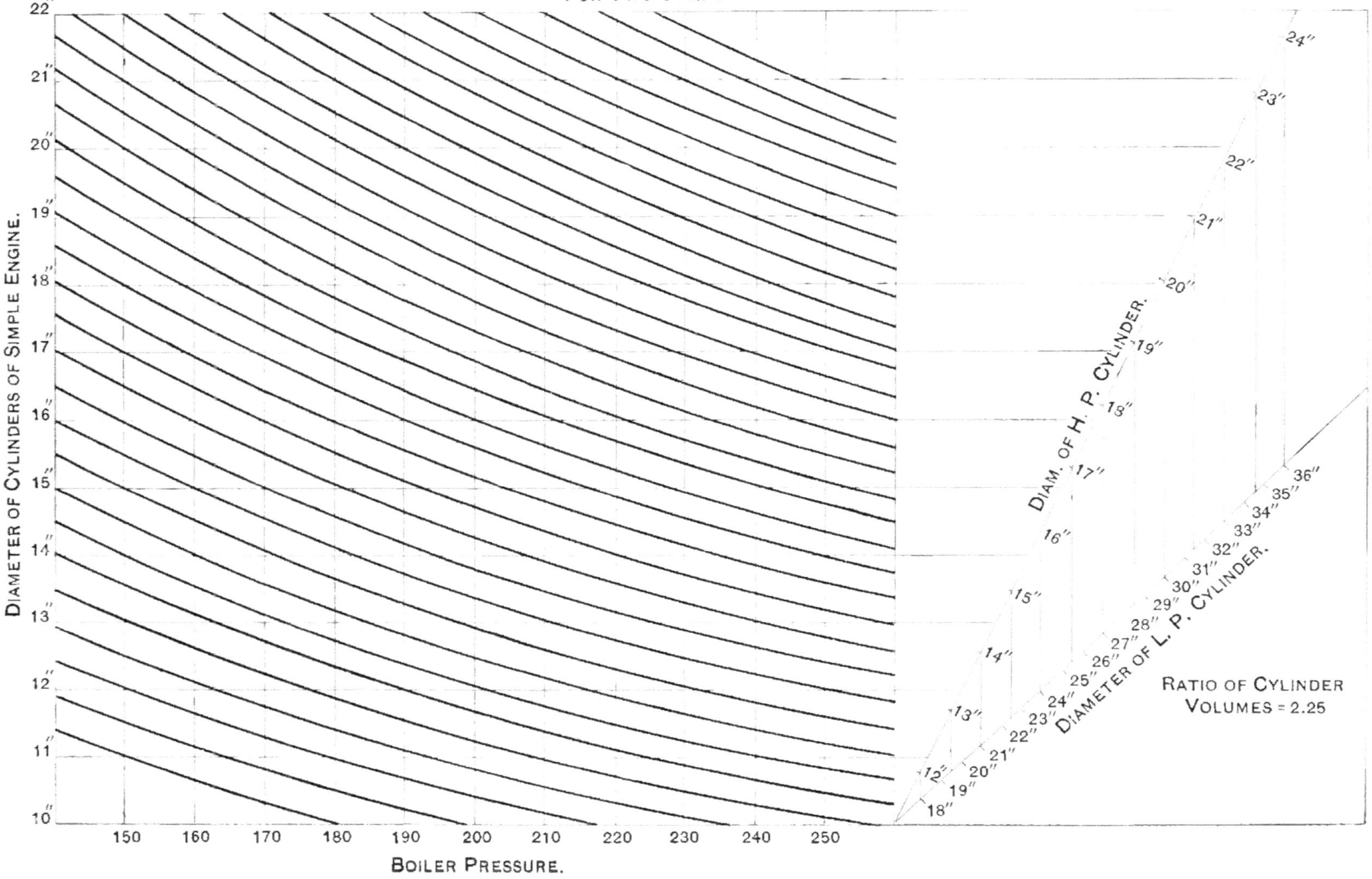

Diameter of Cylinders of Simple Engine.
22″ 21″ 20″ 19″ 18″ 17″ 16″ 15″ 14″ 13″ 12″ 11″ 10″

Boiler Pressure.
150 160 170 180 190 200 210 220 230 240 250

Diam. of H. P. Cylinder.
12″ 13″ 14″ 15″ 16″ 17″ 18″ 19″ 20″ 21″ 22″ 23″ 24″

Diameter of L. P. Cylinder.
18″ 19″ 20″ 21″ 22″ 23″ 24″ 25″ 26″ 27″ 28″ 29″ 30″ 31″ 32″ 33″ 34″ 35″ 36″

Ratio of Cylinder Volumes = 2.25

Table C.

Relative Diameters of Cylinders.

For Four Cylinder Compound.

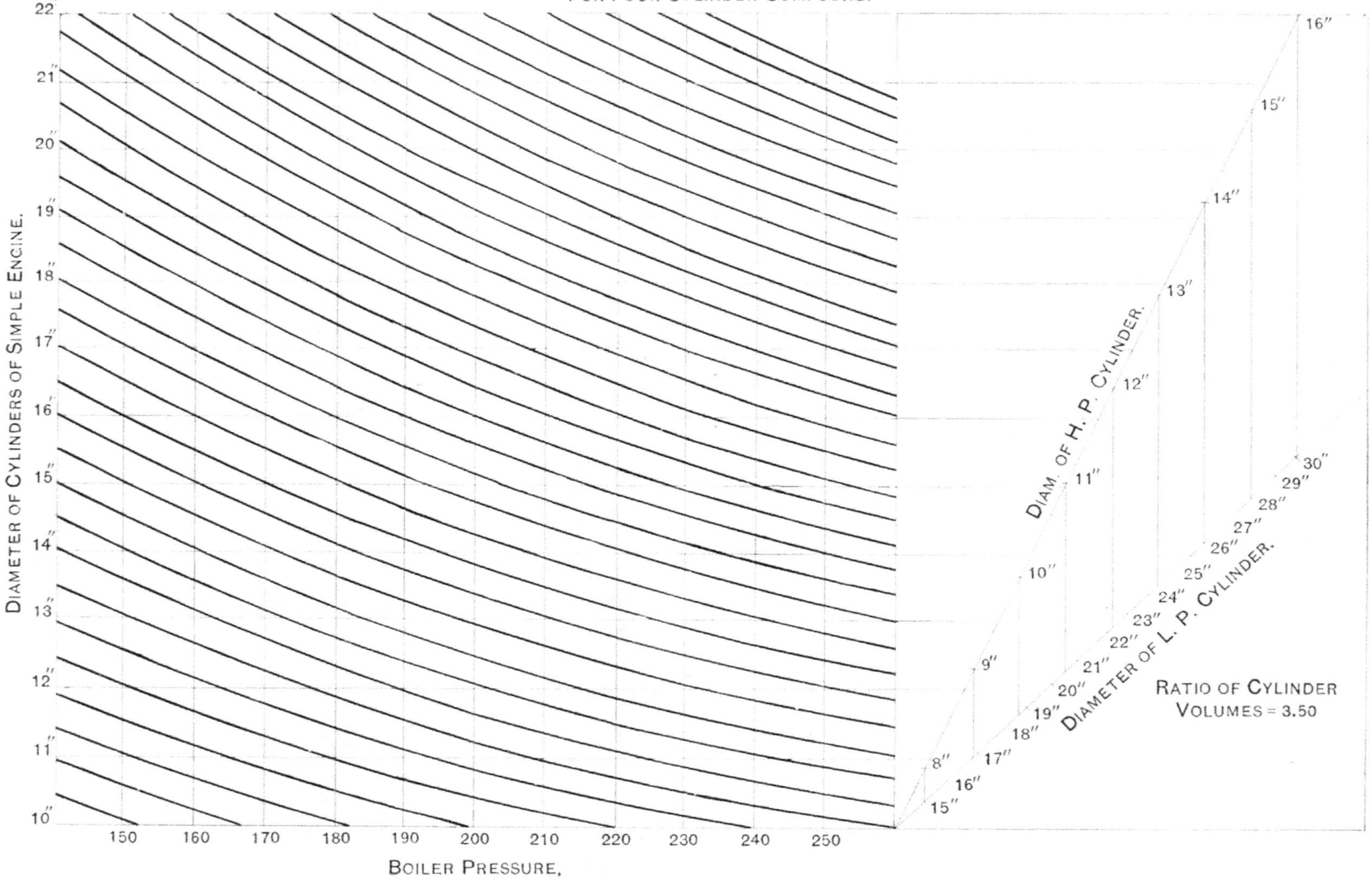

Diameter of Cylinders of Simple Engine.

Boiler Pressure.

Diam. of H. P. Cylinder.

Diameter of L. P. Cylinder.

Ratio of Cylinder Volumes = 3.50

SPECIFICATIONS.

We give below the form of specification used by the Brooks Locomotive Works. It will be noted that this does not elaborate on specific methods of construction, it being well known that these vary with different conditions and in the various localities for which our locomotives are constructed. It is our aim to meet the views of our patrons and to furnish locomotives well designed, properly proportioned and carefully constructed, in *all* their parts, of the best material and finish, in a workmanlike manner. We are constantly making improvements, and do not hesitate to immediately adopt the latest and best features. By so doing our locomotives are always up to date and as efficient as it is possible to make them.

BROOKS LOCOMOTIVE WORKS,

DUNKIRK, N. Y., U. S. A.,

DESIGNERS AND BUILDERS OF STRICTLY HIGH-GRADE LOCOMOTIVES.

SPECIFICATION

OF A

LOCOMOTIVE ENGINE.

NO. .... 189 .

FOR THE ....

TYPE .... CLASS ....

WITH ..... WHEELED TENDER .... TANK .... CAPACITY .... U. S. GALLONS AND ...... TONS FUEL.

CYLINDERS			WHEELS								BOILER		FIRE BOX		
			TENDER		TRAILING		COUPLED DRIVERS		LEADING						
TYPE	DIA.	STROKE	NO.	DIA	NO.	DIA	NO.	DIA	NO.	DIA	TYPE	DIA	TYPE	LENGTH	WIDTH

FLUES			WHEEL BASE				AVERAGE WEIGHT IN WORKING ORDER, POUNDS				
NO.	DIA	LENGTH	DRIVING	RIGID	ENGINE	ENGINE AND TENDER	TENDER	TRAILING WHEELS	DRIVERS	LEADING WHEELS	TOTAL ENGINE

BOILER PRESSURE	FUEL	LIMITATIONS							GAUGE OF TRACK	
POUNDS	KIND	WEIGHT PER AXLE	WEIGHT ON DRIVERS	TOTAL WEIGHT	HEIGHT	WIDTH	LENGTH	TOTAL WHEEL BASE	FEET	INCHES

GENERAL DESIGN SHOWN BELOW.

PHOTO. OF ENGINE NO. ....

CATALOGUE PAGE NO. ....

DIAGRAM SHEET NO. ....

CARD OR SKETCH NO. ....

....

....

....

DETAILED SPECIFICATION.

BOILER.	Of the "Crown Bar," "Radial Stayed," or Improved "Belpaire" type, built straight or wagon top with conical connection. Dome of suitable size, located to suit construction........................Waist..................inches diameter.
MATERIAL.	Material of shell, best homogeneous boiler steel...........................Thickness of plates..
CONSTRUCTION.	Boiler well designed, carefully constructed, substantially riveted and thoroughly braced in all its parts, having an ample factor of safety to carry the working pressure, plates planed at edge and caulked with round nosed pneumatic tool,
TEST.	tested by water to 40 per cent. and by steam to 25 per cent. above the working pressure.
RIVETING.	Longitudinal seams quadruple, quintuple or sextuple riveted, according to location, size and pressure; rivets of suitable sizes for the thickness of plates.
FIRE-BOX.	Of the deep, sloping or long type, between or over frames................................ ....long and ....wide inside sheets.
MATERIAL.	Plates of best homogeneous fire box steel, thoroughly annealed after flanging... Flue sheet..................½, crown sheet..................⅜, side sheets................. $\frac{5}{16}$ or ⅜, back sheet..................$\frac{5}{16}$ or ⅜ inches thick.
MUD RING.	Accurately fitted and substantially..................riveted, water space................. inches front, ...inches sides and..................inches back at bottom, increasing gradually towards crown...
STAY-BOLTS.	Of best double refined iron..................1-inch diameter, ...spaced not over.........4.........inches from center to center, screwed in and riveted over sheets at both ends, ends drilled with test holes.
....	....
CROWN STAYS.	Crown sheet securely supported by crown bolts with conical neck and head under sheet, radial or direct stays with heads under sheet screwed into sheets from inside and riveted over on outside, and spaced not over ....4¼.......... inches from centre to centre.
	Crown bars of suitable size, each formed from two bars of iron welded together at ends and spaced not over.........5¼.........inches from centre to centre, raised a suitable distance above crown sheet and separated therefrom by conical thimbles or ferrules, ends of bars having solid bearing on side sheets, bars secured to roof sheet by slings..
FLUES.	Of best lap welded charcoal iron or steel...............in number, ...inches external diameter, thickness No.................B. W. G., length over sheets ....feet..................inches. Spaced in vertical rows and set with copper ferrules on fire box end, both ends carefully beaded with pneumatic tool..
BRICK ARCH.	Fire brick arch supported on studs..
WASHOUT PLUGS, ETC.	Blow off cock in bottom of fire box leg, suitable washout plugs in corners and sides of fire box, in front end and above crown sheet.
....	....
....	....
....	....
THROTTLE VALVE AND STEAM PIPES.	Cast iron balanced throttle valve in dome, ...large wrought iron dry pipe attached to suitable tee head and cast iron steam pipes in smoke box..
EXHAUST PIPE.	Exhaust pipe in smoke box of cast iron, with suitable nozzles..........................
SMOKE BOX.	Short extension smoke box, with suitable netting, deflector and cinder valve, front and door flanged steel..
STACK.	Straight or taper pattern of cast iron or sheet steel with flanged base..................
GRATES.	Suitable for the fuel. Cast iron, rocking pattern; operated from cab.................
ASH PAN.	Suitable for the fuel. Arranged with suitable cleaning holes; dampers front and rear operated from cab.
....	....
....	....
....	....
....	....

FRAMES.	Of best hammered iron. Main frames and pedestals forged solid, accurately planed and slotted. Front frames securely spliced to main frames. Pedestal tie bars well secured to frames......
BRACES.	Frames thoroughly braced together and to boiler by suitable castings, braces, expansion plates and pads......
......	......
TRUCKS.	Leading truck of the......wheel type, with swiveling and swing centre or swing centre and radial bar.
LEADING WHEELS.	Leading truck wheels......inches nominal diameter......
	Axles of hammered iron or steel, journals......inches diameter, inches long......
	Trailing truck of the......wheel type, with swiveling and swing centre and radial bar.
TRAILING WHEELS.	Trailing truck wheels......inches nominal diameter......
	Axles of hammered iron or steel, journals......inches diameter......inches long.
TRUCK FRAMES.	Of wrought iron, pedestals of wrought or cast iron. Boxes of cast iron with heavy brass or bronze bearings......
DRIVERS.	Driving wheels......in number, ...inches diameter outside of tires.
WHEEL CENTRES.	Of cast iron or steel......inches diameter, well designed, properly proportioned and carefully counterbalanced......
TIRES.	Driving tires of best open hearth steel......3......inches thick when finished.
	1st, 2d, 3d, 4th pairs flanged 5½......inches wide......
	1st 2d, 3d, 4th pairs plain 6......inches wide......
AXLES.	Driving axles of hammered iron or steel, ...journals......inches diameter, ...inches long......
BOXES.	Driving boxes of cast iron or steel......with heavy brass or bronze bearings carefully fitted, provided with shoes and adjustable wedges.
SPRINGS.	All springs under engine of the best crucible cast steel properly proportioned for their loads......
EQUALIZATION.	Spring rigging and equalization of the best design to secure easy riding. All bearings thoroughly hardened.
CYLINDERS.	Slide valve pattern or improved piston valve type. Horizontal, outside connected ......high pressure......inches diameter, ...low pressure......inches diameter, ...inches stroke, of close grained hard cast iron, each with half saddle, carefully fitted together and perfectly interchangeable......
HEADS AND CHESTS.	Cylinder heads of cast iron......, steam chests of cast iron......, covers of cast iron......
PISTONS.	Of cast iron or steel......fitted with approved form of cast iron packing rings.
PISTON RODS.	Of hammered steel......carefully ground and securely fastened to pistons and crossheads......
PACKING.	Metallic packing on piston rods and valve stems......
VALVE MOTION.	Approved shifting link type, graduated to cut off equally at all points.
	Valves......balanced slide valve or improved piston type......
	Links, blocks, lifters, jaws and pins of hammered iron......thoroughly case hardened.
	Rockers hammered iron or cast steel, reverse shaft wrought iron or cast steel, reverse lever with finely graduated quadrant......
ECCENTRICS.	Of cast iron keyed to axles, straps of cast iron...... ......carefully fitted......
GUIDES.	Of hammered iron or steel case hardened, securely bolted to cylinder heads and to heavy hammered iron guide yoke extending across frames. Guides and cross-heads......type.
CROSS-HEADS.	Of cast steel with heavy brass or bronze bearings......
RODS.	Connecting rods of hammered iron or steel, with straps, wedges or keys and brasses.
	Coupling rods of hammered iron or steel, with straps, wedges or keys and brasses ......or solid ends with heavy bushings properly secured.
CRANK PINS.	Of hammered steel of ample proportions......
......	......

CAB.	Engine cab well designed and substantially built of seasoned hard wood........... roof of pine covered with tin plate, or constructed of steel with double roof, ...well arranged sash and doors of cherry, glazed with double thick American crystal glass; well braced and securely fastened to engine.
	Cab conveniently arranged for engineman and fireman, with roomy deck.......... ....and provided with comfortable seats, seat cushions and arm rests, clothes and tool boxes and signal gong.
Run-Boards.	Suitable run-boards of hard wood, or run-plates of steel with steel nosings, extending from cab to front end.
Steps.	Engine provided with convenient and safe steps and grab handles wherever required.
Handrails.	Neat, well arranged and safe handrails of suitable size.
BUMPERS.	Substantial bumper beams, securely attached to frames, of oak, iron or steel, neatly finished, on front and rear ends..
Pilot.	Made of well seasoned hard wood.........................well bolted to bumper and thoroughly braced...
COUPLERS.	Suitable drawheads or couplers, securely attached to bumpers front................. and rear..
....	....
MOUNTINGS.	Engine provided with.........sand box.........with suitable pipes......................... ....operated from cab.
	Bell..., whistle, and necessary attachments for headlights, signal lamps and flag holders...
FITTINGS.	Steam gauge, ...water gauge, gauge cocks, steam and water gauge lamps, blower valve...................., cylinder cocks, port cocks and drain cocks in all exposed pipes. All cocks and valves in cab attached to separate turret connected to dome. All fittings, handles and levers in cab arranged in the most convenient manner.
Lubrication.	All bearings on engine provided with suitable means for their proper lubrication, adjustable oil cups of ample capacity provided where required.
	Cylinders and valves oiled from cab through copper pipes under jacket by improved..................sight feed lubricator..
Feed Water.	Supplied by two improved injectors of proper capacity, with suitable steam, feed and check valves and well arranged piping...
Safety Valves.	Two...............improved locomotive pop valves of suitable size, located in dome cover or auxiliary turret, ...carefully tested and set to blow at two and three pounds above working pressure.
....	....
....	....
TOOLS.	A complete set of engine tools provided. Two screw jacks with levers, ... heavy steel pinch bar, small bar, machinists' hammer, soft hammers, two monkey wrenches, complete set of spanner wrenches to fit all nuts on engine, plug and flat wrenches, injector and packing wrenches, packing tools, chisels, pin punches.
	One set of engine oilers and oil cans, torch, torch holder, etc. One set firing tools, scoop shovel, coal pick, slice bar, clinker hook, ash hoe, pail and broom.
....	....
Lagging.	Boiler and dome lagged with.., cylinders and chests lagged with.......................................
FINISH.	Boiler jacket and bands.............planished iron. Neat dome casing with painted iron body with cast iron top and bottom rings, or flanged steel casing, sand box casings to match dome..
	Cylinder head casings, pressed steel painted...
	Steam chest, cover casings cast iron or pressed steel painted. Cylinder and steam chest side casings of sheet iron or steel painted..
Painting.	Engine to be well painted and varnished, and lettered and numbered, as required.
....	....
....	....
....	....

DETAILED SPECIFICATION.—(Continued.)

TENDER. TRUCKS.	Tender of the eight............wheeled type............having two four-wheeled centre bearing trucks of improved construction, ...side bearings on rear truck.
WHEELS.	Wheels..................inches nominal diameter..
AXLES	Of hammered iron or steel... journals.................. inches diameter, ...inches long..
BOXES.	Of.................cast iron, with heavy brass bearings...
SPRINGS.	Of best crucible cast steel, ...equalized brakes with metal beams, and M. C. B. shoes on all wheels............ ....
TENDER FRAME.	Of.....................well designed, carefully constructed, and thoroughly braced, and provided with heavy draw-bar, chafing blocks and safety chains between engine and tender, and suitable draw-gear on rear end.
TOOL BOXES.	Set of 3.................boxes, strongly made and provided with good locks.
....	....
TANK.	Water carried in.........................tank..constructed of tank steel plates...................inch thick, strongly built, well riveted and thoroughly stayed and braced.
WATER.	Capacity........................U. S. gallons..
FUEL.	Capacity of fuel space about.................U. S. tons...
....	....
CONSTRUCTION.	Engine well designed, properly proportioned and carefully constructed in all its parts, and finished in a workmanlike manner. All material entering into construction of the best quality. All work and material thoroughly inspected and tested before and after working. Engine after completion fired up and tested under steam on our own tracks.
GAUGES.	All principal parts liable to depreciation in service accurately made to standard gauges and templets, interchangeable with similar parts on our engines of same types and dimensions.
THREADS.	All threads U. S. standard unless otherwise specified......................................
....	....
PATENTS.	All patented devices, which we do not control, not provided for in this specification are excepted.
....	....
EXTRAS.	....
BRAKES.	....
....	....
TRAIN SIGNAL.	....
HEADLIGHT.	....
....	....
....	....
....	....
....	....
....	....
....	....
....	....
....	....
....	....
....	....
....	....
....	....

BROOKS LOCOMOTIVE WORKS,

DUNKIRK, N. Y., U. S. A.

PHYSICAL AND CHEMICAL TESTS OF MATERIAL.

GENERAL. All material used in constructing locomotives which does not fill the following requirements will be rejected. Notwithstanding these tests, should any defects develop in process of working the material will be rejected.

NOTE. Tensile strength is in pounds per square inch. Elongation is percentage in a test strip 8 inches long.

BOILER SHELL STEEL. All plates must be made of open hearth process steel: Tensile strength desired 56,000 pounds, minimum 52,000 pounds, maximum 60,000; elongation desired 27 per cent., minimum 25 per cent.; reduction of area 50 per cent.

FIRE BOX STEEL. All plates must be made of open hearth process steel: Tensile strength desired 55,000 pounds, minimum 52,000 pounds, maximum 58,000 pounds; elongation desired 28 per cent., minimum 26 per cent.; reduction of area 56 per cent.

ANALYSIS. Chemical analysis for fire box steel:

	Carbon.	Phosphorous.	Manganese.	Sulphur.	Silicon.
Desired,	.18	.03	.40	.02	.02
Maximum,	.25	.03	.45	.03	.035
Minimum,	.15				

TESTS. Shell and fire box plates must be free from all mechanical defects, and a test piece must, without annealing, bend over on itself, cold, and after being heated to a cherry red and quenched in water, at 80 degrees, show no signs of cracks or flaws on outside edge.

BOILER FLUES. All iron or steel flues must conform to specification, must be free from all imperfections, and must be rolled accurately to size. A test piece, 1¼ inches long, cut from any flue, set on end and hammered down to ⅞-inch, must show no longitudinal cracks and must show no transverse cracks when solid. Each and every flue must be tested by the makers to an internal hydraulic pressure of at least 500 pounds per square inch.

STAY BOLT IRON. All iron for stay-bolts must be double refined, rolled perfectly round, and true to standard gauges and permit cutting a clean sharp thread. Minimum tensile strength 48,000 pounds; minimum elongation 25 per cent. A test piece, 24 inches long, must stand bending double, both ways, without showing fracture or flaw.

BAR IRON. All bar iron not exceeding 1⅝ inches diameter and rectangular sections not exceeding 2 square inches area; tensile strength desired 49,000 pounds, minimum 48,000 pounds; elongation desired 22 per cent., minimum 20 per cent. and must not show granular fracture.

Bar iron of larger size; tensile strength, minimum 46,000 pounds; elongation, minimum 20 per cent.

STEEL FORGINGS. All steel forgings must be made from blooms of open hearth process steel, containing not over 5 per cent. phosphorous; test strips to be cut from forgings 2 inches square, hammered from blooms.

AXLES AND PINS. Steel for axles, crank pins, etc.: Tensile strength desired 80,000 pounds, minimum 75,000 pounds, maximum 85,000 pounds; elongation desired 18 per cent., minimum 14 per cent.

RODS. Steel for rods: Tensile strength, minimum 70,000 pounds, maximum, 80,000 pounds; elongation, minimum 16 per cent.

STEEL CASTINGS. All steel castings must be made by the open hearth process, must have smooth, uniform surface, must be entirely free from blow holes, sand, shrinkage and cracks; tensile strength desired 70,000 pounds, minimum 60,000 pounds; elongation desired 18 per cent, minimum 13 per cent.

CHILLED WHEELS. All chilled wheels must conform to specifications of the M. C. B. and A. R. M. M. Associations, and be guaranteed 40,000 miles for 28-inch wheels, 45,000 miles for 30-inch wheels, 50,000 miles for 33-inch wheels.

CLASSIFICATION OF LOCOMOTIVES.

We give below classification of locomotives adopted by the Brooks Locomotive Works. Whilst the classification symbols are not arranged consecutively on account of their being an outgrowth of an earlier designation, yet it will be found by reference to the key that all engines having a similar arrangement of machinery are designated by the same fundamental symbol, the suffixes as noted below being explanatory of additional rear truck or trailers and the type of water tank employed when a separate tender is not used.

CLASSIFICATION.

The first capital letter designates the class of locomotive and indicates the general construction of the engine.

The second capital letter indicates that the engine is arranged with trailing wheels or truck.

The letter "P" represents one pair trailers or two-wheel truck, "Q" four-wheel trailing truck, and "R" a six-wheel trailing truck.

When only capital letters are used to designate the class, this indicates that the engine is provided with a separate tender.

The small letters represent that the engine has no tender, but that the water and fuel is carried in tank and coal bunk attached to engine.

The letter "T" represents a saddle tank, "X" a rear tank, "Y" side tanks.

When any two of these letters are used in combination they represent that the engine is provided with tanks of both kinds which these letters designate.

There are twelve primary classes represented by the letters A to L inclusive, as under noted.

A.	8-Wheel	Engine	with	4 Coupled	Wheels	and	4-Wheel	Leading	Truck.
D.	10-Wheel	"	"	6 Coupled	"	"	4-Wheel	"	"
F.	12-Wheel	"	"	8 Coupled	"	"	4-Wheel	"	"
G.	14-Wheel	"	"	10 Coupled	"	"	4-Wheel	"	"
J.	6-Wheel	Engine	with	4 Coupled	Wheels	and	2-Wheel	Leading	Truck.
B.	8-Wheel	"	"	6 Coupled	"	"	2-Wheel	"	"
C.	10-Wheel	"	"	8 Coupled	"	"	2-Wheel	"	"
K.	12-Wheel	"	"	10 Coupled	"	"	2-Wheel	"	"
E.	4-Wheel	Engine	with	4 Coupled	Wheels	and	No	Leading	Truck.
H.	6-Wheel	"	"	6 Coupled	"	"	"	"	"
I.	8-Wheel	"	"	8 Coupled	"	"	"	"	"
L.	10-Wheel	"	"	10 Coupled	"	"	"	"	"

MONON ROUTE

BUILT BY

BROOKS LOCOMOTIVE WORKS

DUNKIRK, N. Y., U.S.A.

1897

FOR THE CHICAGO, INDIANAPOLIS & LOUISVILLE RAILWAY.

CODE WORD, QUAGGA. SERIES, 604.

TYPE, 8-WHEELED PASSENGER. CLASS, $18\frac{1}{2}$ A.

WITH 8-WHEELED TENDER

TANK CAPACITY 4000 U. S. GALLONS AND $8\frac{1}{2}$ TONS FUEL.

CYLINDERS			WHEELS								BOILER		FIRE BOX		
TYPE	DIA.	STROKE	TENDER		TRAILING		COUPLED DRIVERS		LEADING		TYPE	DIA.	TYPE	LENGTH	WIDTH
			NO.	DIA.	NO.	DIA.	NO.	DIA.	NO.	DIA.					
Simple	$18\frac{1}{2}''$	24″	8	33″	—	—	4	72″	4	$33\frac{1}{4}''$	Rad. Stay, Wagon Top	62″	Long, Wide Sloping	97″	41″

FLUES			WHEEL BASE				AVERAGE WEIGHT IN WORKING ORDER, POUNDS				
NO.	DIA.	LENGTH	DRIVING	RIGID	ENGINE	ENGINE AND TENDER	TENDER	TRAILING WHEELS	DRIVERS	LEADING WHEELS	TOTAL ENGINE
300	2″	$11'$-$6\frac{1}{4}''$	8′-6″	8′-6″	23′-5″	48′-4″	89000	—	79000	42800	121800

BOILER PRESSURE	FUEL	HEATING SURFACE, SQ. FT.				GRATE AREA	GAUGE OF TRACK	
POUNDS PER SQ. INCH ABOVE ATMOSPHERE	KIND	FLUES	FIRE BOX	ARCH PIPES	TOTAL	SQUARE FEET	METRES	FEET INCHES
190	Bituminous Coal	1804.4	145.6	—	1950	26.8	1.435	$4'$-$8\frac{1}{2}''$

FOR HAULING CAPACITY SEE PAGE 290.

ADIRONDACK
5
5

BUILT BY

BROOKS LOCOMOTIVE WORKS

DUNKIRK, N. Y., U.S.A.

1897

FOR THE ST. LAWRENCE & ADIRONDACK RAILWAY.

CODE WORD, QUAHOG. SERIES, 606.

TYPE, 8-WHEELED PASSENGER. CLASS, 18 A.

WITH 8-WHEELED TENDER TANK CAPACITY 4200 U. S. GALLONS AND 8½ TONS FUEL.

CYLINDERS			WHEELS								BOILER		FIRE BOX		
TYPE	DIA.	STROKE	TENDER		TRAILING		COUPLED DRIVERS		LEADING		TYPE	DIA.	TYPE	LENGTH	WIDTH
			NO.	DIA.	NO.	DIA.	NO.	DIA.	NO.	DIA.					
Simple	18″	26″	8	33″	—	—	4	64″	4	28″	Improved Belpaire	60″	Long, Wide Sloping	107⅝″	40⅞″

FLUES			WHEEL BASE				AVERAGE WEIGHT IN WORKING ORDER, POUNDS				
NO.	DIA.	LENGTH	DRIVING	RIGID	ENGINE	ENGINE AND TENDER	TENDER	TRAILING WHEELS	DRIVERS	LEADING WHEELS	TOTAL ENGINE
274	2″	11′-7⅛″	8′-6″	8′-6″	23′-7″	49′-4″	89000	—	80000	42300	122300

BOILER PRESSURE	FUEL	HEATING SURFACE, SQ. FT.				GRATE AREA	GAUGE OF TRACK	
POUNDS PER SQ. INCH ABOVE ATMOSPHERE	KIND	FLUES	FIRE BOX	ARCH PIPES	TOTAL	SQUARE FEET	METRES	FEET INCHES
200	Bituminous Coal	1646.7	154.2	13.26	1814.16	30.4	1.435	4′-8½″

FOR HAULING CAPACITY SEE PAGE 290.

961
I. C. R. R.
961

BUILT BY

BROOKS LOCOMOTIVE WORKS

DUNKIRK, N. Y., U.S.A.

1896

FOR THE ILLINOIS CENTRAL RAILROAD.

CODE WORD, QUAIL.

TYPE, 8-WHEELED PASSENGER.

WITH 8-WHEELED TENDER

SERIES, 590.

CLASS, 18 A.

TANK CAPACITY 4200 U. S. GALLONS AND $8\frac{1}{2}$ TONS FUEL.

CYLINDERS			WHEELS								BOILER		FIRE BOX		
			TENDER		TRAILING		COUPLED DRIVERS		LEADING						
TYPE	DIA.	STROKE	NO.	DIA.	NO.	DIA.	NO.	DIA.	NO.	DIA.	TYPE	DIA.	TYPE	LENGTH	WIDTH
Simple	18″	26″	8	38″	—	—	4	75″	4	36″	Improved Belpaire	62″	Long, Sloping	$107\frac{5}{8}$″	$36\frac{3}{8}$″

FLUES			WHEEL BASE				AVERAGE WEIGHT IN WORKING ORDER, POUNDS				
NO.	DIA.	LENGTH	DRIVING	RIGID	ENGINE	ENGINE AND TENDER	TENDER	TRAILING WHEELS	DRIVERS	LEADING WHEELS	TOTAL ENGINE
274	2″	11′-$7\frac{1}{8}$″	8′-9″	8′-9″	23′-7″	50′-6″	90000	—	80000	40000	120000

BOILER PRESSURE	FUEL	HEATING SURFACE, SQ. FT.				GRATE AREA	GAUGE OF TRACK	
POUNDS PER SQ. INCH ABOVE ATMOSPHERE	KIND	FLUES	FIRE BOX	ARCH PIPES	TOTAL	SQUARE FEET	METRES	FEET INCHES
200	Bituminous Coal	1649.4	152.2	—	1801.6	27.2	1.435	4′-$8\frac{1}{2}$″

FOR HAULING CAPACITY SEE PAGE 290.

210
210
CH&D
CH&D

BUILT BY

BROOKS LOCOMOTIVE WORKS

DUNKIRK, N. Y., U.S.A.

1893

FOR THE CINCINNATI, HAMILTON & DAYTON RAILWAY.

CODE WORD, QUAKER.

TYPE, 8-WHEELED PASSENGER.

WITH 8-WHEELED TENDER

SERIES, 486.

CLASS, 18 A.

TANK CAPACITY 4200 U. S. GALLONS AND 8½ TONS FUEL.

CYLINDERS			WHEELS								BOILER		FIRE BOX		
			TENDER		TRAILING		COUPLED DRIVERS		LEADING						
TYPE	DIA.	STROKE	NO.	DIA.	NO.	DIA.	NO.	DIA.	NO.	DIA.	TYPE	DIA.	TYPE	LENGTH	WIDTH
Simple	18″	26″	8	33″	—	—	4	73″	4	33″	Improved Belpaire	58″	Long, Sloping	102″	32″

FLUES			WHEEL BASE				AVERAGE WEIGHT IN WORKING ORDER, POUNDS				
NO.	DIA.	LENGTH	DRIVING	RIGID	ENGINE	ENGINE AND TENDER	TENDER	TRAILING WHEELS	DRIVERS	LEADING WHEELS	TOTAL ENGINE
226	2″	11′-7″	8′-0″	8′-0″	22′-8″	46′-8″	90000	——	74000	38000	112000

BOILER PRESSURE	FUEL	HEATING SURFACE, SQ. FT.				GRATE AREA	GAUGE OF TRACK	
POUNDS PER SQ. INCH ABOVE ATMOSPHERE	KIND	FLUES	FIRE BOX	ARCH PIPES	TOTAL	SQUARE FEET	METRES	FEET INCHES
180	Bituminous Coal	1372	133	19	1524	22.6	1.435	4′-8½″

FOR HAULING CAPACITY SEE PAGE 290.

785
785
785

BUILT BY

BROOKS LOCOMOTIVE WORKS

DUNKIRK, N. Y., U.S.A.

1888

FOR THE UNION PACIFIC RAILROAD.

CODE WORD, QUAMOR. SERIES, 293.

TYPE, 8-WHEELED PASSENGER. CLASS, 18 A.

WITH 8-WHEELED TENDER

TANK CAPACITY 2900 U. S. GALLONS AND 6 TONS FUEL.

CYLINDERS			WHEELS								BOILER		FIRE BOX		
TYPE	DIA.	STROKE	TENDER		TRAILING		COUPLED DRIVERS		LEADING		TYPE	DIA.	TYPE	LENGTH	WIDTH
			NO.	DIA.	NO.	DIA.	NO.	DIA.	NO	DIA.					
Simple	18″	26″	8	33″	—	—	4	63″	4	30″	Crown Bar, Wagon Top	55″	Deep	73″	35″

FLUES			WHEEL BASE				AVERAGE WEIGHT IN WORKING ORDER, POUNDS				
NO.	DIA.	LENGTH	DRIVING	RIGID	ENGINE	ENGINE AND TENDER	TENDER	TRAILING WHEELS	DRIVERS	LEADING WHEELS	TOTAL ENGINE
201	2″	12′-6″	8′-10″	8′-10″	24′-9″	46′-2¼″	67000	—	63000	37000	100000

BOILER PRESSURE	FUEL	HEATING SURFACE, SQ. FT.				GRATE AREA	GAUGE OF TRACK	
POUNDS PER SQ. INCH ABOVE ATMOSPHERE	KIND	FLUES	FIRE BOX	ARCH PIPES	TOTAL	SQUARE FEET	METRES	FEET INCHES
150	Bituminous Coal	1315	111.	—	1426	17.55	1.435	4′-8½″

FOR HAULING CAPACITY SEE PAGE 290.

33
L. I. R. R.

BUILT BY

BROOKS LOCOMOTIVE WORKS

DUNKIRK, N. Y., U.S.A.

1898

FOR THE LONG ISLAND RAILROAD.

CODE WORD, QUARRY. SERIES, 639.

TYPE, 8-WHEELED PASSENGER. CLASS, 18 A.

WITH 8-WHEELED TENDER

TANK CAPACITY 4000 U. S. GALLONS AND $8\frac{1}{2}$ TONS FUEL.

CYLINDERS			WHEELS								BOILER		FIRE BOX		
			TENDER		TRAILING		COUPLED DRIVERS		LEADING						
TYPE	DIA.	STROKE	NO.	DIA.	NO.	DIA.	NO.	DIA	NO.	DIA.	TYPE	DIA	TYPE	LENGTH	WIDTH
Simple	18″	24″	8	33″	—	—	4	67″	4	30″	Rad. Stay, Wagon Top	56″	Long, Wide Sloping	$132\frac{3}{4}$″	$42\frac{3}{4}$″

FLUES			WHEEL BASE				AVERAGE WEIGHT IN WORKING ORDER, POUNDS				
NO.	DIA.	LENGTH	DRIVING	RIGID	ENGINE	ENGINE AND TENDER	TENDER	TRAILING WHEELS	DRIVERS	LEADING WHEELS	TOTAL ENGINE
225	2″	11′-$5\frac{1}{8}$″	7′-6″	7′-6″	22′-0″	48′-5″	85000	——	81500	33500	115000

BOILER PRESSURE	FUEL	HEATING SURFACE, SQ. FT.				GRATE AREA	GAUGE OF TRACK	
POUNDS PER SQ. INCH ABOVE ATMOSPHERE	KIND	FLUES	FIRE BOX	ARCH PIPES	TOTAL	SQUARE FEET	METRES	FEET INCHES
180	Anthracite Coal	1343	160.9	——	1503.9	38.5	1.435	4′-$8\frac{1}{2}$″

FOR HAULING CAPACITY SEE PAGE 290.

PECOS VALLEY & NORTHEASTERN
7

BUILT BY

BROOKS LOCOMOTIVE WORKS

DUNKIRK, N. Y., U.S.A.

1898

FOR THE PECOS VALLEY & NORTHEASTERN RAILWAY.

CODE WORD, QUARTAN. SERIES, 664.

TYPE, 8-WHEELED PASSENGER. CLASS, 18 A.

WITH 8-WHEELED TENDER TANK CAPACITY 4000 U. S. GALLONS AND $8\frac{1}{2}$ TONS FUEL.

CYLINDERS			WHEELS								BOILER		FIRE BOX		
TYPE	DIA.	STROKE	TENDER NO.	TENDER DIA.	TRAILING NO.	TRAILING DIA.	COUPLED DRIVERS NO.	COUPLED DRIVERS DIA.	LEADING NO.	LEADING DIA.	TYPE	DIA.	TYPE	LENGTH	WIDTH
Simple	18″	24″	8	33″	—	—	4	62″	4	30″	Rad. Stay, Wagon Top	58″	Long, Sloping	103″	33″

FLUES			WHEEL BASE				AVERAGE WEIGHT IN WORKING ORDER, POUNDS				
NO.	DIA.	LENGTH	DRIVING	RIGID	ENGINE	ENGINE AND TENDER	TENDER	TRAILING WHEELS	DRIVERS	LEADING WHEELS	TOTAL ENGINE
225	2″	11′-7⅛″	8′-0″	8′-0″	22′-8″	48′-11⅜″	84000	—	72000	37000	109000

BOILER PRESSURE	FUEL	HEATING SURFACE, SQ. FT.				GRATE AREA	GAUGE OF TRACK	
POUNDS PER SQ. INCH ABOVE ATMOSPHERE	KIND	FLUES	FIRE BOX	ARCH PIPES	TOTAL	SQUARE FEET	METRES	FEET INCHES
180	Bituminous Coal	1355	140	—	1495	23.1	1.435	4′-8½″

FOR HAULING CAPACITY SEE PAGE 290.

WASHINGTON COUNTY
1
1
1
BROOKS

BUILT BY

BROOKS LOCOMOTIVE WORKS

DUNKIRK, N. Y., U.S.A.

1898

FOR THE WASHINGTON COUNTY RAILROAD.

CODE WORD, QUARTIC. SERIES, 647.

TYPE, 8-WHEELED PASSENGER. CLASS, 18 A.

WITH 8-WHEELED TENDER TANK CAPACITY 4000 U. S. GALLONS AND $8\frac{1}{2}$ TONS FUEL.

CYLINDERS			WHEELS								BOILER		FIRE BOX			
TYPE	DIA	STROKE	TENDER		TRAILING		COUPLED DRIVERS		LEADING		TYPE	DIA.	TYPE	LENGTH	WIDTH
			NO.	DIA.	NO.	DIA.	NO.	DIA.	NO.	DIA.					
Simple	18″	24″	8	33″	—	—	4	62″	4	30″	Rad. Stay, Wagon Top	56″	Long, Sloping	97″	33″

FLUES			WHEEL BASE				AVERAGE WEIGHT IN WORKING ORDER, POUNDS				
NO.	DIA.	LENGTH	DRIVING	RIGID	ENGINE	ENGINE AND TENDER	TENDER	TRAILING WHEELS	DRIVERS	LEADING WHEELS	TOTAL ENGINE
225	2″	$11'\text{-}7\frac{1}{8}''$	8′-0″	8′-0″	22′-8″	48′-11″	85000	—	70800	36200	107000

BOILER PRESSURE	FUEL	HEATING SURFACE, SQ. FT.				GRATE AREA	GAUGE OF TRACK	
POUNDS PER SQ. INCH ABOVE ATMOSPHERE	KIND	FLUES	FIRE BOX	ARCH PIPES	TOTAL	SQUARE FEET	METRES	FEET INCHES
180	Bituminous Coal	1356	134	—	1490	21.8	1.435	$4'\text{-}8\frac{1}{2}''$

FOR HAULING CAPACITY SEE PAGE 290.

The locomotive described above was used by the Lake Shore & Michigan Southern Railway Co. during the Chicago Exposition in regular daily service on the "Exposition Flyer" or twenty-hour train between New York and Chicago, a distance of 980 miles.

Near Elkhart, Ind., this engine attained a speed of **10.2** miles in less than six minutes, or at the rate of over **102** miles per hour.

"THE EXPOSITION FLYER."

BUILT BY

BROOKS LOCOMOTIVE WORKS

DUNKIRK, N. Y., U.S.A.

1893

FOR THE LAKE SHORE & MICHIGAN SOUTHERN RAILWAY.

CODE WORD, QUARTO. SERIES, 472.

TYPE, 8-WHEELED PASSENGER. CLASS, 17 A.

WITH 8-WHEELED TENDER TANK CAPACITY 3100 U. S. GALLONS AND 7 TONS FUEL.

CYLINDERS			WHEELS								BOILER		FIRE BOX		
			TENDER		TRAILING		COUPLED DRIVERS		LEADING						
TYPE	DIA.	STROKE	NO.	DIA.	NO.	DIA.	NO.	DIA.	NO.	DIA.	TYPE	DIA.	TYPE	LENGTH	WIDTH
Simple	17″	24″	8	33″	—	—	4	72″	4	33″	Improved Belpaire	52″	Deep	78″	34″

FLUES			WHEEL BASE				AVERAGE WEIGHT IN WORKING ORDER, POUNDS				
NO.	DIA.	LENGTH	DRIVING	RIGID	ENGINE	ENGINE AND TENDER	TENDER	TRAILING WHEELS	DRIVERS	LEADING WHEELS	TOTAL ENGINE
202	2″	12′-0″	9′-0″	9′-0″	23′-9″	45′-8″	70000	—	65100	39500	104600

BOILER PRESSURE	FUEL	HEATING SURFACE, SQ. FT.				GRATE AREA	GAUGE OF TRACK	
POUNDS PER SQ. INCH ABOVE ATMOSPHERE	KIND	FLUES	FIRE BOX	ARCH PIPES	TOTAL	SQUARE FEET	METRES	FEET INCHES
180	Bituminous Coal	1258	140	—	1398	18.4	1.435	4′-8½″

FOR HAULING CAPACITY SEE PAGE 290.

15
15
15
15
PECOS VALLEY & NORTHEASTERN

BUILT BY

BROOKS LOCOMOTIVE WORKS

DUNKIRK, N. Y., U.S.A.

1898

FOR THE PECOS VALLEY & NORTHEASTERN RAILWAY.

CODE WORD, QUATRAIN. SERIES, 680.

TYPE, 8-WHEELED PASSENGER. CLASS, 17 A.

WITH 8-WHEELED TENDER TANK CAPACITY 4000 U. S. GALLONS AND 8½ TONS FUEL.

CYLINDERS			WHEELS								BOILER		FIRE BOX		
			TENDER		TRAILING		COUPLED DRIVERS		LEADING						
TYPE	DIA.	STROKE	NO.	DIA.	NO.	DIA.	NO.	DIA.	NO.	DIA.	TYPE	DIA.	TYPE	LENGTH	WIDTH
Simple	17″	24″	8	33″	—	—	4	62″	4	30″	Rad. Stay, Wagon Top	52″	Long, Sloping	96″	33″

FLUES			WHEEL BASE				AVERAGE WEIGHT IN WORKING ORDER, POUNDS				
NO.	DIA.	LENGTH	DRIVING	RIGID	ENGINE	ENGINE AND TENDER	TENDER	TRAILING WHEELS	DRIVERS	LEADING WHEELS	TOTAL ENGINE
196	2″	11′-1″	8′-0″	8′-0″	22′-1½″	44′-0″	86000	—	64000	32000	96000

BOILER PRESSURE	FUEL	HEATING SURFACE, SQ. FT.				GRATE AREA	GAUGE OF TRACK	
POUNDS PER SQ. INCH ABOVE ATMOSPHERE	KIND	FLUES	FIRE BOX	ARCH PIPES	TOTAL	SQUARE FEET	METRES	FEET INCHES
180	Bituminous Coal	1129	115	—	1244	22	1.435	4′-8½″

FOR HAULING CAPACITY SEE PAGE 290.

F. S. R. R.
25

BUILT BY

BROOKS LOCOMOTIVE WORKS

DUNKIRK, N. Y., U.S.A.

1894

FOR THE FLORIDA SOUTHERN RAILWAY.

CODE WORD, QUAVER.

TYPE, 8-WHEELED PASSENGER.

WITH 8-WHEELED TENDER

SERIES, 525.

CLASS 17 A.

TANK CAPACITY 3500 U. S. GALLONS AND 6 TONS FUEL.

CYLINDERS			WHEELS								BOILER		FIRE BOX		
TYPE	DIA.	STROKE	TENDER NO.	TENDER DIA.	TRAILING NO.	TRAILING DIA.	COUPLED DRIVERS NO.	COUPLED DRIVERS DIA.	LEADING NO.	LEADING DIA.	TYPE	DIA.	TYPE	LENGTH	WIDTH
Simple	17″	24″	8	33″	—	—	4	62″	4	28″	Crown Bar, Wagon Top	52″	Deep	72″	35″

FLUES			WHEEL BASE				AVERAGE WEIGHT IN WORKING ORDER, POUNDS				
NO.	DIA.	LENGTH	DRIVING	RIGID	ENGINE	ENGINE AND TENDER	TENDER	TRAILING WHEELS	DRIVERS	LEADING WHEELS	TOTAL ENGINE
186	2″	10′-11″	8′-6″	8′-6″	22′-6″	44′-9″	67000	—	58600	35000	93600

BOILER PRESSURE	FUEL	HEATING SURFACE, SQ. FT.				GRATE AREA	GAUGE OF TRACK	
POUNDS PER SQ. INCH ABOVE ATMOSPHERE	KIND	FLUES	FIRE BOX	ARCH PIPES	TOTAL	SQUARE FEET	METRES	FEET INCHES
160	Wood	1055.7	1110.7	—	1166	17	1.435	4′-8½″

FOR HAULING CAPACITY SEE PAGE 290.

16
16
16

BUILT BY

BROOKS LOCOMOTIVE WORKS

DUNKIRK, N. Y., U.S.A.

1894

FOR THE NORTH PACIFIC COAST RAILROAD.

CODE WORD, QUAY. SERIES, 523.

TYPE, 8-WHEELED PASSENGER. CLASS, 15 A.

WITH 8-WHEELED TENDER

TANK CAPACITY 2200 U. S. GALLONS AND 6 TONS FUEL.

CYLINDERS			WHEELS								BOILER		FIRE BOX		
			TENDER		TRAILING		COUPLED DRIVERS		LEADING						
TYPE	DIA.	STROKE	NO.	DIA.	NO.	DIA.	NO.	DIA.	NO.	DIA.	TYPE	DIA.	TYPE	LENGTH	WIDTH
Simple	15″	20″	8	28″	—	—	4	48″	4	28″	Crown Bar, Wagon Top	50¼″	Long, Wide Sloping	84″	24″

FLUES			WHEEL BASE				AVERAGE WEIGHT IN WORKING ORDER, POUNDS				
NO.	DIA.	LENGTH	DRIVING	RIGID	ENGINE	ENGINE AND TENDER	TENDER	TRAILING WHEELS	DRIVERS	LEADING WHEELS	TOTAL ENGINE
164	2″	9′-0″	7′-0″	7′-0″	18′-5″	40′-10″	64000	——	48000	20000	68000

BOILER PRESSURE	FUEL	HEATING SURFACE, SQ. FT.				GRATE AREA	GAUGE OF TRACK	
POUNDS PER SQ. INCH ABOVE ATMOSPHERE	KIND	FLUES	FIRE BOX	ARCH PIPES	TOTAL	SQUARE FEET	METRES	FEET INCHES
165	Bituminous Coal	772	83	——	855	13.6	.914	3′-0″

FOR HAULING CAPACITY SEE PAGE 290.

51
P. B. & L. E.
51
BESSEMER.

BUILT BY

BROOKS LOCOMOTIVE WORKS

DUNKIRK, N. Y., U.S.A.

1897

FOR THE PITTSBURG, BESSEMER & LAKE ERIE RAILROAD.

CODE WORD, QUEACH. SERIES, 607.

TYPE, MOGUL FREIGHT. CLASS, 20 B.

WITH 8-WHEELED TENDER TANK CAPACITY 4000 U. S. GALLONS AND $8\frac{1}{2}$ TONS FUEL.

CYLINDERS			WHEELS								BOILER		FIRE BOX		
			TENDER		TRAILING		COUPLED DRIVERS		LEADING						
TYPE	DIA.	STROKE	NO.	DIA.	NO.	DIA.	NO.	DIA.	NO.	DIA.	TYPE	DIA.	TYPE	LENGTH	WIDTH
Simple	20″	26″	8	33″	—	—	6	56″	2	33″	Rad. Stay, Straight Top	72″	Long, Wide	108″	$37\frac{3}{4}$″

FLUES			WHEEL BASE				AVERAGE WEIGHT IN WORKING ORDER, POUNDS				
NO.	DIA.	LENGTH	DRIVING	RIGID	ENGINE	ENGINE AND TENDER	TENDER	TRAILING WHEELS	DRIVERS	LEADING WHEELS	TOTAL ENGINE
300	2″	12′-$0\frac{3}{8}$″	14′-0″	14′-0″	22′-5″	52′-4″	85000	—	145400	22450	167850

BOILER PRESSURE	FUEL	HEATING SURFACE, SQ. FT.				GRATE AREA	GAUGE OF TRACK	
POUNDS PER SQ. INCH ABOVE ATMOSPHERE	KIND	FLUES	FIRE BOX	ARCH PIPES	TOTAL	SQUARE FEET	METRES	FEET INCHES
180	Bituminous Coal	1871	186	—	2057	28.4	1.435	4′-$8\frac{1}{2}$″

FOR HAULING CAPACITY SEE PAGE 290.

GREAT NORTHERN
371

BUILT BY

BROOKS LOCOMOTIVE WORKS

DUNKIRK, N. Y., U. S. A.

1896

FOR THE GREAT NORTHERN RAILWAY.

CODE WORD, QUEAN. SERIES, 587.

TYPE, MOGUL FREIGHT. CLASS, 19 B.

WITH 8-WHEELED TENDER TANK CAPACITY 4000 U. S. GALLONS AND $8\frac{1}{2}$ TONS FUEL.

CYLINDERS			WHEELS								BOILER		FIRE BOX		
TYPE	DIA.	STROKE	TENDER		TRAILING		COUPLED DRIVERS		LEADING		TYPE	DIA.	TYPE	LENGTH	WIDTH
			NO.	DIA.	NO.	DIA.	NO.	DIA.	NO.	DIA.					
Simple	19″	26″	8	33″	—	—	6	55″	2	30″	Improved Belpaire	63″	Long, Sloping	98″	32″

FLUES			WHEEL BASE				AVERAGE WEIGHT IN WORKING ORDER, POUNDS				
NO.	DIA.	LENGTH	DRIVING	RIGID	ENGINE	ENGINE AND TENDER	TENDER	TRAILING WHEELS	DRIVERS	LEADING WHEELS	TOTAL ENGINE
250	2″	11′-1⅛″	14′-0″	14′-0″	21′-6″	48′-4″	85000	—	114000	16000	130000

BOILER PRESSURE	FUEL	HEATING SURFACE, SQ. FT.				GRATE AREA	GAUGE OF TRACK	
POUNDS PER SQ. INCH ABOVE ATMOSPHERE	KIND	FLUES	FIRE BOX	ARCH PIPES	TOTAL	SQUARE FEET	METRES	FEET INCHES
180	Bituminous Coal	1450	151	—	1601	21.1	1.435	4′-8½″

FOR HAULING CAPACITY SEE PAGE 290.

N.Y.C.&H.R.R.R.
720

BUILT BY

BROOKS LOCOMOTIVE WORKS

DUNKIRK, N. Y., U.S.A.

1889

FOR THE NEW YORK CENTRAL & HUDSON RIVER RAILROAD.

CODE WORD, QUEBECK. SERIES, 345.

TYPE, MOGUL FREIGHT. CLASS, 19 B.

WITH 8-WHEELED TENDER TANK CAPACITY 3500 U. S. GALLONS AND 7 TONS FUEL.

CYLINDERS			WHEELS								BOILER		FIRE BOX		
TYPE	DIA.	STROKE	TENDER NO.	TENDER DIA.	TRAILING NO.	TRAILING DIA.	COUPLED DRIVERS NO.	COUPLED DRIVERS DIA.	LEADING NO.	LEADING DIA.	TYPE	DIA.	TYPE	LENGTH	WIDTH
Simple	19″	26″	8	33″	—	—	6	64″	2	30″	Crown Bar, Wagon Top	58″	Long, Wide	102″	43″

FLUES			WHEEL BASE				AVERAGE WEIGHT IN WORKING ORDER, POUNDS					
NO.	DIA.	LENGTH	DRIVING	RIGID	ENGINE	ENGINE AND TENDER	TENDER	TRAILING WHEELS	DRIVERS	LEADING WHEELS	TOTAL ENGINE
270	2″	11′-6$\frac{1}{8}$″	14′-0″	14′-0″	21′-9″	46′-2″	73000	—	106000	16000	122000

BOILER PRESSURE	FUEL	HEATING SURFACE, SQ. FT.				GRATE AREA	GAUGE OF TRACK		
POUNDS PER SQ. INCH ABOVE ATMOSPHERE	KIND	FLUES	FIRE BOX	ARCH PIPES	TOTAL	SQUARE FEET	METRES	FEET	INCHES
160	Bituminous Coal	1590	144	—	1734	29.75	1.435	4′-8$\frac{1}{2}$″	

FOR HAULING CAPACITY SEE PAGE 290.

255

BUILT BY

BROOKS LOCOMOTIVE WORKS

DUNKIRK, N. Y., U.S.A.

1895

FOR THE MISSOURI, KANSAS & TEXAS RAILWAY.

CODE WORD, QUECK. SERIES, 546.

TYPE, MOGUL FREIGHT. CLASS, 19 B.

WITH 8-WHEELED TENDER TANK CAPACITY 4000 U. S. GALLONS AND 8 TONS FUEL.

CYLINDERS			WHEELS								BOILER		FIRE BOX		
TYPE	DIA.	STROKE	TENDER		TRAILING		COUPLED DRIVERS		LEADING		TYPE	DIA.	TYPE	LENGTH	WIDTH
			NO.	DIA.	NO.	DIA.	NO.	DIA.	NO.	DIA.					
Simple	19″	24″	8	33″	—	—	6	56″	2	30″	Crown Bar, Straight Top	60″	Long	96$\frac{7}{16}$″	34$\frac{3}{8}$″

FLUES			WHEEL BASE				AVERAGE WEIGHT IN WORKING ORDER, POUNDS				
NO.	DIA.	LENGTH	DRIVING	RIGID	ENGINE	ENGINE AND TENDER	TENDER	TRAILING WHEELS	DRIVERS	LEADING WHEELS	TOTAL ENGINE
228	2″	11′-6″	12′-8″	12′-8″	20′-1$\frac{1}{2}$″	44′-11$\frac{3}{4}$″	85000	—	105000	16000	121000

BOILER PRESSURE	FUEL	HEATING SURFACE, SQ. FT.				GRATE AREA	GAUGE OF TRACK	
POUNDS PER SQ. INCH ABOVE ATMOSPHERE	KIND	FLUES	FIRE BOX	ARCH PIPES	TOTAL	SQUARE FEET	METRES	FEET INCHES
170	Bituminous Coal	1357.77	134.5	—	1492.27	22.6	1.435	4′-8$\frac{1}{2}$″

FOR HAULING CAPACITY SEE PAGE 290.

106
106
F. & P. M.
F. & P. M.
105

BUILT BY

BROOKS LOCOMOTIVE WORKS

DUNKIRK, N. Y., U.S.A.

1898

FOR THE FLINT & PERE MARQUETTE RAILROAD.

CODE WORD, QUELQUE. SERIES, 679.

TYPE, MOGUL FREIGHT. CLASS, 18 B.

WITH 8-WHEELED TENDER TANK CAPACITY 4500 U. S. GALLONS AND 12½ TONS FUEL.

CYLINDERS			WHEELS								BOILER		FIRE BOX		
TYPE	DIA.	STROKE	TENDER NO.	TENDER DIA.	TRAILING NO.	TRAILING DIA.	COUPLED DRIVERS NO.	COUPLED DRIVERS DIA.	LEADING NO.	LEADING DIA.	TYPE	DIA.	TYPE	LENGTH	WIDTH
Simple Piston Valve	18″	30″	8	33″	—	—	6	56″	2	30″	Improved Belpaire	62″	Long, Sloping	108″	42″

FLUES			WHEEL BASE				AVERAGE WEIGHT IN WORKING ORDER, POUNDS				
NO.	DIA.	LENGTH	DRIVING	RIGID	ENGINE	ENGINE AND TENDER	TENDER	TRAILING WHEELS	DRIVERS	LEADING WHEELS	TOTAL ENGINE
272	2″	12′-1¼″	15′-0″	15′-0″	23′-5″	51′-6″	90000	—	120000	17000	137000

BOILER PRESSURE	FUEL	HEATING SURFACE, SQ. FT.				GRATE AREA	GAUGE OF TRACK	
POUNDS PER SQ. INCH ABOVE ATMOSPHERE	KIND	FLUES	FIRE BOX	ARCH PIPES	TOTAL	SQUARE FEET	METRES	FEET INCHES
180	Bituminous Coal	1708	157	21	1886	30.8	1.435	4′-8½″

FOR HAULING CAPACITY SEE PAGE 290.

B., St. M. & S. W. R.R.
5

BUILT BY

BROOKS LOCOMOTIVE WORKS

DUNKIRK, N. Y., U.S.A.

1897

FOR THE BUFFALO, ST. MARY'S & SOUTHWESTERN RAILROAD.

CODE WORD, QUEME. SERIES, 597.

TYPE, MOGUL FREIGHT. CLASS, 18 B.

WITH 8-WHEELED TENDER TANK CAPACITY 3100 U. S. GALLONS AND 4 TONS FUEL.

CYLINDERS			WHEELS								BOILER		FIRE BOX		
TYPE	DIA.	STROKE	TENDER		TRAILING		COUPLED DRIVERS		LEADING		TYPE	DIA.	TYPE	LENGTH	WIDTH
			NO.	DIA.	NO.	DIA.	NO.	DIA.	NO.	DIA.					
Simple	18″	24″	8	33″	—	—	6	57″	2	30″	Crown Bar, Wagon Top	60″	Long, Sloping	102″	33″

FLUES			WHEEL BASE				AVERAGE WEIGHT IN WORKING ORDER, POUNDS				
NO.	DIA.	LENGTH	DRIVING	RIGID	NE	ENGINE AND TENDER	TENDER	TRAILING WHEELS	DRIVERS	LEADING WHEELS	TOTAL ENGINE
250	2″	11′-1¼″	13′-0″	13′-0″	20′-6″	47′-2″	72000	——	108000	16000	124000

BOILER PRESSURE	FUEL	HEATING SURFACE, SQ. FT.				GRATE AREA	GAUGE OF TRACK		
POUNDS PER SQ. INCH ABOVE ATMOSPHERE	KIND	FLUES	FIRE BOX	ARCH PIPES	TOTAL	SQUARE FEET	METRES	FEET	INCHES
180	Bituminous Coal	1455	168	——	1623	23.3	1.435	4′-8½″	

FOR HAULING CAPACITY SEE PAGE 290.

D. M. R. & N. R. R.
8
D.M.R.&N.R.R.

BUILT BY

BROOKS LOCOMOTIVE WORKS

DUNKIRK, N. Y., U.S.A.

1895

FOR THE DULUTH, MISSISSIPPI RIVER & NORTHERN RAILROAD.

CODE WORD, QUENCH. SERIES, 547.

TYPE, MOGUL FREIGHT. CLASS, 18 B.

WITH 8-WHEELED TENDER

TANK CAPACITY 3500 U. S. GALLONS AND 7 TONS FUEL.

CYLINDERS			WHEELS								BOILER		FIRE BOX		
TYPE	DIA.	STROKE	TENDER NO.	TENDER DIA.	TRAILING NO.	TRAILING DIA.	COUPLED DRIVERS NO.	COUPLED DRIVERS DIA.	LEADING NO.	LEADING DIA.	TYPE	DIA.	TYPE	LENGTH	WIDTH
Simple	18″	24″	8	33″	—	—	6	51″	2	28″	Crown Bar, Wagon Top	56″	Long, Sloping	96″	34″

FLUES			WHEEL BASE				AVERAGE WEIGHT IN WORKING ORDER, POUNDS				
NO.	DIA.	LENGTH	DRIVING	RIGID	ENGINE	ENGINE AND TENDER	TENDER	TRAILING WHEELS	DRIVERS	LEADING WHEELS	TOTAL ENGINE
212	2″	11′-1″	14′-0″	14′-0″	21′-6″	48′-0″	74000	—	96000	14500	110500

BOILER PRESSURE	FUEL	HEATING SURFACE, SQ. FT.				GRATE AREA	GAUGE OF TRACK	
POUNDS PER SQ. INCH ABOVE ATMOSPHERE	KIND	FLUES	FIRE BOX	ARCH PIPES	TOTAL	SQUARE FEET	METRES	FEET INCHES
180	Bituminous Coal	1214	133.5	—	1347.5	22.2	1.435	4′-8½″

FOR HAULING CAPACITY SEE PAGE 290.

85
N.Y.C. & St. L. R.R.
New York Chicago & St. Louis R.R

BUILT BY

BROOKS LOCOMOTIVE WORKS

DUNKIRK, N. Y., U.S.A.

1889

FOR THE NEW YORK, CHICAGO & ST. LOUIS RAILROAD.

CODE WORD, QUENELLA. SERIES, 361.

TYPE, MOGUL FREIGHT. CLASS, 18 B.

WITH 8-WHEELED TENDER TANK CAPACITY 3000 U. S. GALLONS AND 6 TONS FUEL.

CYLINDERS			WHEELS								BOILER		FIRE BOX		
			TENDER		TRAILING		COUPLED DRIVERS		LEADING						
TYPE	DIA.	STROKE	NO.	DIA.	NO.	DIA.	NO.	DIA.	NO.	DIA.	TYPE	DIA.	TYPE	LENGTH	WIDTH
Simple	18″	24″	8	33″	—	—	6	56″	2	30″	Rad. Stay, Straight Top	56″	Long, Sloping	112″	$34\frac{1}{2}$″

FLUES			WHEEL BASE				AVERAGE WEIGHT IN WORKING ORDER, POUNDS				
NO.	DIA.	LENGTH	DRIVING	RIGID	ENGINE	ENGINE AND TENDER	TENDER	TRAILING WHEELS	DRIVERS	LEADING WHEELS	TOTAL ENGINE
201	2″	11′-$1\frac{1}{16}$″	15′-0″	15′-0″	22′-6″	44′-$5\frac{1}{4}$″	60000	—	85000	15000	100000

BOILER PRESSURE	FUEL	HEATING SURFACE, SQ. FT.				GRATE AREA	GAUGE OF TRACK	
POUNDS PER SQ. INCH ABOVE ATMOSPHERE	KIND	FLUES	FIRE BOX	ARCH PIPES	TOTAL	SQUARE FEET	METRES	FEET INCHES
175	Bituminous Coal	1157	117	—	1274	26.25	1.435	4′-$8\frac{1}{2}$″

FOR HAULING CAPACITY SEE PAGE 290.

MUNISING RAILWAY.

BUILT BY

BROOKS LOCOMOTIVE WORKS

DUNKIRK, N. Y., U.S.A.

1896

FOR THE MUNISING RAILWAY.

CODE WORD, QUERCITE. — SERIES, 579.

TYPE, MOGUL FREIGHT. — CLASS, 16 B.

WITH 8-WHEELED TENDER — TANK CAPACITY 3000 U. S. GALLONS AND 6 TONS FUEL.

CYLINDERS			WHEELS								BOILER		FIRE BOX		
TYPE	DIA.	STROKE	TENDER NO.	TENDER DIA.	TRAILING NO.	TRAILING DIA.	COUPLED DRIVERS NO.	COUPLED DRIVERS DIA.	LEADING NO.	LEADING DIA.	TYPE	DIA.	TYPE	LENGTH	WIDTH
Simple	16″	24″	8	33″	—	—	6	50″	2	30″	Crown Bar, Wagon Top	50¼″	Deep	66″	34½″

FLUES			WHEEL BASE				AVERAGE WEIGHT IN WORKING ORDER, POUNDS				
NO.	DIA.	LENGTH	DRIVING	RIGID	ENGINE	ENGINE AND TENDER	TENDER	TRAILING WHEELS	DRIVERS	LEADING WHEELS	TOTAL ENGINE
156	2″	10′-0″	13′-9″	13′-9″	21′-3″	43′-1″	65000	—	76000	14000	90000

BOILER PRESSURE	FUEL	HEATING SURFACE, SQ. FT.				GRATE AREA	GAUGE OF TRACK	
POUNDS PER SQ. INCH ABOVE ATMOSPHERE	KIND	FLUES	FIRE BOX	ARCH PIPES	TOTAL	SQUARE FEET	METRES	FEET INCHES
165	Bituminous Coal	810.7	95	—	905.7	15.3	1.435	4′-8½″

FOR HAULING CAPACITY SEE PAGE 290.

ITASCA No. 2
ITASCA RAILROAD.

BUILT BY

BROOKS LOCOMOTIVE WORKS

DUNKIRK, N. Y., U.S.A.

1898

FOR THE ITASCA RAILROAD.

CODE WORD, QUERCUS. SERIES, 651.

TYPE, MOGUL FREIGHT. CLASS, 14 B.

WITH 8-WHEELED TENDER TANK CAPACITY 3000 U. S. GALLONS AND 6 TONS FUEL.

CYLINDERS			WHEELS								BOILER		FIRE BOX		
			TENDER		TRAILING		COUPLED DRIVERS		LEADING						
TYPE	DIA.	STROKE	NO.	DIA.	NO.	DIA.	NO.	DIA.	NO.	DIA.	TYPE	DIA.	TYPE	LENGTH	WIDTH
Simple	14″	22″	8	30″	—	—	6	42″	2	24″	Crown Bar, Wagon Top	46″	Long, Sloping	54″	33″

FLUES			WHEEL BASE				AVERAGE WEIGHT IN WORKING ORDER, POUNDS				
NO.	DIA.	LENGTH	DRIVING	RIGID	ENGINE	ENGINE AND TENDER	TENDER	TRAILING WHEELS	DRIVERS	LEADING WHEELS	TOTAL ENGINE
126	2″	9′-0″	11′-0″	11′-0″	17′-8″	40′-0½″	63000	—	56000	10500	66500

BOILER PRESSURE	FUEL	HEATING SURFACE, SQ. FT.				GRATE AREA	GAUGE OF TRACK	
POUNDS PER SQ. INCH ABOVE ATMOSPHERE	KIND	FLUES	FIRE BOX	ARCH PIPES	TOTAL	SQUARE FEET	METRES	FEET INCHES
150	Bituminous Coal	589	75	—	664	12.1	1.435	4′-8½″

FOR HAULING CAPACITY SEE PAGE 290.

3
Q.& T.L.R.R.
3

BUILT BY

BROOKS LOCOMOTIVE WORKS

DUNKIRK, N. Y., U.S.A.

1894

FOR THE QUINCY & TORCH LAKE RAILROAD.

CODE WORD, QUERENT. SERIES, 537.

TYPE, MOGUL FREIGHT. CLASS, 17 B.

WITH 8-WHEELED TENDER TANK CAPACITY 3100 U. S. GALLONS AND 7 TONS FUEL.

CYLINDERS			WHEELS								BOILER		FIRE BOX		
TYPE	DIA.	STROKE	TENDER		TRAILING		COUPLED DRIVERS		LEADING		TYPE	DIA.	TYPE	LENGTH	WIDTH
			NO.	DIA.	NO.	DIA.	NO.	DIA.	NO.	DIA.					
Simple	17″	22″	8	28″	—	—	6	44″	2	28″	Rad. Stay, Straight Top	58″	Long, Wide, Sloping	108″	24″

FLUES			WHEEL BASE				AVERAGE WEIGHT IN WORKING ORDER, POUNDS				
NO.	DIA.	LENGTH	DRIVING	RIGID	ENGINE	ENGINE AND TENDER	TENDER	TRAILING WHEELS	DRIVERS	LEADING WHEELS	TOTAL ENGINE
200	2″	10′-1⅛″	11′-0″	11′-0″	18′-0″	43′-6″	72000	—	79000	11000	90000

BOILER PRESSURE	FUEL	HEATING SURFACE, SQ. FT.				GRATE AREA	GAUGE OF TRACK	
POUNDS PER SQ. INCH ABOVE ATMOSPHERE	KIND	FLUES	FIRE BOX	ARCH PIPES	TOTAL	SQUARE FEET	METRES	FEET INCHES
160	Bituminous Coal	1050	114	—	1164	17.5	.914	3′-0″

FOR HAULING CAPACITY SEE PAGE 290.

1
C. & N-W.
1
COLORADO & NORTH-WESTERN RY.

BUILT BY

BROOKS LOCOMOTIVE WORKS

DUNKIRK, N. Y., U.S.A.

1897

FOR THE COLORADO & NORTH-WESTERN RAILWAY.

CODE WORD, QUERIST.

TYPE, MOGUL FREIGHT.

WITH 8-WHEELED TENDER

SERIES, 624.

CLASS, 15 B.

TANK CAPACITY 2000 U. S. GALLONS AND 6 TONS FUEL.

CYLINDERS			WHEELS								BOILER		FIRE BOX		
TYPE	DIA.	STROKE	TENDER		TRAILING		COUPLED DRIVERS		LEADING		TYPE	DIA.	TYPE	LENGTH	WIDTH
			NO.	DIA.	NO.	DIA.	NO.	DIA.	NO.	DIA.					
Simple	15″	22″	8	28″	—	—	6	42″	2	28″	Rad. Stay, Straight Top	54″	Long, Wide	84″	24″

FLUES			WHEEL BASE				AVERAGE WEIGHT IN WORKING ORDER, POUNDS				
NO.	DIA.	LENGTH	DRIVING	RIGID	ENGINE	ENGINE AND TENDER	TENDER	TRAILING WHEELS	DRIVERS	LEADING WHEELS	TOTAL ENGINE
170	2″	$8'\text{-}2\frac{1}{16}''$	10′-4″	10′-4″	16′-10″	41′-1″	52000	—	61000	9000	70000

BOILER PRESSURE	FUEL	HEATING SURFACE, SQ. FT.				GRATE AREA	GAUGE OF TRACK	
POUNDS PER SQ. INCH ABOVE ATMOSPHERE	KIND	FLUES	FIRE BOX	ARCH PIPES	TOTAL	SQUARE FEET	METRES	FEET INCHES
165	Bituminous Coal	720	88	—	808	13.5	.914	3′-0″

FOR HAULING CAPACITY SEE PAGE 290.

2
W. F. PLEAS
2
SISKIWIT & SOUTHERN R. R.

BUILT BY

BROOKS LOCOMOTIVE WORKS

DUNKIRK, N. Y., U.S.A.

1895

FOR THE SISKIWIT & SOUTHERN RAILROAD.

CODE WORD, QUERKIN. SERIES, 562.

TYPE, MOGUL FREIGHT. CLASS, 15 B.

WITH 8-WHEELED TENDER

TANK CAPACITY 2700 U. S. GALLONS AND 6 TONS FUEL.

CYLINDERS			WHEELS								BOILER		FIRE BOX		
TYPE	DIA.	STROKE	TENDER		TRAILING		COUPLED DRIVERS		LEADING		TYPE	DIA.	TYPE	LENGTH	WIDTH
			NO.	DIA.	NO.	DIA.	NO.	DIA.	NO.	DIA.					
Simple	15″	20″	8	28″	—	—	6	36″	2	24″	Crown Bar, Wagon Top	50″	Long, Wide over Frames	84″	24″

FLUES			WHEEL BASE				AVERAGE WEIGHT IN WORKING ORDER, POUNDS				
NO.	DIA.	LENGTH	DRIVING	RIGID	ENGINE	ENGINE AND TENDER	TENDER	TRAILING WHEELS	DRIVERS	LEADING WHEELS	TOTAL ENGINE
164	2″	8′-2″	10′-4″	10′-4″	16′-10″	41′-4″	56000	—	58000	10000	68000

BOILER PRESSURE	FUEL	HEATING SURFACE, SQ. FT.				GRATE AREA	GAUGE OF TRACK	
POUNDS PER SQ. INCH ABOVE ATMOSPHERE	KIND	FLUES	FIRE BOX	ARCH PIPES	TOTAL	SQUARE FEET	METRES	FEET INCHES
150	Bituminous Coal	695	85.5	—	780.5	13.6	.914	3′-0″

FOR HAULING CAPACITY SEE PAGE 290.

6
T. V. Ry.
6

BUILT BY

BROOKS LOCOMOTIVE WORKS

DUNKIRK, N. Y., U.S.A.

1898

FOR THE TIONESTA VALLEY RAILWAY.

CODE WORD, QUERLE. SERIES, 661.

TYPE, MOGUL FREIGHT. CLASS, 15 B.

WITH 8-WHEELED TENDER TANK CAPACITY 2000 U. S. GALLONS AND 6 TONS FUEL.

CYLINDERS			WHEELS								BOILER		FIRE BOX		
TYPE	DIA.	STROKE	TENDER		TRAILING		COUPLED DRIVERS		LEADING		TYPE	DIA.	TYPE	LENGTH	WIDTH
			NO.	DIA.	NO.	DIA.	NO.	DIA.	NO.	DIA.					
Simple	15″	18″	8	26″	—	—	6	38″	2	24″	Rad. Stay, Straight Top	52″	Long, Wide over Frames	78″	24″

FLUES			WHEEL BASE				AVERAGE WEIGHT IN WORKING ORDER, POUNDS				
NO.	DIA.	LENGTH	DRIVING	RIGID	ENGINE	ENGINE AND TENDER	TENDER	TRAILING WHEELS	DRIVERS	LEADING WHEELS	TOTAL ENGINE
150	2″	7′-5½″	10′-0″	10′-0″	15′-9″	39′-5½″	50000	——	51000	7000	58000

BOILER PRESSURE	FUEL	HEATING SURFACE, SQ. FT.				GRATE AREA	GAUGE OF TRACK	
POUNDS PER SQ. INCH ABOVE ATMOSPHERE	KIND	FLUES	FIRE BOX	ARCH PIPES	TOTAL	SQUARE FEET	METRES	FEET INCHES
165	Bituminous Coal	579	79	——	658	12.5	.914	3′-0″

FOR HAULING CAPACITY SEE PAGE 290.

81
81
P. B. & L. E.
81
BESSEMER.

BUILT BY

BROOKS LOCOMOTIVE WORKS

DUNKIRK, N. Y., U.S.A.

1899

FOR THE PITTSBURGH, BESSEMER & LAKE ERIE RAILROAD.

CODE WORD, QUERPO. SERIES, 685.

TYPE, CONSOLIDATION FREIGHT. CLASS, 22 C.

WITH 8-WHEELED TENDER TANK CAPACITY 5000 U. S. GALLONS AND 12½ TONS FUEL.

CYLINDERS			WHEELS								BOILER		FIRE BOX		
TYPE	DIA.	STROKE	TENDER		TRAILING		COUPLED DRIVERS		LEADING		TYPE	DIA.	TYPE	LENGTH	WIDTH
			NO.	DIA.	NO.	DIA.	NO.	DIA.	NO.	DIA.					
Simple Piston Valve	22″	28″	8	33″	—	—	8	54″	2	30″	Rad. Stay, Straight Top	72″	Long, Wide over Frames	114″	42″

FLUES			WHEEL BASE				AVERAGE WEIGHT IN WORKING ORDER, POUNDS				
NO.	DIA.	LENGTH	DRIVING	RIGID	ENGINE	ENGINE AND TENDER	TENDER	TRAILING WHEELS	DRIVERS	LEADING WHEELS	TOTAL ENGINE
242	2¼″	14′-9¼″	15′-4″	15′-4″	23′-9″	54′-0″	107000	——	159000	20000	179000

BOILER PRESSURE	FUEL	HEATING SURFACE, SQ. FT.				GRATE AREA	GAUGE OF TRACK	
POUNDS PER SQ. INCH ABOVE ATMOSPHERE	KIND	FLUES	FIRE BOX	ARCH PIPES	TOTAL	SQUARE FEET	METRES	FEET INCHES
180	Bituminous Coal	2091	192	——	2283	32.4	1.435	4′-8½″

FOR HAULING CAPACITY SEE PAGE 290.

ERIE
1401

BUILT BY

BROOKS LOCOMOTIVE WORKS

DUNKIRK, N. Y., U.S.A.

1899

FOR THE ERIE RAILROAD.

CODE WORD, QUESAL.

TYPE, CONSOLIDATION FREIGHT.

WITH 8-WHEELED TENDER

SERIES, 701.

CLASS, 21 C.

TANK CAPACITY 6000 U. S. GALLONS AND 15 TONS FUEL.

CYLINDERS			WHEELS								BOILER		FIRE BOX		
TYPE	DIA.	STROKE	TENDER NO.	TENDER DIA.	TRAILING NO.	TRAILING DIA.	COUPLED DRIVERS NO.	COUPLED DRIVERS DIA.	LEADING NO	LEADING DIA.	TYPE	DIA.	TYPE	LENGTH	WIDTH
Simple	21″	28″	8	36″	—	—	8	57″	2	30″	Rad. Stay, Wagon Top	68″	Long, Wide over Frames	120″	42″

FLUES			WHEEL BASE				AVERAGE WEIGHT IN WORKING ORDER, POUNDS				
NO.	DIA.	LENGTH	DRIVING	RIGID	ENGINE	ENGINE AND TENDER	TENDER	TRAILING WHEELS	DRIVERS	LEADING WHEELS	TOTAL ENGINE
304	2″	13′-2$\frac{3}{8}$″	15′-9″	15′-9″	24′-0″	53′-6″	132000	—	150000	20000	170000

BOILER PRESSURE	FUEL	HEATING SURFACE, SQ. FT.				GRATE AREA	GAUGE OF TRACK	
POUNDS PER SQ. INCH ABOVE ATMOSPHERE	KIND	FLUES	FIRE BOX	ARCH PIPES	TOTAL	SQUARE FEET	METRES	FEET INCHES
200	Bituminous Coal	2082	193	—	2275	41.4	1.435	4′-8$\frac{1}{2}$″

FOR HAULING CAPACITY SEE PAGE 290.

153
153
L. I. R. R.

BUILT BY

BROOKS LOCOMOTIVE WORKS

DUNKIRK, N. Y., U.S.A.

1898

FOR THE LONG ISLAND RAILROAD.

CODE WORD QUESQUE. SERIES, 677.

TYPE, CONSOLIDATION FREIGHT. CLASS, 21 C.

WITH 8-WHEELED TENDER

TANK CAPACITY 4000 U. S. GALLONS AND 8½ TONS FUEL.

CYLINDERS			WHEELS								BOILER		FIRE BOX		
TYPE	DIA.	STROKE	TENDER		TRAILING		COUPLED DRIVERS		LEADING		TYPE	DIA	TYPE	LENGTH	WIDTH
			NO.	DIA.	NO.	DIA.	NO.	DIA.	NO.	DIA.					
Simple	21″	28″	8	30″	—	—	8	51″	2	30″	Rad. Stay, Straight Top	72″	Wide over Wheels	120″	84″

FLUES			WHEEL BASE				AVERAGE WEIGHT IN WORKING ORDER, POUNDS				
NO.	DIA.	LENGTH	DRIVING	RIGID	ENGINE	ENGINE AND TENDER	TENDER	TRAILING WHEELS	DRIVERS	LEADING WHEELS	TOTAL ENGINE
294	2″	11′-7$\frac{3}{16}$″	14′-6″	14′-6″	22′-9″	50′-2″	86000	—	135000	20000	155000

BOILER PRESSURE	FUEL	HEATING SURFACE, SQ. FT.				GRATE AREA	GAUGE OF TRACK	
POUNDS PER SQ. INCH ABOVE ATMOSPHERE	KIND	FLUES	FIRE BOX	ARCH PIPES	TOTAL	SQUARE FEET	METRES	FEET INCHES
180	Anthracite Coal	1773	172	—	1945	69.5	1.435	4′-8½″

FOR HAULING CAPACITY SEE PAGE 290.

L. & N. R. R.
891
891
891

BUILT BY

BROOKS LOCOMOTIVE WORKS

DUNKIRK, N. Y., U.S.A.

1898

FOR THE LOUISVILLE & NASHVILLE RAILROAD.

CODE WORD, QUESTANT. SERIES, 668.

TYPE, CONSOLIDATION FREIGHT. CLASS, 21 C.

WITH 8-WHEELED TENDER TANK CAPACITY 4200 U. S. GALLONS AND $12\frac{1}{2}$ TONS FUEL.

CYLINDERS			WHEELS								BOILER		FIRE BOX		
			TENDER		TRAILING		COUPLED DRIVERS		LEADING						
TYPE	DIA.	STROKE	NO.	DIA.	NO.	DIA.	NO.	DIA.	NO.	DIA.	TYPE	DIA.	TYPE	LENGTH	WIDTH
Simple	21″	26″	8	33″	—	—	8	55″	2	33″	Improved Belpaire	$65\frac{15}{16}$″	Long between Frames	$123\frac{1}{2}$″	34″

FLUES			WHEEL BASE				AVERAGE WEIGHT IN WORKING ORDER, POUNDS				
NO.	DIA.	LENGTH	DRIVING	RIGID	ENGINE	ENGINE AND TENDER	TENDER	TRAILING WHEELS	DRIVERS	LEADING WHEELS	TOTAL ENGINE
222	$2\frac{1}{4}$″	14′-0″	15′-11″	15′-11″	23′-8″	51′-11″	94000	—	139000	17000	156000

BOILER PRESSURE	FUEL	HEATING SURFACE, SQ. FT.				GRATE AREA	GAUGE OF TRACK		
POUNDS PER SQ. INCH ABOVE ATMOSPHERE	KIND	FLUES	FIRE BOX	ARCH PIPES	TOTAL	SQUARE FEET	METRES	FEET	INCHES
170	Bituminous Coal	1820	185	—	2005	29.8	1.435	4′-$8\frac{1}{2}$″	

FOR HAULING CAPACITY SEE PAGE 290.

316
316
L. S. & M. S. R'y.

BUILT BY

BROOKS LOCOMOTIVE WORKS

DUNKIRK, N. Y., U.S.A.

1899

FOR THE LAKE SHORE & MICHIGAN SOUTHERN RAILWAY.

CODE WORD, QUESTMAN. SERIES, 683.

TYPE, CONSOLIDATION FREIGHT. CLASS, 20½ C.

WITH 8-WHEELED TENDER TANK CAPACITY 5000 U. S. GALLONS AND 12½ TONS FUEL.

CYLINDERS			WHEELS								BOILER		FIRE BOX		
TYPE	DIA.	STROKE	TENDER		TRAILING		COUPLED DRIVERS		LEADING		TYPE	DIA.	TYPE	LENGTH	WIDTH
			NO.	DIA.	NO.	DIA.	NO.	DIA.	NO.	DIA.					
Simple	20½″	28″	8	33″	—	—	8	56″	2	33″	Rad. Stay, Wagon Top	64⅛″	Long, Wide over Frames	114″	42″

FLUES			WHEEL BASE				AVERAGE WEIGHT IN WORKING ORDER, POUNDS				
NO.	DIA.	LENGTH	DRIVING	RIGID	ENGINE	ENGINE AND TENDER	TENDER	TRAILING WHEELS	DRIVERS	LEADING WHEELS	TOTAL ENGINE
286	2″	13′-3″	15′-3″	15′-3″	23′-3″	51′-6″	94000	—	138500	18000	156500

BOILER PRESSURE	FUEL	HEATING SURFACE, SQ. FT.				GRATE AREA	GAUGE OF TRACK	
POUNDS PER SQ. INCH ABOVE ATMOSPHERE	KIND	FLUES	FIRE BOX	ARCH PIPES	TOTAL	SQUARE FEET	METRES	FEET INCHES
180	Bituminous Coal	1971	188	24	2183	324	1.435	4′-8½″

FOR HAULING CAPACITY SEE PAGE 290.

St. M. & S. W. R. R.
7

BUILT BY

BROOKS LOCOMOTIVE WORKS

DUNKIRK, N. Y., U.S.A.

1896

FOR THE ST. MARY'S & SOUTHWESTERN RAILROAD.

CODE WORD, QUESTOR. SERIES, 575.

TYPE, CONSOLIDATION FREIGHT. CLASS, 20 C.

WITH 8-WHEELED TENDER TANK CAPACITY 4000 U. S. GALLONS AND $8\frac{1}{2}$ TONS FUEL.

CYLINDERS			WHEELS								BOILER		FIRE BOX		
			TENDER		TRAILING		COUPLED DRIVERS		LEADING						
TYPE	DIA.	STROKE	NO.	DIA.	NO.	DIA.	NO.	DIA.	NO.	DIA.	TYPE	DIA.	TYPE	LENGTH	WIDTH
Simple	20″	26″	8	33″	—	—	8	51″	2	30″	Crown Bar, Wagon Top	68″	Long, Wide	$107\frac{5}{8}$″	$37\frac{7}{8}$″

FLUES			WHEEL BASE				AVERAGE WEIGHT IN WORKING ORDER, POUNDS				
NO.	DIA.	LENGTH	DRIVING	RIGID	ENGINE	ENGINE AND TENDER	TENDER	TRAILING WHEELS	DRIVERS	LEADING WHEELS	TOTAL ENGINE
308	2″	11′-$1\frac{5}{16}$″	14′-8″	14′-8″	22′-8″	50′-4″	86000	—	142000	16750	158750

BOILER PRESSURE	FUEL	HEATING SURFACE, SQ. FT.				GRATE AREA	GAUGE OF TRACK		
POUNDS PER SQ. INCH ABOVE ATMOSPHERE	KIND	FLUES	FIRE BOX	ARCH PIPES	TOTAL	SQUARE FEET	METRES	FEET	INCHES
180	Bituminous Coal	1765	196	—	1961	28.2	1.435	4′-$8\frac{1}{2}$″	

FOR HAULING CAPACITY SEE PAGE 290.

SOUTHERN.
231

BUILT BY

BROOKS LOCOMOTIVE WORKS

DUNKIRK, N. Y., U.S.A.

1896

FOR THE SOUTHERN RAILWAY.

CODE WORD, QUETTE. SERIES, 582.

TYPE, CONSOLIDATION FREIGHT. CLASS, 20 C.

WITH 8-WHEELED TENDER

TANK CAPACITY 4200 U. S. GALLONS AND 8½ TONS FUEL.

CYLINDERS			WHEELS								BOILER		FIRE BOX		
			TENDER		TRAILING		COUPLED DRIVERS		LEADING						
TYPE	DIA.	STROKE	NO.	DIA.	NO.	DIA.	NO.	DIA.	NO.	DIA.	TYPE	DIA.	TYPE	LENGTH	WIDTH
Simple	20″	26″	8	33″	—	—	8	56″	2	30″	Rad. Stay, Wagon Top	60″	Long, Wide Sloping	102¾″	41⅞″

FLUES			WHEEL BASE				AVERAGE WEIGHT IN WORKING ORDER, POUNDS				
NO.	DIA.	LENGTH	DRIVING	RIGID	ENGINE	ENGINE AND TENDER	TENDER	TRAILING WHEELS	DRIVERS	LEADING WHEELS	TOTAL ENGINE
234	2″	13′-10″	15′-0″	15′-0″	22′-9½″	49′-6″	86000	—	120100	20000	140100

BOILER PRESSURE	FUEL	HEATING SURFACE, SQ. FT.				GRATE AREA	GAUGE OF TRACK		
POUNDS PER SQ. INCH ABOVE ATMOSPHERE	KIND	FLUES	FIRE BOX	ARCH PIPES	TOTAL	SQUARE FEET	METRES	FEET	INCHES
175	Bituminous Coal	1684	143	—	1827	30	1.448	4′-9″	

FOR HAULING CAPACITY SEE PAGE 290.

1316
Union Pacific
1316

BUILT BY

BROOKS LOCOMOTIVE WORKS

DUNKIRK, N. Y., U.S.A.

1898

FOR THE UNION PACIFIC RAILWAY.

CODE WORD, QUEYOR. SERIES, 673.

TYPE, CONSOLIDATION FREIGHT. CLASS, 20 C.

WITH 8-WHEELED TENDER TANK CAPACITY 4000 U. S. GALLONS AND 8½ TONS FUEL.

CYLINDERS			WHEELS								BOILER		FIRE BOX		
TYPE	DIA.	STROKE	TENDER		TRAILING		COUPLED DRIVERS		LEADING		TYPE	DIA.	TYPE	LENGTH	WIDTH
			NO.	DIA.	NO.	DIA.	NO.	DIA.	NO.	DIA.					
Simple	20″	24″	8	33″	—	—	8	51″	2	28″	Crown Bar, Wagon Top	64″	Long, Wide	107⅞″	41½″

FLUES			WHEEL BASE				AVERAGE WEIGHT IN WORKING ORDER, POUNDS				
NO.	DIA.	LENGTH	DRIVING	RIGID	ENGINE	ENGINE AND TENDER	TENDER	TRAILING WHEELS	DRIVERS	LEADING WHEELS	TOTAL ENGINE
272	2″	13′-6″	15′-5″	15′-5″	23′-0″	52′-10¼″	89000	—	131000	14000	145000

BOILER PRESSURE	FUEL	HEATING SURFACE, SQ. FT.				GRATE AREA	GAUGE OF TRACK	
POUNDS PER SQ. INCH ABOVE ATMOSPHERE	KIND	FLUES	FIRE BOX	ARCH PIPES	TOTAL	SQUARE FEET	METRES	FEET INCHES
180	Bituminous Coal	1911	170	23	2104	30.3	1.435	4′-8½″

FOR HAULING CAPACITY SEE PAGE 290.

201
O.R.&N.Co.
201

BUILT BY

BROOKS LOCOMOTIVE WORKS

DUNKIRK, N. Y., U.S.A.

1898

FOR THE OREGON RAILROAD & NAVIGATION COMPANY.

CODE WORD, QUIBBLE. SERIES, 674.

TYPE, CONSOLIDATION FREIGHT. CLASS, 19 C.

WITH 8-WHEELED TENDER TANK CAPACITY 4500 U. S. GALLONS AND 12½ TONS FUEL.

CYLINDERS			WHEELS								BOILER		FIRE BOX		
TYPE	DIA.	STROKE	TENDER		TRAILING		COUPLED DRIVERS		LEADING		TYPE	DIA.	TYPE	LENGTH	WIDTH
			NO.	DIA.	NO.	DIA.	NO.	DIA.	NO.	DIA.					
Simple Piston Valve	19″	30″	8	33″	—	—	8	55″	2	30″	Improved Belpaire	64″	Long, Wide	114″	42″

FLUES			WHEEL BASE				AVERAGE WEIGHT IN WORKING ORDER, POUNDS				
NO.	DIA.	LENGTH	DRIVING	RIGID	ENGINE	ENGINE AND TENDER	TENDER	TRAILING WHEELS	DRIVERS	LEADING WHEELS	TOTAL ENGINE
286	2″	13′-2¼″	14′-6″	14′-6″	23′-2″	51′-8¾″	103000	—	136200	17800	154000

BOILER PRESSURE	FUEL	HEATING SURFACE, SQ. FT.				GRATE AREA	GAUGE OF TRACK		
POUNDS PER SQ. INCH ABOVE ATMOSPHERE	KIND	FLUES	FIRE BOX	ARCH TUBES	TOTAL	SQUARE FEET	METRES	FEET	INCHES
200	Bituminous Coal	1958	182	22	2162	32	1.435	4′-8½″	

FOR HAULING CAPACITY SEE PAGE 290.

80
St. Joseph & Grand Island
80

BUILT BY

BROOKS LOCOMOTIVE WORKS

DUNKIRK, N. Y., U.S.A.

1899

FOR THE ST. JOSEPH & GRAND ISLAND RAILWAY.

CODE WORD, QUICA. SERIES, 694.

TYPE, CONSOLIDATION FREIGHT. CLASS, 19 C.

WITH 8-WHEELED TENDER TANK CAPACITY 4500 U. S. GALLONS AND $8\frac{1}{2}$ TONS FUEL.

CYLINDERS			WHEELS								BOILER		FIRE BOX		
TYPE	DIA.	STROKE	TENDER		TRAILING		COUPLED DRIVERS		LEADING		TYPE	DIA.	TYPE	LENGTH	WIDTH
			NO.	DIA.	NO.	DIA.	NO.	DIA.	NO.	DIA.					
Simple Piston Valve	19″	30″	8	33″	—	—	8	54″	2	30″	Rad. Stay, Wagon Top	66″	Long, Wide	114″	42″

FLUES			WHEEL BASE				AVERAGE WEIGHT IN WORKING ORDER, POUNDS				
NO.	DIA.	LENGTH	DRIVING	RIGID	ENGINE	ENGINE AND TENDER	TENDER	TRAILING WHEELS	DRIVERS	LEADING WHEELS	TOTAL ENGINE
306	2″	13′-2$\frac{5}{16}$″	14′-6″	14′-6″	23′-2″	51′-3″	95000	—	135000	17000	152000

BOILER PRESSURE	FUEL	HEATING SURFACE, SQ. FT.				GRATE AREA	GAUGE OF TRACK	
POUNDS PER SQ. INCH ABOVE ATMOSPHERE	KIND	FLUES	FIRE BOX	ARCH PIPES	TOTAL	SQUARE FEET	METRES	FEET INCHES
200	Bituminous Coal	2096	162	—	2258	32	1.435	4′-8$\frac{1}{2}$″

FOR HAULING CAPACITY SEE PAGE 290.

GREAT NORTHERN
515

BUILT BY

BROOKS LOCOMOTIVE WORKS

DUNKIRK, N. Y., U.S.A.

1893

FOR THE GREAT NORTHERN RAILWAY.

CODE WORD, QUICKEN. SERIES, 482.

TYPE, CONSOLIDATION FREIGHT. CLASS, $B\frac{13}{22}$ C.

WITH 8-WHEELED TENDER TANK CAPACITY 4000 U. S. GALLONS AND 8 TONS FUEL.

CYLINDERS			WHEELS								BOILER		FIRE BOX		
			TENDER		TRAILING		COUPLED DRIVERS		LEADING						
TYPE	DIA.	STROKE	NO.	DIA.	NO.	DIA.	NO.	DIA.	NO.	DIA.	TYPE	DIA.	TYPE	LENGTH	WIDTH
Tandem Compound	13″ 22″	26″	8	33″	—	—	8	55″	2	30″	Improved Belpaire	63″	Long	114″	32″

FLUES			WHEEL BASE				AVERAGE WEIGHT IN WORKING ORDER, POUNDS				
NO.	DIA.	LENGTH	DRIVING	RIGID	ENGINE	ENGINE AND TENDER	TENDER	TRAILING WHEELS	DRIVERS	LEADING WHEELS	TOTAL ENGINE
208	2¼″	11′-7″	15′-6″	15′-6″	23′-0″	50′-0″	85000	——	130000	17000	147000

BOILER PRESSURE	FUEL	HEATING SURFACE, SQ. FT.				GRATE AREA	GAUGE OF TRACK	
POUNDS PER SQ. INCH ABOVE ATMOSPHERE	KIND	FLUES	FIRE BOX	ARCH PIPES	TOTAL	SQUARE FEET	METRES	FEET INCHES
180	Bituminous Coal	1419	177	——	1596	25.3	1.435	4′-8½″

FOR HAULING CAPACITY SEE PAGE 290.

B. R. & P. Ry.
129
129

BUILT BY

BROOKS LOCOMOTIVE WORKS

DUNKIRK, N. Y., U.S.A.

1894

FOR THE BUFFALO, ROCHESTER & PITTSBURG RAILWAY.

CODE WORD, QUICKSET. SERIES, 519.

TYPE, CONSOLIDATION FREIGHT. CLASS, 18 C.

WITH 8-WHEELED TENDER TANK CAPACITY 3900 U. S. GALLONS AND $6\frac{1}{2}$ TONS FUEL.

CYLINDERS			WHEELS								BOILER		FIRE BOX		
TYPE	DIA.	STROKE	TENDER		TRAILING		COUPLED DRIVERS		LEADING		TYPE	DIA.	TYPE	LENGTH	WIDTH
			NO.	DIA.	NO.	DIA.	NO.	DIA.	NO.	DIA.					
Simple	18″	26″	8	33″	—	—	8	48″	2	30″	Improved Belpaire	58″	Long	108″	33″

FLUES			WHEEL BASE				AVERAGE WEIGHT IN WORKING ORDER, POUNDS				
NO.	DIA.	LENGTH	DRIVING	RIGID	ENGINE	ENGINE AND TENDER	TENDER	TRAILING WHEELS	DRIVERS	LEADING WHEELS	TOTAL ENGINE
212	2″	13′-2″	13′-4″	13′-4″	20′-10″	47′-10″	78000	—	115000	13000	128000

BOILER PRESSURE	FUEL	HEATING SURFACE, SQ. FT.				GRATE AREA	GAUGE OF TRACK		
POUNDS PER SQ. INCH ABOVE ATMOSPHERE	KIND	FLUES	FIRE BOX	ARCH PIPES	TOTAL	SQUARE FEET	METRES	FEET	INCHES
180	Bituminous Coal	1452	158	15.7	1625.7	24	1.435	4′-$8\frac{1}{2}$″	

FOR HAULING CAPACITY SEE PAGE 290.

10
10
M.St.P.& A.Ry.
10
MINNEAPOLIS, ST. PAUL & ASHLAND RAILWAY

BUILT BY

BROOKS LOCOMOTIVE WORKS

DUNKIRK, N. Y., U.S.A.

1899

FOR THE MINNEAPOLIS, ST. PAUL & ASHLAND RAILWAY.

CODE WORD, QUICKSTEP. SERIES, 696.

TYPE, CONSOLIDATION LOGGING. CLASS, 18 C.

WITH 8-WHEELED TENDER TANK CAPACITY 4000 U. S. GALLONS AND 9½ TONS FUEL.

CYLINDERS			WHEELS								BOILER		FIRE BOX		
TYPE	DIA.	STROKE	TENDER		TRAILING		COUPLED DRIVERS		LEADING		TYPE	DIA.	TYPE	LENGTH	WIDTH
			NO.	DIA.	NO.	DIA.	NO.	DIA.	NO.	DIA.					
Simple	18″	26″	8	33″	—	—	8	50″	2	30″	Rad. Stay, Wagon Top	58″	Long, Sloping	$107\frac{3}{16}$″	$32\frac{3}{8}$″

FLUES			WHEEL BASE				AVERAGE WEIGHT IN WORKING ORDER, POUNDS				
NO.	DIA.	LENGTH	DRIVING	RIGID	ENGINE	ENGINE AND TENDER	TENDER	TRAILING WHEELS	DRIVERS	LEADING WHEELS	TOTAL ENGINE
230	2″	13′-$10\frac{1}{8}$″	14′-6″	14′-6″	22′-1″	48′-1″	90000	—	118800	12000	130800

BOILER PRESSURE	FUEL	HEATING SURFACE, SQ. FT.				GRATE AREA	GAUGE OF TRACK	
POUNDS PER SQ. INCH ABOVE ATMOSPHERE	KIND	FLUES	FIRE BOX	ARCH PIPES	TOTAL	SQUARE FEET	METRES	FEET INCHES
180	Bituminous Coal	1657	150	—	1807	24.3	1.435	4′-8½″

FOR HAULING CAPACITY SEE PAGE 290.

BUILT BY

BROOKS LOCOMOTIVE WORKS

DUNKIRK, N. Y., U.S.A.

1898

FOR THE COLORADO & NORTHWESTERN RAILWAY.

CODE WORD, QUIDAM. SERIES, 656.

TYPE, CONSOLIDATION FREIGHT. CLASS, 16 C.

WITH 8-WHEELED TENDER

TANK CAPACITY 3100 U. S. GALLONS AND 7 TONS FUEL.

CYLINDERS			WHEELS								BOILER		FIRE BOX		
			TENDER		TRAILING		COUPLED DRIVERS		LEADING						
TYPE	DIA.	STROKE	NO.	DIA.	NO.	DIA.	NO.	DIA.	NO.	DIA.	TYPE	DIA.	TYPE	LENGTH	WIDTH
Simple Piston Valve	16″	20″	8	28″	—	—	8	37″	2	24″	Rad. Stay, Wagon Top	58″	Long, Wide	120″	24″

FLUES			WHEEL BASE				AVERAGE WEIGHT IN WORKING ORDER, POUNDS				
NO.	DIA.	LENGTH	DRIVING	RIGID	ENGINE	ENGINE AND TENDER	TENDER	TRAILING WHEELS	DRIVERS	LEADING WHEELS	TOTAL ENGINE
221	2″	10′-1$\frac{1}{8}$″	10′-8″	10′-8″	18′-4″	43′-9″	67000	——	86000	8500	94500

BOILER PRESSURE	FUEL	HEATING SURFACE, SQ. FT.				GRATE AREA	GAUGE OF TRACK	
POUNDS PER SQ. INCH ABOVE ATMOSPHERE	KIND	FLUES	FIRE BOX	ARCH TUBES	TOTAL	SQUARE FEET	METRES	FEET INCHES
180	Bituminous Coal	1159	130	——	1289	19.3	0.9144	3′-0″

FOR HAULING CAPACITY SEE PAGE 290.

BUILT BY

BROOKS LOCOMOTIVE WORKS

DUNKIRK, N. Y., U.S.A.

1898

FOR THE COLORADO & NORTHWESTERN RAILWAY.

CODE WORD, QUIDDIT. SERIES, 648.

TYPE, CONSOLIDATION FREIGHT. CLASS, 16 C.

WITH 8-WHEELED TENDER TANK CAPACITY 3100 U. S. GALLONS AND 7 TONS FUEL.

CYLINDERS			WHEELS								BOILER		FIRE BOX		
			TENDER		TRAILING		COUPLED DRIVERS		LEADING						
TYPE	DIA.	STROKE	NO.	DIA.	NO.	DIA.	NO.	DIA.	NO.	DIA.	TYPE	DIA.	TYPE	LENGTH	WIDTH
Simple	16″	20″	8	28″	—	—	8	37″	2	24″	Rad. Stay, Wagon Top	58″	Long, Wide	120″	24″

FLUES			WHEEL BASE				AVERAGE WEIGHT IN WORKING ORDER, POUNDS				
NO.	DIA.	LENGTH	DRIVING	RIGID	ENGINE	ENGINE AND TENDER	TENDER	TRAILING WHEELS	DRIVERS	LEADING WHEELS	TOTAL ENGINE
221	2″	10′-1⅛″	10′-8″	10′-8″	18′-4″	43′-9″	67000	—	86000	9000	95000

BOILER PRESSURE	FUEL	HEATING SURFACE, SQ. FT.				GRATE AREA	GAUGE OF TRACK	
POUNDS PER SQ. INCH ABOVE ATMOSPHERE	KIND	FLUES	FIRE BOX	ARCH PIPES	TOTAL	SQUARE FEET	METRES	FEET INCHES
180	Bituminous Coal	1159	130	—	1289	19.3	0.9144	3′-0″

FOR HAULING CAPACITY SEE PAGE 290.

726
DENVER & RIO GRANDE

BUILT BY

BROOKS LOCOMOTIVE WORKS

DUNKIRK, N. Y., U.S.A.

1899

FOR THE DENVER & RIO GRANDE RAILROAD.

CODE WORD, QUIDDLE.

SERIES, 698.

TYPE, 10-WHEELED PASSENGER.

CLASS, 21 D.

WITH 8-WHEELED TENDER

TANK CAPACITY 5500 U. S. GALLONS AND 10 TONS FUEL.

CYLINDERS			WHEELS								BOILER		FIRE BOX		
TYPE	DIA.	STROKE	TENDER NO.	TENDER DIA.	TRAILING NO.	TRAILING DIA.	COUPLED DRIVERS NO.	COUPLED DRIVERS DIA.	LEADING NO.	LEADING DIA.	TYPE	DIA.	TYPE	LENGTH	WIDTH
Simple Piston Valve	21″	26″	8	38″	—	—	6	63″	4	33″	Rad. Stay, Wagon Top	68″	Long, Wide Sloping	121″	41″

FLUES			WHEEL BASE				AVERAGE WEIGHT IN WORKING ORDER, POUNDS				
NO.	DIA.	LENGTH	DRIVING	RIGID	ENGINE	ENGINE AND TENDER	TENDER	TRAILING WHEELS	DRIVERS	LEADING WHEELS	TOTAL ENGINE
326	2″	13′-3$\frac{13}{16}$″	13′-0″	13′-0″	23′-7″	53′-10$\frac{3}{4}$″	115000	—	124000	36000	160000

BOILER PRESSURE	FUEL	HEATING SURFACE, SQ. FT.				GRATE AREA	GAUGE OF TRACK	
POUNDS PER SQ. INCH ABOVE ATMOSPHERE	KIND	FLUES	FIRE BOX	ARCH PIPES	TOTAL	SQUARE FEET	METRES	FEET INCHES
210	Bituminous Coal	2257	165	—	2422	33.5	1.435	4′-8$\frac{1}{2}$″

FOR HAULING CAPACITY SEE PAGE 290.

L. I. R. R.
128

BUILT BY

BROOKS LOCOMOTIVE WORKS

DUNKIRK, N. Y., U.S.A.

1899

FOR THE LONG ISLAND RAILROAD.

CODE WORD, QUIDNUNC.

SERIES, 692.

TYPE, 10-WHEELED FREIGHT.

CLASS, 21 D.

WITH 8-WHEELED TENDER

TANK CAPACITY 4000 U. S. GALLONS AND $8\frac{1}{2}$ TONS FUEL.

CYLINDERS			WHEELS								BOILER		FIRE BOX		
			TENDER		TRAILING		COUPLED DRIVERS		LEADING						
TYPE	DIA.	STROKE	NO.	DIA.	NO.	DIA.	NO.	DIA.	NO.	DIA.	TYPE	DIA.	TYPE	LENGTH	WIDTH
Simple	21″	26″	8	33″	—	—	6	$60\frac{1}{2}$″	4	30″	Straight	$66\frac{1}{8}$″	Wide over Wheels	120″	84″

FLUES			WHEEL BASE				AVERAGE WEIGHT IN WORKING ORDER, POUNDS				
NO.	DIA.	LENGTH	DRIVING	RIGID	ENGINE	ENGINE AND TENDER	TENDER	TRAILING WHEELS	DRIVERS	LEADING WHEELS	TOTAL ENGINE
272	2″	$13'\text{-}4\frac{3}{16}$″	13′-0″	6′-6″	23′-5″	51′-1″	90000	—	115000	36000	151000

BOILER PRESSURE	FUEL	HEATING SURFACE, SQ. FT.				GRATE AREA	GAUGE OF TRACK	
POUNDS PER SQ. INCH ABOVE ATMOSPHERE	KIND	FLUES	FIRE BOX	ARCH TUBES	TOTAL	SQUARE FEET	METRES	FEET INCHES
180	Fine Anthracite Coal	1889	141	—	2030	69.5	1.435	$4'\text{-}8\frac{1}{2}$″

FOR HAULING CAPACITY SEE PAGE 290.

150
GREAT NORTHERN.
GREAT NORTHERN.
150

BUILT BY

BROOKS LOCOMOTIVE WORKS

DUNKIRK, N. Y., U.S.A.

1898

FOR THE GREAT NORTHERN RAILWAY.

CODE WORD, QUIESCE. SERIES, 654.

TYPE, 10-WHEELED PASSENGER. CLASS, 20 D.

WITH 8-WHEELED TENDER

TANK CAPACITY 4500 U. S. GALLONS AND 8½ TONS FUEL.

CYLINDERS			WHEELS								BOILER		FIRE BOX		
TYPE	DIA.	STROKE	TENDER		TRAILING		COUPLED DRIVERS		LEADING		TYPE	DIA.	TYPE	LENGTH	WIDTH
			NO.	DIA.	NO.	DIA.	NO.	DIA.	NO.	DIA.					
Simple Piston Valve	20″	30″	8	33″	—	—	6	63″	4	30″	Improved Belpaire	70″	Long, Wide Sloping	123″	41¼″

FLUES			WHEEL BASE				AVERAGE WEIGHT IN WORKING ORDER, POUNDS				
NO.	DIA.	LENGTH	DRIVING	RIGID	ENGINE	ENGINE AND TENDER	TENDER	TRAILING WHEELS	DRIVERS	LEADING WHEELS	TOTAL ENGINE
303	2¼″	13′-10¼″	14′-6″	14′-6″	25′-4″	53′-6″	90000	—	129500	36500	166000

BOILER PRESSURE	FUEL	HEATING SURFACE, SQ. FT.				GRATE AREA	GAUGE OF TRACK	
POUNDS PER SQ. INCH ABOVE ATMOSPHERE	KIND	FLUES	FIRE BOX	ARCH PIPES	TOTAL	SQUARE FEET	METRES	FEET INCHES
210	Bituminous Coal	2452	201	24	2677	35.4	1.435	4′-8½″

FOR HAULING CAPACITY SEE PAGE 290.

THE HEAVIEST EXPRESS PASSENGER LOCOMOTIVE EVER BUILT

BUILT BY

BROOKS LOCOMOTIVE WORKS

DUNKIRK, N. Y., U.S.A.

October, 1899.

FOR THE LAKE SHORE & MICHIGAN SOUTHERN RAILWAY.

CODE WORD, QUIET. SERIES, 720.

TYPE, 10-WHEELED EXPRESS PASSENGER. CLASS, 20 D.

WITH 8-WHEELED TENDER TANK CAPACITY 5000 U. S. GALLONS AND $9\frac{1}{2}$ TONS FUEL.

CYLINDERS			WHEELS								BOILER		FIRE BOX		
TYPE	DIA.	STROKE	TENDER NO.	TENDER DIA.	TRAILING NO.	TRAILING DIA.	COUPLED DRIVERS NO.	COUPLED DRIVERS DIA.	LEADING NO.	LEADING DIA.	TYPE	DIA.	TYPE	LENGTH	WIDTH
Simple	20″	28″	8	36″	—	—	6	80″	4	36″	Rad. Stay, Wagon Top	66″	Long, Wide, Sloping	121″	41″

FLUES			WHEEL BASE				AVERAGE WEIGHT IN WORKING ORDER, POUNDS				
NO.	DIA.	LENGTH	DRIVING	RIGID	ENGINE	ENGINE AND TENDER	TENDER	TRAILING WHEELS	DRIVERS	LEADING WHEELS	TOTAL ENGINE
345	2″	15′-0¼″	16′-6″	16′-6″	27′-4″	55′-2¼″	112000	—	133000	38600	171600

BOILER PRESSURE	FUEL	HEATING SURFACE, SQ. FT.				GRATE AREA	GAUGE OF TRACK	
POUNDS PER SQ. INCH ABOVE ATMOSPHERE	KIND	FLUES	FIRE BOX	ARCH PIPES	TOTAL	SQUARE FEET	METRES	FEET INCHES
210	Bituminous Coal	2694	191	32	2917	33.6	1.435	4′-8½″

FOR HAULING CAPACITY SEE PAGE 290.

L. S. & M. S.
601
COMPOUND.
L. S. & M. S.
601
601

BUILT BY

BROOKS LOCOMOTIVE WORKS

DUNKIRK, N. Y., U.S.A.

1893

FOR THE LAKE SHORE & MICHIGAN SOUTHERN RAILWAY.

CODE WORD, QUIETUS.

TYPE, 10-WHEELED FREIGHT.

WITH 8-WHEELED TENDER

SERIES, 489.

CLASS, $A^{18}_{28\frac{1}{2}}$ D.

TANK CAPACITY 3700 U. S. GALLONS AND 7 TONS FUEL.

CYLINDERS			WHEELS								BOILER		FIRE BOX		
TYPE	DIA.	STROKE	TENDER		TRAILING		COUPLED DRIVERS		LEADING		TYPE	DIA.	TYPE	LENGTH	WIDTH
			NO.	DIA.	NO.	DIA.	NO.	DIA.	NO.	DIA.					
2 Cyl. Compound	18″ H. P. 28½″ L. P.	24″	8	33″	—	—	6	56″	4	28″	Crown Bar, Wagon Top	52″	Long, Sloping	96″	34½″

FLUES			WHEEL BASE				AVERAGE WEIGHT IN WORKING ORDER, POUNDS				
NO.	DIA.	LENGTH	DRIVING	RIGID	ENGINE	ENGINE AND TENDER	TENDER	TRAILING WHEELS	DRIVERS	LEADING WHEELS	TOTAL ENGINE
186	2″	12′-0$\frac{1}{16}$″	13′-3″	8′-0″	23′-1½″	45′-6½″	78000	—	80000	25000	105000

BOILER PRESSURE	FUEL	HEATING SURFACE, SQ. FT.				GRATE AREA	GAUGE OF TRACK	
POUNDS PER SQ. INCH ABOVE ATMOSPHERE	KIND	FLUES	FIRE BOX	ARCH PIPES	TOTAL	SQUARE FEET	METRES	FEET INCHES
180	Bituminous Coal	1168	112	18	1298	23.0	1.435	4′-8½″

FOR HAULING CAPACITY SEE PAGE 290.

1703
Union Pacific
1703

BUILT BY

BROOKS LOCOMOTIVE WORKS

DUNKIRK, N. Y., U.S.A.

1899

FOR THE UNION PACIFIC RAILROAD.

CODE WORD, QUILL.

TYPE, 10-WHEELED FREIGHT.

WITH 8-WHEELED TENDER

SERIES, 700.

CLASS, 20 D.

TANK CAPACITY 5000 U. S. GALLONS AND 12½ TONS FUEL.

CYLINDERS			WHEELS								BOILER		FIRE BOX		
TYPE	DIA.	STROKE	TENDER		TRAILING		COUPLED DRIVERS		LEADING		TYPE	DIA.	TYPE	LENGTH	WIDTH
			NO.	DIA.	NO.	DIA.	NO.	DIA.	NO.	DIA.					
Simple	20″	28″	8	33″	—	—	6	57″	4	30″	Crown Bar, Wagon Top	68″	Long, Wide	114″	41″

FLUES			WHEEL BASE				AVERAGE WEIGHT IN WORKING ORDER, POUNDS				
NO.	DIA.	LENGTH	DRIVING	RIGID	ENGINE	ENGINE AND TENDER	TENDER	TRAILING WHEELS	DRIVERS	LEADING WHEELS	TOTAL ENGINE
342	2″	13′-2⅜″	14′-6″	14′-6″	24′-9″	52′-4½″	102000	—	130000	35000	165000

BOILER PRESSURE	FUEL	HEATING SURFACE, SQ. FT.				GRATE AREA	GAUGE OF TRACK	
POUNDS PER SQ. INCH ABOVE ATMOSPHERE	KIND	FLUES	FIRE BOX	ARCH PIPES	TOTAL	SQUARE FEET	METRES	FEET INCHES
200	Bituminous Coal	2343	211	20	2574	31.3	1.435	4′-8½″

FOR HAULING CAPACITY SEE PAGE 290.

13
I. C. R. R.

BUILT BY

BROOKS LOCOMOTIVE WORKS

DUNKIRK, N. Y., U.S.A.

1898

FOR THE ILLINOIS CENTRAL RAILROAD.

CODE WORD, QUILLETOR. SERIES, 669.

TYPE, 10-WHEELED FREIGHT. CLASS, 20 D.

WITH 8-WHEELED TENDER TANK CAPACITY 5000 U. S. GALLONS AND 9½ TONS FUEL.

CYLINDERS			WHEELS								BOILER		FIRE BOX		
TYPE	DIA.	STROKE	TENDER		TRAILING		COUPLED DRIVERS		LEADING		TYPE	DIA.	TYPE	LENGTH	WIDTH
			NO.	DIA.	NO.	DIA.	NO.	DIA.	NO.	DIA.					
Simple	20″	28″	8	36″	—	—	6	63″	4	33″	Rad. Stay, Wagon Top	66″	Long, Sloping	121″	33½″

FLUES			WHEEL BASE				AVERAGE WEIGHT IN WORKING ORDER, POUNDS				
NO.	DIA.	LENGTH	DRIVING	RIGID	ENGINE	ENGINE AND TENDER	TENDER	TRAILING WHEELS	DRIVERS	LEADING WHEELS	TOTAL ENGINE
304	2″	14′-0″	13′-6″	13′-6″	24′-4″	51′-3″	102000	—	123000	32000	155000

BOILER PRESSURE	FUEL	HEATING SURFACE, SQ. FT.				GRATE AREA	GAUGE OF TRACK	
POUNDS PER SQ. INCH ABOVE ATMOSPHERE	KIND	FLUES	FIRE BOX	ARCH PIPES	TOTAL	SQUARE FEET	METRES	FEET INCHES
180	Bituminous Coal	2204	197	—	2401	27.2	1.435	4′-8½″

FOR HAULING CAPACITY SEE PAGE 290.

ST. LAWRENCE & ADIRONDACK RY.
KUSHAQUA
2

BUILT BY

BROOKS LOCOMOTIVE WORKS

DUNKIRK, N. Y., U.S.A.

1896

FOR THE ST. LAWRENCE & ADIRONDACK RAILWAY.

CODE WORD, QUILTED. SERIES, 578.

TYPE, 10-WHEELED PASSENGER. CLASS, 20 D.

WITH 8-WHEELED TENDER TANK CAPACITY 4500 U. S. GALLONS AND $8\frac{1}{2}$ TONS FUEL.

CYLINDERS			WHEELS								BOILER		FIRE BOX		
TYPE	DIA.	STROKE	TENDER NO.	TENDER DIA.	TRAILING NO.	TRAILING DIA.	COUPLED DRIVERS NO.	COUPLED DRIVERS DIA.	LEADING NO.	LEADING DIA.	TYPE	DIA.	TYPE	LENGTH	WIDTH
Simple	20″	26″	8	33″	—	—	6	57″	4	28″	Improved Belpaire	64″	Long, Wide Sloping	113″	$40\frac{1}{2}$″

FLUES			WHEEL BASE				AVERAGE WEIGHT IN WORKING ORDER, POUNDS				
NO.	DIA.	LENGTH	DRIVING	RIGID	ENGINE	ENGINE AND TENDER	TENDER	TRAILING WHEELS	DRIVERS	LEADING WHEELS	TOTAL ENGINE
278	2″	12′-$7\frac{1}{4}$″	14′-6″	14′-6″	24′-8″	52′-7″	90000	——	126000	28000	154000

BOILER PRESSURE	FUEL	HEATING SURFACE, SQ. FT.				GRATE AREA	GAUGE OF TRACK	
POUNDS PER SQ. INCH ABOVE ATMOSPHERE	KIND	FLUES	FIRE BOX	ARCH PIPES	TOTAL	SQUARE FEET	METRES	FEET INCHES
195	Bituminous Coal	1824	168	24	2016	32.0	1.435	4′-$8\frac{1}{2}$″

FOR HAULING CAPACITY SEE PAGE 290.

771
ERIE RAILROAD

BUILT BY

BROOKS LOCOMOTIVE WORKS

DUNKIRK, N. Y., U.S.A.

1896

FOR THE ERIE RAILROAD.

CODE WORD, QUINATE. SERIES, 586.

TYPE, 10-WHEELED PASSENGER. CLASS, 20 D.

WITH 8-WHEELED TENDER TANK CAPACITY 4500 U. S. GALLONS AND $8\frac{1}{2}$ TONS FUEL.

CYLINDERS			WHEELS								BOILER		FIRE BOX		
			TENDER		TRAILING		COUPLED DRIVERS		LEADING						
TYPE	DIA.	STROKE	NO.	DIA.	NO.	DIA.	NO.	DIA.	NO.	DIA.	TYPE	DIA.	TYPE	LENGTH	WIDTH
Simple	20″	26″	8	36″	—	—	6	62″	4	30″	Rad. Stay, Wagon Top	64″	Long, Wide	$107\frac{1}{8}$″	$40\frac{1}{4}$″

FLUES			WHEEL BASE				AVERAGE WEIGHT IN WORKING ORDER, POUNDS				
NO.	DIA.	LENGTH	DRIVING	RIGID	ENGINE	ENGINE AND TENDER	TENDER	TRAILING WHEELS	DRIVERS	LEADING WHEELS	TOTAL ENGINE
282	2″	13′-2″	13′-6″	13′-6″	24′-2″	50′-6″	93000	—	108000	36750	144750

BOILER PRESSURE	FUEL	HEATING SURFACE, SQ. FT.				GRATE AREA	GAUGE OF TRACK	
POUNDS PER SQ. INCH ABOVE ATMOSPHERE	KIND	FLUES	FIRE BOX	ARCH PIPES	TOTAL	SQUARE FEET	METRES	FEET INCHES
180	Bituminous Coal	1931	121	—	2052	29.7	1.435	4′-$8\frac{1}{2}$″

FOR HAULING CAPACITY SEE PAGE 290.

342
L.S. & M.S. R'y.
342

BUILT BY

BROOKS LOCOMOTIVE WORKS

DUNKIRK, N. Y., U.S.A.

1899

FOR THE LAKE SHORE & MICHIGAN SOUTHERN RAILWAY.

CODE WORD, QUINCE. SERIES, 684.

TYPE, 10-WHEELED FREIGHT. CLASS, $19\frac{1}{2}$ D.

WITH 8-WHEELED TENDER TANK CAPACITY 5000 U. S. GALLONS AND 10 TONS FUEL.

CYLINDERS			WHEELS								BOILER		FIRE BOX		
TYPE	DIA.	STROKE	TENDER		TRAILING		COUPLED DRIVERS		LEADING		TYPE	DIA.	TYPE	LENGTH	WIDTH
			NO.	DIA.	NO.	DIA.	NO.	DIA.	NO.	DIA.					
Simple	$19\frac{1}{2}''$	30″	8	36″	—	—	6	62″	4	33″	Rad. Stay, Wagon Top	$64\frac{1}{8}''$	Long, Wide, Sloping	114″	42″

FLUES			WHEEL BASE				AVERAGE WEIGHT IN WORKING ORDER, POUNDS				
NO.	DIA.	LENGTH	DRIVING	RIGID	ENGINE	ENGINE AND TENDER	TENDER	TRAILING WHEELS	DRIVERS	LEADING WHEELS	TOTAL ENGINE
286	2″	$13'\text{-}3\frac{5}{16}''$	15′-0″	15′-0″	25′-6″	$52'\text{-}9\frac{1}{4}''$	103000	——	120000	34000	154000

BOILER PRESSURE	FUEL	HEATING SURFACE, SQ. FT.				GRATE AREA	GAUGE OF TRACK	
POUNDS PER SQ. INCH ABOVE ATMOSPHERE	KIND	FLUES	FIRE BOX	ARCH PIPES	TOTAL	SQUARE FEET	METRES	FEET INCHES
180	Bituminous Coal	1971	178	24	2173	32.4	1.435	$4'\text{-}8\frac{1}{2}''$

FOR HAULING CAPACITY SEE PAGE 290.

WISCONSIN CENTRAL
227

BUILT BY

BROOKS LOCOMOTIVE WORKS

DUNKIRK, N. Y., U.S.A.

1898

FOR THE WISCONSIN CENTRAL LINES.

CODE WORD, QUINIC.

SERIES, 637.

TYPE, 10-WHEELED PASSENGER.

CLASS, 19 D.

WITH 8-WHEELED TENDER

TANK CAPACITY 4500 U. S. GALLONS AND 10 TONS FUEL.

CYLINDERS			WHEELS								BOILER		FIRE BOX		
TYPE	DIA.	STROKE	TENDER		TRAILING		COUPLED DRIVERS		LEADING		TYPE	DIA.	TYPE	LENGTH	WIDTH
			NO.	DIA.	NO.	DIA.	NO.	DIA.	NO.	DIA.					
Simple Piston Valve	19″	26″	8	33″	—	—	6	69″	4	33″	Improved Belpaire	66″	Long, Wide, Sloping	113″	41⅜″

FLUES			WHEEL BASE				AVERAGE WEIGHT IN WORKING ORDER, POUNDS				
NO.	DIA.	LENGTH	DRIVING	RIGID	ENGINE	ENGINE AND TENDER	TENDER	TRAILING WHEELS	DRIVERS	LEADING WHEELS	TOTAL ENGINE
308	2″	13′-2¼″	14′-6″	14′-6″	24′-9″	52′-1″	94000	—	115000	34000	149000

BOILER PRESSURE	FUEL	HEATING SURFACE, SQ. FT.				GRATE AREA	GAUGE OF TRACK		
POUNDS PER SQ. INCH ABOVE ATMOSPHERE	KIND	FLUES	FIRE BOX	ARCH PIPES	TOTAL	SQUARE FEET	METRES	FEET	INCHES
200	Bituminous Coal	2111	165	24	2300	32.4	1.435	4′-8½″	

FOR HAULING CAPACITY SEE PAGE 290.

GREAT NORTHERN
668
GREAT NORTHERN

BUILT BY

BROOKS LOCOMOTIVE WORKS

DUNKIRK, N. Y., U.S.A.

1893

FOR THE GREAT NORTHERN RAILWAY.

CODE WORD, QUININE.

TYPE, 10-WHEELED PASSENGER.

WITH 8-WHEELED TENDER

SERIES, 485.

CLASS, 19 D.

TANK CAPACITY 4000 U. S. GALLONS AND 8½ TONS FUEL.

CYLINDERS			WHEELS								BOILER		FIRE BOX		
TYPE	DIA.	STROKE	TENDER		TRAILING		COUPLED DRIVERS		LEADING		TYPE	DIA.	TYPE	LENGTH	WIDTH
			NO.	DIA.	NO.	DIA.	NO.	DIA.	NO.	DIA.					
Simple	19″	26″	8	33″	—	—	6	72″	4	33″	Improved Belpaire	60″	Long, Sloping	114″	32″

FLUES			WHEEL BASE				AVERAGE WEIGHT IN WORKING ORDER, POUNDS				
NO.	DIA.	LENGTH	DRIVING	RIGID	ENGINE	ENGINE AND TENDER	TENDER	TRAILING WHEELS	DRIVERS	LEADING WHEELS	TOTAL ENGINE
202	$2\frac{1}{4}$″	13′-10″	14′-6″	14′-6″	25′-0″	52′-4″	86000	—	111000	27000	138000

BOILER PRESSURE	FUEL	HEATING SURFACE, SQ. FT.				GRATE AREA	GAUGE OF TRACK	
POUNDS PER SQ. INCH ABOVE ATMOSPHERE	KIND	FLUES	FIRE BOX	ARCH PIPES	TOTAL	SQUARE FEET	METRES	FEET INCHES
180	Bituminous Coal	1646	152	—	1798	25.3	1.435	4′-$8\frac{1}{2}$″

FOR HAULING CAPACITY SEE PAGE 290.

815
C.R.I.&P.RY.

BUILT BY

BROOKS LOCOMOTIVE WORKS

DUNKIRK, N. Y., U. S. A.

1892

FOR THE CHICAGO, ROCK ISLAND & PACIFIC RAILWAY.

CODE WORD, QUINISM. SERIES, 439.

TYPE, 10-WHEELED FREIGHT. CLASS, 19 D.

WITH 8-WHEELED TENDER TANK CAPACITY 3600 U. S. GALLONS AND 7 TONS FUEL.

CYLINDERS			WHEELS								BOILER		FIRE BOX		
			TENDER		TRAILING		COUPLED DRIVERS		LEADING						
TYPE	DIA.	STROKE	NO.	DIA.	NO.	DIA.	NO.	DIA.	NO.	DIA.	TYPE	DIA.	TYPE	LENGTH	WIDTH
Simple	19″	24″	8	33″	—	—	6	$63\frac{3}{4}$″	4	30″	Rad. Stay, Wagon Top	60″	Long, Sloping	103″	$34\frac{1}{2}$″

FLUES			WHEEL BASE				AVERAGE WEIGHT IN WORKING ORDER, POUNDS				
NO.	DIA.	LENGTH	DRIVING	RIGID	ENGINE	ENGINE AND TENDER	TENDER	TRAILING WHEELS	DRIVERS	LEADING WHEELS	TOTAL ENGINE
254	2″	13′-1″	12′-4″	12′-4″	23′-0″	46′-10″	76000	——	106500	25500	132000

BOILER PRESSURE	FUEL	HEATING SURFACE, SQ. FT.				GRATE AREA	GAUGE OF TRACK	
POUNDS PER SQ. INCH ABOVE ATMOSPHERE	KIND	FLUES	FIRE BOX	ARCH PIPES	TOTAL	SQUARE FEET	METRES	FEET INCHES
160	Bituminous Coal	1740	140	18	1898	24	1.435	4′-$8\frac{1}{2}$″

FOR HAULING CAPACITY SEE PAGE 290.

P & E
11

BUILT BY

BROOKS LOCOMOTIVE WORKS

DUNKIRK, N. Y., U.S.A.

1898

FOR THE PRESCOTT & EASTERN RAILROAD.

CODE WORD, QUINNAT. SERIES, 504 C.

TYPE, 10-WHEELED FREIGHT. CLASS, 19 D.

WITH 8-WHEELED TENDER

TANK CAPACITY 4500 U. S. GALLONS AND 8½ TONS FUEL.

CYLINDERS			WHEELS								BOILER		FIRE BOX		
TYPE	DIA.	STROKE	TENDER		TRAILING		COUPLED DRIVERS		LEADING		TYPE	DIA.	TYPE	LENGTH	WIDTH
			NO.	DIA.	NO.	DIA.	NO.	DIA.	NO.	DIA.					
Simple	19″	24″	8	33″	—	—	6	56″	4	28″	Crown Bar, Wagon Top	58″	Long, Sloping	108″	33″

FLUES			WHEEL BASE				AVERAGE WEIGHT IN WORKING ORDER, POUNDS				
NO.	DIA.	LENGTH	DRIVING	RIGID	ENGINE	ENGINE AND TENDER	TENDER	TRAILING WHEELS	DRIVERS	LEADING WHEELS	TOTAL ENGINE
224	2″	12′-7⅛″	12′-0″	12′-0″	21′-10″	48′-10¾″	90000	—	106000	24000	130000

BOILER PRESSURE	FUEL	HEATING SURFACE, SQ. FT.				GRATE AREA	GAUGE OF TRACK	
POUNDS PER SQ. INCH ABOVE ATMOSPHERE	KIND	FLUES	FIRE BOX	ARCH PIPES	TOTAL	SQUARE FEET	METRES	FEET INCHES
180	Bituminous Coal	1464	142	—	1606	24	1.435	4′-8½″

FOR HAULING CAPACITY SEE PAGE 290.

205
C.C.C. & STL.

BUILT BY

BROOKS LOCOMOTIVE WORKS

DUNKIRK, N. Y., U.S.A.

1893

FOR THE CLEVELAND, CINCINNATI, CHICAGO & ST. LOUIS RAILWAY.

CODE WORD, QUINOGEN. SERIES, 517.

TYPE, 10-WHEELED PASSENGER. CLASS, 18½ D.

WITH 8-WHEELED TENDER. TANK CAPACITY 4000 U. S. GALLONS AND 8 TONS FUEL.

CYLINDERS			WHEELS								BOILER		FIRE BOX		
			TENDER		TRAILING		COUPLED DRIVERS		LEADING						
TYPE	DIA.	STROKE	NO.	DIA.	NO.	DIA.	NO.	DIA.	NO.	DIA.	TYPE	DIA.	TYPE	LENGTH	WIDTH
Simple	18½″	24″	8	33″	—	—	6	68″	4	30″	Crown Bar, Wagon Top	58″	Long, Wide, Sloping	102″	42″

FLUES			WHEEL BASE				AVERAGE WEIGHT IN WORKING ORDER, POUNDS				
NO.	DIA.	LENGTH	DRIVING	RIGID	ENGINE	ENGINE AND TENDER	TENDER	TRAILING WHEELS	DRIVERS	LEADING WHEELS	TOTAL ENGINE
252	2″	13′-10⅛″	15′-6″	9′-0″	25′-8″	49′-0″	90000	——	109500	26000	135500

BOILER PRESSURE	FUEL	HEATING SURFACE, SQ. FT.				GRATE AREA	GAUGE OF TRACK	
POUNDS PER SQ. INCH ABOVE ATMOSPHERE	KIND	FLUES	FIRE BOX	ARCH PIPES	TOTAL	SQUARE FEET	METRES	FEET INCHES
180	Bituminous Coal	1819	155	—	1974	29.1	1.435	4′-8½″

FOR HAULING CAPACITY SEE PAGE 290.

194
194
B. R. & P. RY

BUILT BY

BROOKS LOCOMOTIVE WORKS

DUNKIRK, N. Y., U.S.A.

1898

FOR THE BUFFALO, ROCHESTER & PITTSBURG RAILWAY.

CODE WORD, QUINOME. SERIES, 681.

TYPE, 10-WHEELED PASSENGER. CLASS, 18 D.

WITH 8-WHEELED TENDER TANK CAPACITY 4500 U. S. GALLONS AND $10\frac{1}{2}$ TONS FUEL.

CYLINDERS			WHEELS								BOILER		FIRE BOX		
TYPE	DIA.	STROKE	TENDER		TRAILING		COUPLED DRIVERS		LEADING		TYPE	DIA.	TYPE	LENGTH	WIDTH
			NO.	DIA.	NO.	DIA.	NO.	DIA.	NO.	DIA.					
Simple Piston Valve	18″	26″	8	$33\frac{1}{2}$″	—	—	6	69″	4	$30\frac{1}{2}$″	Improved Belpaire	62″	Long, Wide, Sloping	108″	42″

FLUES			WHEEL BASE				AVERAGE WEIGHT IN WORKING ORDER, POUNDS				
NO.	DIA.	LENGTH	DRIVING	RIGID	ENGINE	ENGINE AND TENDER	TENDER	TRAILING WHEELS	DRIVERS	LEADING WHEELS	TOTAL ENGINE
272	2″	13′-$2\frac{1}{4}$″	14′-0″	14′-0″	24′-3″	51′-$10\frac{3}{4}$″	103000	—	109000	33000	142000

BOILER PRESSURE	FUEL	HEATING SURFACE, SQ. FT.				GRATE AREA	GAUGE OF TRACK	
POUNDS PER SQ. INCH ABOVE ATMOSPHERE	KIND	FLUES	FIRE BOX	ARCH PIPES	TOTAL	SQUARE FEET	METRES	FEET INCHES
200	Bituminous Coal	1862	157	—	2019	30.8	1.435	4′-$8\frac{1}{2}$″

FOR HAULING CAPACITY SEE PAGE 290.

D.M.R.&N.R.R.
D. M. R. & N. R. R.
9

BUILT BY

BROOKS LOCOMOTIVE WORKS

DUNKIRK, N. Y., U.S.A.

1898

FOR THE DULUTH, MISSISSIPPI RIVER & NORTHERN RAILROAD.

CODE WORD, QUINOVIC. SERIES, 658.

TYPE, 10-WHEELED PASSENGER. CLASS, 18 D.

WITH 8-WHEELED TENDER TANK CAPACITY 4000 U. S. GALLONS AND 8½ TONS FUEL.

CYLINDERS			WHEELS								BOILER		FIRE BOX		
			TENDER		TRAILING		COUPLED DRIVERS		LEADING						
TYPE	DIA.	STROKE	NO.	DIA.	NO.	DIA.	NO.	DIA.	NO.	DIA.	TYPE	DIA.	TYPE	LENGTH	WIDTH
Simple	18″	24″	8	33″	—	—	6	63″	4	30″	Improved Belpaire	56″	Long, Sloping	97″	32″

FLUES			WHEEL BASE				AVERAGE WEIGHT IN WORKING ORDER, POUNDS				
NO.	DIA.	LENGTH	DRIVING	RIGID	ENGINE	ENGINE AND TENDER	TENDER	TRAILING WHEELS	DRIVERS	LEADING WHEELS	TOTAL ENGINE
225	2″	13′-4⅛″	14′-0″	14′-0″	24′-4″	51′-1⅛″	85000	—	97800	30000	127800

BOILER PRESSURE	FUEL	HEATING SURFACE, SQ. FT.				GRATE AREA	GAUGE OF TRACK		
POUNDS PER SQ. INCH ABOVE ATMOSPHERE	KIND	FLUES	FIRE BOX	ARCH PIPES	TOTAL	SQUARE FEET	METRES	FEET	INCHES
180	Bituminous Coal	1562	119	—	1681	20.92	1.435	4′-8½″	

FOR HAULING CAPACITY SEE PAGE 290.

B. R. & P. RY
9

BUILT BY

BROOKS LOCOMOTIVE WORKS

DUNKIRK, N. Y., U.S.A.

1897

FOR THE BUFFALO, ROCHESTER & PITTSBURG RAILWAY.

CODE WORD, QUINOYL. SERIES, 619.

TYPE, 10-WHEELED PASSENGER. CLASS, 18 D.

WITH 8-WHEELED TENDER TANK CAPACITY 4000 U. S. GALLONS AND 8½ TONS FUEL.

CYLINDERS			WHEELS								BOILER		FIRE BOX		
TYPE	DIA.	STROKE	TENDER NO.	TENDER DIA.	TRAILING NO.	TRAILING DIA.	COUPLED DRIVERS NO.	COUPLED DRIVERS DIA.	LEADING NO.	LEADING DIA.	TYPE	DIA.	TYPE	LENGTH	WIDTH
Simple	18″	24″	8	33″	—	—	6	68″	4	30″	Improved Belpaire	57″	Long, Sloping	97″	32″

FLUES			WHEEL BASE				AVERAGE WEIGHT IN WORKING ORDER, POUNDS				
NO.	DIA.	LENGTH	DRIVING	RIGID	ENGINE	ENGINE AND TENDER	TENDER	TRAILING WHEELS	DRIVERS	LEADING WHEELS	TOTAL ENGINE
225	2″	13′-4$\frac{1}{8}$″	13′-0″	13′-0″	23′-2″	50′-7″	89000	—	96000	29000	125000

BOILER PRESSURE	FUEL	HEATING SURFACE, SQ. FT.				GRATE AREA	GAUGE OF TRACK	
POUNDS PER SQ. INCH ABOVE ATMOSPHERE	KIND	FLUES	FIRE BOX	ARCH PIPES	TOTAL	SQUARE FEET	METRES	FEET INCHES
180	Bituminous Coal	1563	122	—	1685	21.2	1.435	4′-8½″

FOR HAULING CAPACITY SEE PAGE 290.

5
5
5
5
WASHINGTON COUNTY

BUILT BY

BROOKS LOCOMOTIVE WORKS

DUNKIRK, N. Y., U.S.A.

1898

FOR THE WASHINGTON COUNTY RAILROAD.

CODE WORD, QUINQUE. SERIES, 646.

TYPE, 10-WHEELED FREIGHT. CLASS, 18 D.

WITH 8-WHEELED TENDER TANK CAPACITY 4000 U. S. GALLONS AND 8½ TONS FUEL.

CYLINDERS			WHEELS								BOILER		FIRE BOX		
TYPE	DIA.	STROKE	TENDER		TRAILING		COUPLED DRIVERS		LEADING		TYPE	DIA.	TYPE	LENGTH	WIDTH
			NO.	DIA.	NO.	DIA.	NO.	DIA.	NO.	DIA.					
Simple	18″	24″	8	33″	—	—	6	56″	4	30″	Rad. Stay, Wagon Top	56″	Long, Sloping	97″	33″

FLUES			WHEEL BASE				AVERAGE WEIGHT IN WORKING ORDER, POUNDS				
NO.	DIA.	LENGTH	DRIVING	RIGID	ENGINE	ENGINE AND TENDER	TENDER	TRAILING WHEELS	DRIVERS	LEADING WHEELS	TOTAL ENGINE
225	2″	12′-7″	13′-6″	13′-6″	23′-4″	50′-1″	84000	—	94400	24400	118800

BOILER PRESSURE	FUEL	HEATING SURFACE, SQ. FT.				GRATE AREA	GAUGE OF TRACK		
POUNDS PER SQ. INCH ABOVE ATMOSPHERE	KIND	FLUES	FIRE BOX	ARCH PIPES	TOTAL	SQUARE FEET	METRES	FEET	INCHES
180	Bituminous Coal	1474	134	—	1608	21.8	1.435	4′-8½″	

FOR HAULING CAPACITY SEE PAGE 290.

I. & I. S. R. R.
40

BUILT BY

BROOKS LOCOMOTIVE WORKS

DUNKIRK, N. Y., U.S.A.

1898

FOR THE INDIANA & ILLINOIS SOUTHERN RAILROAD.

CODE WORD, QUINSY. SERIES, 649.

TYPE, 10-WHEELED FREIGHT. CLASS, 18 D.

WITH 8-WHEELED TENDER TANK CAPACITY 3700 U. S. GALLONS AND 7 TONS FUEL.

CYLINDERS			WHEELS								BOILER		FIRE BOX		
TYPE	DIA.	STROKE	TENDER NO.	TENDER DIA.	TRAILING NO.	TRAILING DIA.	COUPLED DRIVERS NO.	COUPLED DRIVERS DIA.	LEADING NO.	LEADING DIA.	TYPE	DIA.	TYPE	LENGTH	WIDTH
Simple	18″	24″	8	33″	—	—	6	56″	4	28″	Improved Belpaire	56″	Long, Sloping	96″	34″

FLUES			WHEEL BASE				AVERAGE WEIGHT IN WORKING ORDER, POUNDS				
NO.	DIA.	LENGTH	DRIVING	RIGID	ENGINE	ENGINE AND TENDER	TENDER	TRAILING WHEELS	DRIVERS	LEADING WHEELS	TOTAL ENGINE
225	2″	12′-7⅛″	13′-6″	13′-6″	23′-4″	49′-10″	77000	—	95700	26550	122250

BOILER PRESSURE	FUEL	HEATING SURFACE, SQ. FT.				GRATE AREA	GAUGE OF TRACK	
POUNDS PER SQ. INCH ABOVE ATMOSPHERE	KIND	FLUES	FIRE BOX	ARCH PIPES	TOTAL	SQUARE FEET	METRES	FEET INCHES
180	Bituminous Coal	1472	130	16.5	1618.5	21	1.435	4′-8½″

FOR HAULING CAPACITY SEE PAGE 290.

28

BUILT BY

BROOKS LOCOMOTIVE WORKS

DUNKIRK, N. Y., U.S.A.

1896

FOR THE OHIO RIVER RAILROAD.

CODE WORD, QUINTAL.

TYPE, 10-WHEELED FREIGHT.

WITH 8-WHEELED TENDER

SERIES, 577.

CLASS, 18 D.

TANK CAPACITY 3000 U. S. GALLONS AND 6 TONS FUEL.

CYLINDERS			WHEELS								BOILER		FIRE BOX		
TYPE	DIA.	STROKE	TENDER		TRAILING		COUPLED DRIVERS		LEADING		TYPE	DIA.	TYPE	LENGTH	WIDTH
			NO.	DIA.	NO.	DIA.	NO.	DIA.	NO.	DIA.					
Simple	18″	24″	8	33″	—	—	6	56″	4	28″	Crown Bar, Wagon Top	54″	Deep	72″	34½″

FLUES			WHEEL BASE				AVERAGE WEIGHT IN WORKING ORDER, POUNDS				
NO.	DIA.	LENGTH	DRIVING	RIGID	ENGINE	ENGINE AND TENDER	TENDER	TRAILING WHEELS	DRIVERS	LEADING WHEELS	TOTAL ENGINE
206	2″	13′-3″	13′-9″	8′-6″	25′-0″	46′-11″	64000	—	78000	28000	106000

BOILER PRESSURE	FUEL	HEATING SURFACE, SQ. FT.				GRATE AREA	GAUGE OF TRACK	
POUNDS PER SQ. INCH ABOVE ATMOSPHERE	KIND	FLUES	FIRE BOX	ARCH PIPES	TOTAL	SQUARE FEET	METRES	FEET INCHES
140	Bituminous Coal	1383	114	—	1497	16.7	1.435	4′-8½″

FOR HAULING CAPACITY SEE PAGE 290.

"THE RECORD BREAKER."

The above locomotive was one of five of our build which made "The Fastest of Fast Runs" from south Chicago to Buffalo on the 24th of October, 1895, over the Lake Shore & Michigan Southern Railway, a distance of 510.1 miles. This locomotive, No. 564, pulled the train from Erie, Pa., to Buffalo, N. Y., a distance of 86 miles, in 70 minutes and 46 seconds.

Maximum speed attained,	92.3 miles per hour.	* Maximum piston speed in feet per minute,	1878
8 consecutive miles at the rate of	85.44 " " "	* Average " " " " "	1484
33 " " " " " "	80.6 " " "	Total amount of coal used,	3250 lbs.
86 " " " " " "	72.92 " " "	Amount of water evaporated,	3700 gals.
* Maximum revolutions of driving wheels per minute,	469	Water evaporated per pound of coal,	9.48 lbs.
* Average " " " " " "	371	Total weight of train including engine,	506500 lbs.

*The diameter of drivers at time of run was 66 inches.

The engine made this remarkable performance without previous preparation, being taken off its regular run for the purpose, after having been in continuous service for over four years, and was in the exact condition shown in the photograph, which was taken in front of our works the day after the run.

BUILT BY

BROOKS LOCOMOTIVE WORKS

DUNKIRK, N. Y., U.S.A.

1891

FOR THE LAKE SHORE & MICHIGAN SOUTHERN RAILWAY.

CODE WORD, QUINTETTE. SERIES, 434.

TYPE, 10-WHEELED PASSENGER. CLASS, 17 D.

WITH 8-WHEELED TENDER

TANK CAPACITY 3700 U. S. GALLONS AND 7 TONS FUEL.

CYLINDERS			WHEELS								BOILER		FIRE BOX		
TYPE	DIA.	STROKE	TENDER		TRAILING		COUPLED DRIVERS		LEADING		TYPE	DIA.	TYPE	LENGTH	WIDTH
			NO.	DIA.	NO.	DIA.	NO.	DIA.	NO.	DIA.					
Simple	17″	24″	8	36″	—	—	6	68″	4	33″	Crown Bar, Wagon Top	52″	Long, Wide, Sloping	96″	42″

FLUES			WHEEL BASE				AVERAGE WEIGHT IN WORKING ORDER, POUNDS				
NO.	DIA.	LENGTH	DRIVING	RIGID	ENGINE	ENGINE AND TENDER	TENDER	TRAILING WHEELS	DRIVERS	LEADING WHEELS	TOTAL ENGINE
202	2″	$13'\text{-}10\frac{1}{16}''$	15′-0″	8′-6″	25′-3″	47′-8″	78000	—	96000	22000	118000

BOILER PRESSURE	FUEL	HEATING SURFACE, SQ. FT.				GRATE AREA	GAUGE OF TRACK	
POUNDS PER SQ. INCH ABOVE ATMOSPHERE	KIND	FLUES	FIRE BOX	ARCH PIPES	TOTAL	SQUARE FEET	METRES	FEET INCHES
180	Bituminous Coal	1462	123	18	1603	28	1.435	$4'\text{-}8\frac{1}{2}''$

FOR HAULING CAPACITY SEE PAGE 290.

118
L.S. & M.S. R'Y.
118

BUILT BY

BROOKS LOCOMOTIVE WORKS

DUNKIRK, N. Y., U.S.A.

1897

FOR THE LAKE SHORE & MICHIGAN SOUTHERN RAILWAY.

CODE WORD, QUINTIC. SERIES, 627.

TYPE, 10-WHEELED FREIGHT. CLASS, 17 D.

WITH 8-WHEELED TENDER

TANK CAPACITY 3100 U. S. GALLONS AND 7 TONS FUEL.

CYLINDERS			WHEELS								BOILER		FIRE BOX		
TYPE	DIA.	STROKE	TENDER NO.	TENDER DIA.	TRAILING NO.	TRAILING DIA.	COUPLED DRIVERS NO.	COUPLED DRIVERS DIA.	LEADING NO.	LEADING DIA.	TYPE	DIA.	TYPE	LENGTH	WIDTH
Simple	17″	24″	8	33″	—	—	6	56″	4	30″	Rad. Stay, Wagon Top	54″	Long, Sloping	96″	34½″

FLUES			WHEEL BASE				AVERAGE WEIGHT IN WORKING ORDER, POUNDS				
NO.	DIA.	LENGTH	DRIVING	RIGID	ENGINE	ENGINE AND TENDER	TENDER	TRAILING WHEELS	DRIVERS	LEADING WHEELS	TOTAL ENGINE
207	2″	12′-0$\frac{3}{16}$″	13′-3″	13′-3″	23′-7½″	45′-10″	73000	—	79500	28500	108000

BOILER PRESSURE	FUEL	HEATING SURFACE, SQ. FT.				GRATE AREA	GAUGE OF TRACK	
POUNDS PER SQ. INCH ABOVE ATMOSPHERE	KIND	FLUES	FIRE BOX	ARCH PIPES	TOTAL	SQUARE FEET	METRES	FEET INCHES
160	Bituminous Coal	1292	123.3	18.6	1433.9	22.6	1.435	4′-8½″

FOR HAULING CAPACITY SEE PAGE 290.

HEAVIEST FREIGHT LOCOMOTIVE IN THE WORLD.

This locomotive is the heaviest ever built, and is designed to haul a train weighing 2,045 tons, exclusive of engine, tender and caboose, up a grade of 38 feet per mile, combined with 3 degree curves, at a speed of 15 miles per hour.

The boiler is of the Player-Belpaire type, and the thickness of the plates, $1\frac{5}{16}''$ and $1''$, is, we believe, the greatest ever used upon locomotive boilers. The diameter at front end is $82''$, connection $88''$, and throat $91\frac{1}{4}''$.

Nearly all parts of this locomotive usually made of cast iron are, with the exception of the cylinders, made of cast or pressed steel or malleable iron.

BUILT BY

BROOKS LOCOMOTIVE WORKS

DUNKIRK, N. Y., U.S.A.

September, 1899,

FOR THE ILLINOIS CENTRAL RAILROAD.

CODE WORD, QUIRANT. | SERIES, 707.

TYPE, 12-WHEELED FREIGHT. | CLASS, 23 F.

WITH 8-WHEELED TENDER

TANK CAPACITY 7000 U. S. GALLONS AND 12 TONS FUEL.

CYLINDERS			WHEELS								BOILER		FIRE BOX		
TYPE	DIA.	STROKE	TENDER		TRAILING		COUPLED DRIVERS		LEADING		TYPE	DIA.	TYPE	LENGTH	WIDTH
			NO.	DIA.	NO.	DIA.	NO.	DIA.	NO.	DIA.					
Simple Piston Valve	23″	30″	8	33″	—	—	8	57″	4	30″	Improved Belpaire	82″	Long, Wide	132″	42″

FLUES			WHEEL BASE				AVERAGE WEIGHT IN WORKING ORDER, POUNDS				
NO.	DIA.	LENGTH	DRIVING	RIGID	ENGINE	ENGINE AND TENDER	TENDER	TRAILING WHEELS	DRIVERS	LEADING WHEELS	TOTAL ENGINE
424	2″	14′-8⅜″	15′-9″	15′-9″	26′-6″	55′-2¾″	132700	—	193200	39000	232200

BOILER PRESSURE	FUEL	HEATING SURFACE, SQ. FT.				GRATE AREA	GAUGE OF TRACK	
POUNDS PER SQ. INCH ABOVE ATMOSPHERE	KIND	FLUES	FIRE BOX	ARCH PIPES	TOTAL	SQUARE FEET	METRES	FEET INCHES
210	Bituminous Coal	3237	263	—	3500	37.5	1.435	4′-8½″

FOR HAULING CAPACITY SEE PAGE 290.

BROOKS
3000
GREAT NORTHERN
103

BUILT BY

BROOKS LOCOMOTIVE WORKS

DUNKIRK, N. Y., U.S.A.

1897

FOR THE GREAT NORTHERN RAILWAY.

CODE WORD, QUIRITE. SERIES, 621.

TYPE, 12-WHEELED FREIGHT. CLASS, 21 F.

WITH 8-WHEELED TENDER

TANK CAPACITY 4500 U. S. GALLONS AND 10 TONS FUEL

CYLINDERS			WHEELS								BOILER		FIRE BOX		
TYPE	DIA.	STROKE	TENDER NO.	TENDER DIA.	TRAILING NO.	TRAILING DIA.	COUPLED DRIVERS NO.	COUPLED DRIVERS DIA.	LEADING NO.	LEADING DIA.	TYPE	DIA.	TYPE	LENGTH	WIDTH
Simple Piston Valve	21″	34″	8	33″	—	—	8	55″	4	33″	Improved Belpaire	78″	Long, Wide	123″	$39\frac{3}{4}$″

FLUES			WHEEL BASE				AVERAGE WEIGHT IN WORKING ORDER, POUNDS				
NO.	DIA.	LENGTH	DRIVING	RIGID	ENGINE	ENGINE AND TENDER	TENDER	TRAILING WHEELS	DRIVERS	LEADING WHEELS	TOTAL ENGINE
376	$2\frac{1}{4}$″	$13'$-$10\frac{3}{8}$″	15′-10″	9′-8″	26′-8″	$54'$-$3\frac{1}{4}$″	96000	—	172000	40750	212750

BOILER PRESSURE	FUEL	HEATING SURFACE, SQ. FT.				GRATE AREA	GAUGE OF TRACK	
POUNDS PER SQ. INCH ABOVE ATMOSPHERE	KIND	FLUES	FIRE BOX	ARCH PIPES	TOTAL	SQUARE FEET	METRES	FEET INCHES
210	Bituminous Coal	3045	235	—	3280	34	1.435	$4'$-$8\frac{1}{2}$″

FOR HAULING CAPACITY SEE PAGE 290.

808
D. L. & W.
808

BUILT BY

BROOKS LOCOMOTIVE WORKS

DUNKIRK, N. Y., U.S.A.

1899

FOR THE DELAWARE, LACKAWANNA & WESTERN RAILROAD.

CODE WORD, QUIRLANE. SERIES, 715.

TYPE, 12-WHEELED FREIGHT. CLASS, 21 F.

WITH 8-WHEELED TENDER

TANK CAPACITY 5000 U. S. GALLONS AND 10 TONS FUEL.

CYLINDERS			WHEELS								BOILER		FIRE BOX		
			TENDER		TRAILING		COUPLED DRIVERS		LEADING						
TYPE	DIA.	STROKE	NO.	DIA.	NO.	DIA.	NO.	DIA.	NO.	DIA.	TYPE	DIA.	TYPE	LENGTH	WIDTH
Simple Piston Valve	21″	32″	8	33″	—	—	8	54″	4	30″	Rad. Stay, Wagon Top	78″	Long, Wide	123″	97″

FLUES			WHEEL BASE				AVERAGE WEIGHT IN WORKING ORDER, POUNDS				
NO.	DIA.	LENGTH	DRIVING	RIGID	ENGINE	ENGINE AND TENDER	TENDER	TRAILING WHEELS	DRIVERS	LEADING WHEELS	TOTAL ENGINE
410	2″	13′-10$\frac{3}{8}$″	15′-0″	15′-0″	25′-9″	50′-4$\frac{1}{4}$″	112000	—	166000	39000	205000

BOILER PRESSURE	FUEL	HEATING SURFACE, SQ. FT.				GRATE AREA	GAUGE OF TRACK	
POUNDS PER SQ. INCH ABOVE ATMOSPHERE	KIND	FLUES	FIRE BOX	ARCH PIPES	TOTAL	SQUARE FEET	METRES	FEET INCHES
200	Fine Anthracite Coal	2950	218	—	3168	82.4	1.435	4′-8$\frac{1}{2}$″

FOR HAULING CAPACITY SEE PAGE 290.

429
C.R.R.of N.J.

BUILT BY

BROOKS LOCOMOTIVE WORKS

DUNKIRK, N. Y., U.S.A.

1899

FOR THE CENTRAL RAILROAD OF NEW JERSEY.

CODE WORD, QUIRLER. — SERIES, 688.

TYPE, 12-WHEELED FREIGHT. — CLASS, 21 F.

WITH 8-WHEELED TENDER — TANK CAPACITY 7000 U. S. GALLONS AND 12½ TONS FUEL.

CYLINDERS			WHEELS								BOILER		FIRE BOX		
			TENDER		TRAILING		COUPLED DRIVERS		LEADING						
TYPE	DIA.	STROKE	NO.	DIA.	NO.	DIA.	NO.	DIA.	NO.	DIA.	TYPE	DIA.	TYPE	LENGTH	WIDTH
Simple Piston Valve	21″	32″	8	33″	—	—	8	55″	4	30″	Rad. Stay, Wagon Top	78″	Long, Wide	123″	97″

FLUES			WHEEL BASE				AVERAGE WEIGHT IN WORKING ORDER, POUNDS				
NO.	DIA.	LENGTH	DRIVING	RIGID	ENGINE	ENGINE AND TENDER	TENDER	TRAILING WHEELS	DRIVERS	LEADING WHEELS	TOTAL ENGINE
410	2″	13′-10¼″	15′-0″	15′-0″	25′-9″	53′-0″	138600	——	159000	42000	201000

BOILER PRESSURE	FUEL	HEATING SURFACE, SQ. FT.				GRATE AREA	GAUGE OF TRACK	
POUNDS PER SQ. INCH ABOVE ATMOSPHERE	KIND	FLUES	FIRE BOX	ARCH PIPES	TOTAL	SQUARE FEET	METRES	FEET INCHES
200	Fine Anthracite Coal	2950	218	—	3168	82.4	1.435	4′-8½″

FOR HAULING CAPACITY SEE PAGE 290.

1502

BUILT BY

BROOKS LOCOMOTIVE WORKS

DUNKIRK, N. Y., U.S.A.

1899

FOR THE UNION PACIFIC RAILROAD.

CODE WORD, QUITTAL. SERIES, 699.

TYPE, 12-WHEELED FREIGHT. CLASS, 21 F.

WITH 8-WHEELED TENDER TANK CAPACITY 5000 U. S. GALLONS AND $10\frac{1}{2}$ TONS FUEL.

CYLINDERS			WHEELS								BOILER		FIRE BOX		
TYPE	DIA.	STROKE	TENDER		TRAILING		COUPLED DRIVERS		LEADING		TYPE	DIA.	TYPE	LENGTH	WIDTH
			NO.	DIA.	NO.	DIA.	NO.	DIA.	NO.	DIA.					
Simple	21″	30″	8	33″	—	—	8	57″	4	30″	Improved Belpaire	76″	Long, Wide	124″	41″

FLUES			WHEEL BASE				AVERAGE WEIGHT IN WORKING ORDER, POUNDS				
NO.	DIA.	LENGTH	DRIVING	RIGID	ENGINE	ENGINE AND TENDER	TENDER	TRAILING WHEELS	DRIVERS	LEADING WHEELS	TOTAL ENGINE
382	2″	13′-$10\frac{3}{8}$″	15′-11″	15′-11″	26′-7″	53′-$10\frac{1}{2}$″	106000	——	163000	34000	197000

BOILER PRESSURE	FUEL	HEATING SURFACE, SQ. FT.				GRATE AREA	GAUGE OF TRACK	
POUNDS PER SQ. INCH ABOVE ATMOSPHERE	KIND	FLUES	FIRE BOX	ARCH PIPES	TOTAL	SQUARE FEET	METRES	FEET INCHES
200	Bituminous Coal	2749	208	23	2980	34	1.435	4′-$8\frac{1}{2}$″

FOR HAULING CAPACITY SEE PAGE 290.

MONON ROUTE
205

BUILT BY

BROOKS LOCOMOTIVE WORKS

DUNKIRK, N. Y., U.S.A.

1898

FOR THE CHICAGO, INDIANAPOLIS & LOUISVILLE RAILROAD.

CODE WORD, QUITTOR. SERIES, 650.

TYPE, 12-WHEELED FREIGHT. CLASS, 21 F.

WITH 8-WHEELED TENDER TANK CAPACITY 4500 U. S. GALLONS AND 10 TONS FUEL.

CYLINDERS			WHEELS								BOILER		FIRE BOX		
TYPE	DIA.	STROKE	TENDER		TRAILING		COUPLED DRIVERS		LEADING		TYPE	DIA.	TYPE	LENGTH	WIDTH
			NO.	DIA.	NO.	DIA.	NO.	DIA.	NO.	DIA.					
Simple Piston Valve	21″	26″	8	33″	—	—	8	54″	4	30″	Improved Belpaire	70″	Long, Wide	121″	42″

FLUES			WHEEL BASE				AVERAGE WEIGHT IN WORKING ORDER, POUNDS				
NO.	DIA.	LENGTH	DRIVING	RIGID	ENGINE	ENGINE AND TENDER	TENDER	TRAILING WHEELS	DRIVERS	LEADING WHEELS	TOTAL ENGINE
300	$2\frac{1}{4}$″	13′-$10\frac{1}{4}$″	15′-4″	15′-4″	25′-11″	54′-$6\frac{1}{2}$″	90000	——	140000	32000	172000

BOILER PRESSURE	FUEL	HEATING SURFACE, SQ. FT.				GRATE AREA	GAUGE OF TRACK	
POUNDS PER SQ. INCH ABOVE ATMOSPHERE	KIND	FLUES	FIRE BOX	ARCH PIPES	TOTAL	SQUARE FEET	METRES	FEET INCHES
200	Bituminous Coal	2436	214	24	2674	34.4	1.435	4′-$8\frac{1}{2}$″

FOR HAULING CAPACITY SEE PAGE 290.

150
150
B. R. & P. RY

BUILT BY

BROOKS LOCOMOTIVE WORKS

DUNKIRK, N. Y., U.S.A.

1898

FOR THE BUFFALO, ROCHESTER & PITTSBURGH RAILROAD.

CODE WORD, QUIVER. SERIES, 663.

TYPE, 12-WHEELED FREIGHT. CLASS, 20 F.

WITH 8-WHEELED TENDER TANK CAPACITY 4500 U. S. GALLONS AND 10 TONS FUEL.

CYLINDERS			WHEELS								BOILER		FIRE BOX		
			TENDER		TRAILING		COUPLED DRIVERS		LEADING						
TYPE	DIA.	STROKE	NO.	DIA.	NO.	DIA.	NO.	DIA.	NO.	DIA.	TYPE	DIA.	TYPE	LENGTH	WIDTH
Simple Piston Valve	20″	26″	8	33½″	—	—	8	55″	4	30½″	Improved Belpaire	66″	Long, Wide	114″	42″

FLUES			WHEEL BASE				AVERAGE WEIGHT IN WORKING ORDER, POUNDS				
NO.	DIA.	LENGTH	DRIVING	RIGID	ENGINE	ENGINE AND TENDER	TENDER	TRAILING WHEELS	DRIVERS	LEADING WHEELS	TOTAL ENGINE
308	2″	13′-2¼″	15′-6″	15′-6″	25′-8″	51′-5¾″	96000	—	126000	30000	156000

BOILER PRESSURE	FUEL	HEATING SURFACE, SQ. FT.				GRATE AREA	GAUGE OF TRACK	
POUNDS PER SQ. INCH ABOVE ATMOSPHERE	KIND	FLUES	FIRE BOX	ARCH PIPES	TOTAL	SQUARE FEET	METRES	FEET INCHES
200	Bituminous Coal	2108	190	—	2298	32.4	1.435	4′-8½″

FOR HAULING CAPACITY SEE PAGE 290.

GREAT NORTHERN.
302
GREAT NORTHERN.
302

BUILT BY

BROOKS LOCOMOTIVE WORKS

DUNKIRK, N. Y., U.S.A.

1898

FOR THE GREAT NORTHERN RAILWAY.

CODE WORD, QUIVOX. — SERIES, 655.

TYPE, 12-WHEELED FREIGHT. — CLASS, 19 F.

WITH 8-WHEELED TENDER — TANK CAPACITY 4500 U. S. GALLONS AND $8\frac{1}{2}$ TONS FUEL.

CYLINDERS			WHEELS								BOILER		FIRE BOX		
TYPE	DIA.	STROKE	TENDER		TRAILING		COUPLED DRIVERS		LEADING		TYPE	DIA.	TYPE	LENGTH	WIDTH
			NO.	DIA.	NO.	DIA.	NO.	DIA.	NO.	DIA.					
Simple Piston Valve	19″	32″	8	33″	—	—	8	55″	4	30″	Improved Belpaire	72″	Long, Wide	124″	42″

FLUES			WHEEL BASE				AVERAGE WEIGHT IN WORKING ORDER, POUNDS				
NO.	DIA.	LENGTH	DRIVING	RIGID	ENGINE	ENGINE AND TENDER	TENDER	TRAILING WHEELS	DRIVERS	LEADING WHEELS	TOTAL ENGINE
324	$2\frac{1}{4}$″	13′-$10\frac{1}{4}$″	15′-4″	9′-8″	26′-1″	53′-$9\frac{1}{4}$″	92000	—	142000	34000	176000

BOILER PRESSURE	FUEL	HEATING SURFACE, SQ. FT.				GRATE AREA	GAUGE OF TRACK	
POUNDS PER SQ. INCH ABOVE ATMOSPHERE	KIND	FLUES	FIRE BOX	ARCH PIPES	TOTAL	SQUARE FEET	METRES	FEET INCHES
200	Bituminous Coal	2622	224	26	2872	35.2	1.435	4′-$8\frac{1}{2}$″

FOR HAULING CAPACITY SEE PAGE 290.

BUFFALO CREEK
8

BUILT BY

BROOKS LOCOMOTIVE WORKS

DUNKIRK, N. Y., U.S.A.

1897

FOR THE BUFFALO CREEK RAILROAD.

CODE WORD, QUODDA. SERIES, 599.

TYPE, 6-WHEELED SWITCHER. CLASS, 20 H.

WITH 8-WHEELED TENDER

TANK CAPACITY 4000 U. S. GALLONS AND 5 TONS FUEL.

CYLINDERS			WHEELS								BOILER		FIRE BOX		
			TENDER		TRAILING		COUPLED DRIVERS		LEADING						
TYPE	DIA.	STROKE	NO.	DIA.	NO.	DIA.	NO.	DIA.	NO.	DIA.	TYPE	DIA.	TYPE	LENGTH	WIDTH
Simple	20″	24″	8	33″	—	—	6	50″	—	—	Rad. Stay, Straight Top	60″	Long, Wide	96″	42″

FLUES			WHEEL BASE				AVERAGE WEIGHT IN WORKING ORDER, POUNDS				
NO.	DIA.	LENGTH	DRIVING	RIGID	ENGINE	ENGINE AND TENDER	TENDER	TRAILING WHEELS	DRIVERS	LEADING WHEELS	TOTAL ENGINE
224	2″	11′-1¼″	10′-8″	10′-8″	10′-8″	42′-6¾″	75000	—	124800	—	124800

BOILER PRESSURE	FUEL	HEATING SURFACE, SQ. FT.				GRATE AREA	GAUGE OF TRACK	
POUNDS PER SQ. INCH ABOVE ATMOSPHERE	KIND	FLUES	FIRE BOX	ARCH PIPES	TOTAL	SQUARE FEET	METRES	FEET INCHES
160	Bituminous Coal	1293	133	—	1426	27.9	1.435	4′-8½″

FOR HAULING CAPACITY SEE PAGE 290.

GREAT NORTHERN
27
GREAT NORTHERN
27

BUILT BY

BROOKS LOCOMOTIVE WORKS

DUNKIRK, N. Y., U.S.A.

1898

FOR THE GREAT NORTHERN RAILWAY.

CODE WORD, QUODIG.

SERIES, 671.

TYPE, 6-WHEELED SWITCHER.

CLASS, 19 H.

WITH 8-WHEELED TENDER

TANK CAPACITY 4000 U. S. GALLONS AND 6 TONS FUEL.

CYLINDERS			WHEELS								BOILER		FIRE BOX		
TYPE	DIA.	STROKE	TENDER		TRAILING		COUPLED DRIVERS		LEADING		TYPE	DIA.	TYPE	LENGTH	WIDTH
			NO.	DIA.	NO.	DIA.	NO.	DIA.	NO.	DIA.					
Simple Piston Valve	19″	28″	8	33″	—	—	6	49″	—	—	Improved Belpaire	66″	Long, Wide	114″	42″

FLUES			WHEEL BASE				AVERAGE WEIGHT IN WORKING ORDER, POUNDS				
NO.	DIA.	LENGTH	DRIVING	RIGID	ENGINE	ENGINE AND TENDER	TENDER	TRAILING WHEELS	DRIVERS	LEADING WHEELS	TOTAL ENGINE
284	2″	11′-1¼″	11′-0″	11′-0″	11′-0″	42′-2¼″	80000	—	137000	—	137000

BOILER PRESSURE	FUEL	HEATING SURFACE, SQ. FT.				GRATE AREA	GAUGE OF TRACK	
POUNDS PER SQ. INCH ABOVE ATMOSPHERE	KIND	FLUES	FIRE BOX	ARCH PIPES	TOTAL	SQUARE FEET	METRES	FEET INCHES
200	Bituminous Coal	1634	188	20	1842	32.4	1.435	4′-8½″

FOR HAULING CAPACITY SEE PAGE 290.

L.S. & M.S. RY
165

BUILT BY

BROOKS LOCOMOTIVE WORKS

DUNKIRK, N. Y., U.S.A.

1899

FOR THE LAKE SHORE & MICHIGAN SOUTHERN RAILWAY.

CODE WORD, QUOIF. SERIES, 682.

TYPE, 6-WHEELED SWITCHER. CLASS, 19 H.

WITH 8-WHEELED TENDER, SLOPING BACK, TANK CAPACITY 3500 U. S. GALLONS AND 5 TONS FUEL.

CYLINDERS			WHEELS								BOILER		FIRE BOX		
			TENDER		TRAILING		COUPLED DRIVERS		LEADING						
TYPE	DIA.	STROKE	NO.	DIA.	NO.	DIA.	NO.	DIA.	NO.	DIA.	TYPE	DIA.	TYPE	LENGTH	WIDTH
Simple	19″	26″	8	30″	—	—	6	52″	—	—	Rad. Stay, Straight Top	64″	Long	80″	34½″

FLUES			WHEEL BASE				AVERAGE WEIGHT IN WORKING ORDER, POUNDS				
NO.	DIA.	LENGTH	DRIVING	RIGID	ENGINE	ENGINE AND TENDER	TENDER	TRAILING WHEELS	DRIVERS	LEADING WHEELS	TOTAL ENGINE
246	2″	14′-6¼″	11′-3″	11′-3″	11′-3″	43′-8¾″	79000	—	122700	—	122700

BOILER PRESSURE	FUEL	HEATING SURFACE, SQ. FT.				GRATE AREA	GAUGE OF TRACK	
POUNDS PER SQ. INCH ABOVE ATMOSPHERE	KIND	FLUES	FIRE BOX	ARCH PIPES	TOTAL	SQUARE FEET	METRES	FEET INCHES
170	Bituminous Coal	1856	145	18	2019	18.6	1.435	4′-8½″

FOR HAULING CAPACITY SEE PAGE 290.

I. C. R. R.
175

BUILT BY

BROOKS LOCOMOTIVE WORKS

DUNKIRK, N. Y., U.S.A.

1898

FOR THE ILLINOIS CENTRAL RAILROAD.

CODE WORD, QUOIFFURE. SERIES, 667.

TYPE, 6-WHEELED SWITCHER. CLASS, 19 H.

WITH 8-WHEELED TENDER, SLOPING BACK, TANK CAPACITY 3000 U. S. GALLONS AND $4\frac{1}{2}$ TONS FUEL.

CYLINDERS			WHEELS								BOILER		FIRE BOX		
TYPE	DIA.	STROKE	TENDER		TRAILING		COUPLED DRIVERS		LEADING		TYPE	DIA.	TYPE	LENGTH	WIDTH
			NO.	DIA.	NO.	DIA.	NO.	DIA.	NO.	DIA.					
Simple	19″	26″	8	33″	—	—	6	51″	—	—	Rad. Stay, Straight Top	62″	Long, Sloping	113″	$34\frac{1}{2}$″

FLUES			WHEEL BASE				AVERAGE WEIGHT IN WORKING ORDER, POUNDS				
NO.	DIA.	LENGTH	DRIVING	RIGID	ENGINE	ENGINE AND TENDER	TENDER	TRAILING WHEELS	DRIVERS	LEADING WHEELS	TOTAL ENGINE
220	2″	10′-$7\frac{1}{16}$″	11′-0″	11′-0″	11′-0″	39′-3″	67000	—	114000	—	114000

BOILER PRESSURE	FUEL	HEATING SURFACE, SQ. FT.				GRATE AREA	GAUGE OF TRACK	
POUNDS PER SQ. INCH ABOVE ATMOSPHERE	KIND	FLUES	FIRE BOX	ARCH PIPES	TOTAL	SQUARE FEET	METRES	FEET INCHES
180	Bituminous Coal	1209	146	—	1355	26	1.435	4′-$8\frac{1}{2}$″

FOR HAULING CAPACITY SEE PAGE 290.

MONON ROUTE

BUILT BY

BROOKS LOCOMOTIVE WORKS

DUNKIRK, N. Y., U.S.A.

1897

FOR THE CHICAGO, INDIANAPOLIS & LOUISVILLE RAILWAY.
(Formerly L., N. A. & C.)

CODE WORD, QUOIN. SERIES, 603.

TYPE, 6-WHEELED SWITCHER. CLASS, 19 H.

WITH 8-WHEELED TENDER, SLOPING BACK, TANK CAPACITY 3500 U. S. GALLONS AND 5 TONS FUEL.

CYLINDERS			WHEELS								BOILER		FIRE BOX		
			TENDER		TRAILING		COUPLED DRIVERS		LEADING						
TYPE	DIA.	STROKE	NO.	DIA.	NO.	DIA.	NO.	DIA.	NO.	DIA.	TYPE	DIA.	TYPE	LENGTH	WIDTH
Simple	19″	24″	8	33″	—	—	6	50″	—	—	Rad. Stay, Straight Top	60″	Long	96½″	32½″

FLUES			WHEEL BASE				AVERAGE WEIGHT IN WORKING ORDER, POUNDS				
NO.	DIA.	LENGTH	DRIVING	RIGID	ENGINE	ENGINE AND TENDER	TENDER	TRAILING WHEELS	DRIVERS	LEADING WHEELS	TOTAL ENGINE
208	2″	11′-0⅛″	11′-0″	11′-0″	11′-0″	41′-5″	70000	—	115500	—	115500

BOILER PRESSURE	FUEL	HEATING SURFACE, SQ. FT.				GRATE AREA	GAUGE OF TRACK	
POUNDS PER SQ. INCH ABOVE ATMOSPHERE	KIND	FLUES	FIRE BOX	ARCH PIPES	TOTAL	SQUARE FEET	METRES	FEET INCHES
180	Bituminous Coal	1189	137	—	1326	21.2	1.435	4′-8½″

FOR HAULING CAPACITY SEE PAGE 290.

34
34
C.C.C.& ST.L.
34
BIG FOUR

BUILT BY

BROOKS LOCOMOTIVE WORKS

DUNKIRK, N. Y., U.S.A.

1898

FOR THE CLEVELAND, CINCINNATI, CHICAGO & ST. LOUIS RAILWAY.

CODE WORD, QUOIT. SERIES, 635.

TYPE, 6-WHEELED SWITCHER. CLASS, 19 H.

WITH 8-WHEELED TENDER, SLOPING BACK, TANK CAPACITY 3500 U. S. GALLONS AND 5 TONS FUEL.

CYLINDERS			WHEELS								BOILER		FIRE BOX		
			TENDER		TRAILING		COUPLED DRIVERS		LEADING						
TYPE	DIA.	STROKE	NO.	DIA.	NO.	DIA.	NO.	DIA.	NO.	DIA.	TYPE	DIA.	TYPE	LENGTH	WIDTH
Simple	19″	24″	8	33″	—	—	6	50″	—	—	Rad. Stay, Straight Top	$60\frac{1}{8}$″	Long	103″	$33\frac{3}{4}$″

FLUES			WHEEL BASE				AVERAGE WEIGHT IN WORKING ORDER, POUNDS				
NO.	DIA.	LENGTH	DRIVING	RIGID	ENGINE	ENGINE AND TENDER	TENDER	TRAILING WHEELS	DRIVERS	LEADING WHEELS	TOTAL ENGINE
232	2″	11′-0″	11′-6″	11′-6″	11′-6″	39′-3″	70000	—	109000	—	109000

BOILER PRESSURE	FUEL	HEATING SURFACE, SQ. FT.				GRATE AREA	GAUGE OF TRACK	
POUNDS PER SQ. INCH ABOVE ATMOSPHERE	KIND	FLUES	FIRE BOX	ARCH PIPES	TOTAL	SQUARE FEET	METRES	FEET INCHES
160	Bituminous Coal	1326	145	—	1471	23.5	1.435	4′-$8\frac{1}{2}$″

FOR HAULING CAPACITY SEE PAGE 290

B. R. & P. RY

BUILT BY

BROOKS LOCOMOTIVE WORKS

DUNKIRK, N. Y., U.S.A.

1898

FOR THE BUFFALO, ROCHESTER & PITTSBURG RAILWAY.

CODE WORD, QUOIX. SERIES, 662.

TYPE, 6-WHEELED SWITCHER. CLASS, 19 H.

WITH 8-WHEELED TENDER, SLOPING BACK, TANK CAPACITY 4000 U. S. GALLONS AND 5 TONS FUEL.

CYLINDERS			WHEELS								BOILER		FIRE BOX		
TYPE	DIA.	STROKE	TENDER NO.	TENDER DIA.	TRAILING NO.	TRAILING DIA.	COUPLED DRIVERS NO.	COUPLED DRIVERS DIA.	LEADING NO.	LEADING DIA.	TYPE	DIA.	TYPE	LENGTH	WIDTH
Simple Piston Valve	19″	24″	8	33″	—	—	6	50″	—	—	Rad. Stay, Wagon Top	58″	Long, Sloping	97″	33″

FLUES			WHEEL BASE				AVERAGE WEIGHT IN WORKING ORDER, POUNDS				
NO.	DIA.	LENGTH	DRIVING	RIGID	ENGINE	ENGINE AND TENDER	TENDER	TRAILING WHEELS	DRIVERS	LEADING WHEELS	TOTAL ENGINE
225	2″	11′-1⅛″	11′-0″	11′-0″	11′-0″	40′-8″	75000	—	108000	—	108000

BOILER PRESSURE	FUEL	HEATING SURFACE, SQ. FT.				GRATE AREA	GAUGE OF TRACK	
POUNDS PER SQ. INCH ABOVE ATMOSPHERE	KIND	FLUES	FIRE BOX	ARCH PIPES	TOTAL	SQUARE FEET	METRES	FEET INCHES
180	Bituminous Coal	1297	134	—	1431	21.7	1.435	4′-8½″

FOR HAULING CAPACITY SEE PAGE 290.

L. E. & W.
4

BUILT BY

BROOKS LOCOMOTIVE WORKS

DUNKIRK, N. Y., U.S.A.

1899

FOR THE LAKE ERIE & WESTERN RAILROAD.

CODE WORD, QUOKE. SERIES, 689.

TYPE, 6-WHEELED SWITCHER. CLASS, 18 H.

WITH 8-WHEELED TENDER, SLOPING BACK, TANK CAPACITY 4000 U. S. GALLONS AND $4\frac{1}{2}$ TONS FUEL.

CYLINDERS			WHEELS								BOILER		FIRE BOX		
TYPE	DIA.	STROKE	TENDER		TRAILING		COUPLED DRIVERS		LEADING		TYPE	DIA.	TYPE	LENGTH	WIDTH
			NO.	DIA.	NO.	DIA.	NO.	DIA.	NO.	DIA.					
Simple	18″	24″	8	33″	—	—	6	50″	—	—	Crown Bar, Wagon Top	56″	Long	84″	33″

FLUES			WHEEL BASE				AVERAGE WEIGHT IN WORKING ORDER, POUNDS				
NO.	DIA.	LENGTH	DRIVING	RIGID	ENGINE	ENGINE AND TENDER	TENDER	TRAILING WHEELS	DRIVERS	LEADING WHEELS	TOTAL ENGINE
213	2″	11′-$1\frac{1}{8}$″	11′-0″	11′-0″	11′-0″	40′-1″	76000	—	110600	—	110600

BOILER PRESSURE	FUEL	HEATING SURFACE, SQ. FT.				GRATE AREA	GAUGE OF TRACK	
POUNDS PER SQ. INCH ABOVE ATMOSPHERE	KIND	FLUES	FIRE BOX	ARCH PIPES	TOTAL	SQUARE FEET	METRES	FEET INCHES
165	Bituminous Coal	1226.6	124	—	1350.6	18.6	1.435	4′-$8\frac{1}{2}$″

FOR HAULING CAPACITY SEE PAGE 290.

BUILT BY

BROOKS LOCOMOTIVE WORKS

DUNKIRK, N. Y., U.S.A.

1898

FOR THE PEORIA & PEKIN UNION RAILWAY.

CODE WORD, QUOLLEG. SERIES, 636.

TYPE, 6-WHEELED SWITCHER. CLASS, 18 H.

WITH 8-WHEELED TENDER, SLOPING BACK, TANK CAPACITY 3100 U. S. GALLONS AND $3\frac{1}{2}$ TONS FUEL.

CYLINDERS			WHEELS								BOILER		FIRE BOX		
TYPE	DIA.	STROKE	TENDER		TRAILING		COUPLED DRIVERS		LEADING		TYPE	DIA.	TYPE	LENGTH	WIDTH
			NO.	DIA.	NO.	DIA.	NO.	DIA.	NO.	DIA.					
Simple	18″	24″	8	33″	—	—	6	52″	—	—	Improved Belpaire	56″	Long	84″	33″

FLUES			WHEEL BASE				AVERAGE WEIGHT IN WORKING ORDER, POUNDS				
NO.	DIA.	LENGTH	DRIVING	RIGID	ENGINE	ENGINE AND TENDER	TENDER	TRAILING WHEELS	DRIVERS	LEADING WHEELS	TOTAL ENGINE
190	2″	11′-1$\frac{1}{8}$″	11′-0″	11′-0″	11′-0″	38′-2″	65000	—	109000	—	109000

BOILER PRESSURE	FUEL	HEATING SURFACE, SQ. FT.				GRATE AREA	GAUGE OF TRACK	
POUNDS PER SQ. INCH ABOVE ATMOSPHERE	KIND	FLUES	FIRE BOX	ARCH PIPES	TOTAL	SQUARE FEET	METRES	FEET INCHES
165	Bituminous Coal	1098	122	—	1220	18.6	1.435	4′-8$\frac{1}{2}$″

FOR HAULING CAPACITY SEE PAGE 290.

BUILT BY

BROOKS LOCOMOTIVE WORKS

DUNKIRK, N. Y., U.S.A.

1898

FOR THE ST. LOUIS NATIONAL STOCK YARDS.

CODE WORD, QUONDAM. SERIES, 678.

TYPE, 6-WHEELED SWITCHER. CLASS, 18 H.

WITH 8-WHEELED TENDER, SLOPING BACK, TANK CAPACITY 2500 U. S. GALLONS AND 4 TONS FUEL.

CYLINDERS			WHEELS								BOILER		FIRE BOX		
			TENDER		TRAILING		COUPLED DRIVERS		LEADING						
TYPE	DIA.	STROKE	NO.	DIA.	NO.	DIA.	NO.	DIA.	NO.	DIA.	TYPE	DIA.	TYPE	LENGTH	WIDTH
Simple	18″	24″	8	33″	—	—	6	50″	—	—	Crown Bar, Straight Top	56″	Long	84″	33″

FLUES			WHEEL BASE				AVERAGE WEIGHT IN WORKING ORDER, POUNDS				
NO.	DIA.	LENGTH	DRIVING	RIGID	ENGINE	ENGINE AND TENDER	TENDER	TRAILING WHEELS	DRIVERS	LEADING WHEELS	TOTAL ENGINE
200	2″	11′-1$\frac{1}{16}$″	11′-0″	11′-0″	11′-0″	38′-5″	62000	—	106000	—	106000

BOILER PRESSURE	FUEL	HEATING SURFACE, SQ. FT.				GRATE AREA	GAUGE OF TRACK	
POUNDS PER SQ. INCH ABOVE ATMOSPHERE	KIND	FLUES	FIRE BOX	ARCH PIPES	TOTAL	SQUARE FEET	METRES	FEET INCHES
165	Bituminous Coal	1153	119	—	1272	18.7	1.435	4′-8½″

FOR HAULING CAPACITY SEE PAGE 290.

CONGRESS GOLD COMPANY.
CONGRESS

OIL BURNING LOCOMOTIVE.

BUILT BY

BROOKS LOCOMOTIVE WORKS

DUNKIRK, N. Y., U.S.A.

1896

FOR THE CONGRESS GOLD COMPANY.

CODE WORD, QUOPLIN.

TYPE, 6-WHEELED SWITCHER.

WITH 8-WHEELED TENDER

SERIES, 584.

CLASS, 17 H.

TANK CAPACITY 3600 U. S. GALLONS AND 5 TONS FUEL (OIL).

CYLINDERS			WHEELS								BOILER		FIRE BOX		
TYPE	DIA.	STROKE	TENDER		TRAILING		COUPLED DRIVERS		LEADING		TYPE	DIA.	TYPE	LENGTH	WIDTH
			NO.	DIA.	NO.	DIA.	NO.	DIA.	NO.	DIA.					
Simple	17″	24″	8	33″	—	—	6	51″	—	—	Crown Bar, Wagon Top	56″	Long	78″	32″

FLUES			WHEEL BASE				AVERAGE WEIGHT IN WORKING ORDER, POUNDS				
NO.	DIA.	LENGTH	DRIVING	RIGID	ENGINE	ENGINE AND TENDER	TENDER	TRAILING WHEELS	DRIVERS	LEADING WHEELS	TOTAL ENGINE
226	2″	11′-1½″	11′-0″	11′-0″	11′-0″	40′-8″	86000	—	112000	—	112000

BOILER PRESSURE	FUEL	HEATING SURFACE, SQ. FT.				GRATE AREA	GAUGE OF TRACK		
POUNDS PER SQ. INCH ABOVE ATMOSPHERE	KIND	FLUES	FIRE BOX	ARCH PIPES	TOTAL	SQUARE FEET	METRES	FEET	INCHES
180	Crude Petroleum	1308	129	—	1437	16.8	1.435	4′-8½″	

FOR HAULING CAPACITY SEE PAGE 290.

ULSTER & DELAWARE. R. R.
13
BROOKS

BUILT BY

BROOKS LOCOMOTIVE WORKS

DUNKIRK, N. Y., U.S.A.

1885

FOR THE ULSTER & DELAWARE RAILROAD.

CODE WORD, QUOPPET. SERIES, 208.

TYPE, 6-WHEELED SADDLE TANK SWITCHER. CLASS, 17 H. T.

TANK CAPACITY 1000 U. S. GALLONS AND 1 TON FUEL.

CYLINDERS			WHEELS								BOILER		FIRE BOX		
TYPE	DIA.	STROKE	TENDER NO.	TENDER DIA.	TRAILING NO.	TRAILING DIA.	COUPLED DRIVERS NO.	COUPLED DRIVERS DIA.	LEADING NO.	LEADING DIA.	TYPE	DIA.	TYPE	LENGTH	WIDTH
Simple	17″	24″	—	—	—	—	6	44″	—	—	Crown Bar, Straight Top	50″	Long, Sloping	96″	34″

FLUES			WHEEL BASE				AVERAGE WEIGHT IN WORKING ORDER, POUNDS				
NO.	DIA.	LENGTH	DRIVING	RIGID	ENGINE	ENGINE AND TENDER	TENDER	TRAILING WHEELS	DRIVERS	LEADING WHEELS	TOTAL ENGINE
143	2″	9′-8″	10′-0″	10′-0″	10′-0″	—	—	—	84000	—	84000

BOILER PRESSURE	FUEL	HEATING SURFACE, SQ. FT.				GRATE AREA	GAUGE OF TRACK	
POUNDS PER SQ. INCH ABOVE ATMOSPHERE	KIND	FLUES	FIRE BOX	ARCH PIPES	TOTAL	SQUARE FEET	METRES	FEET INCHES
135	Anthracite Coal	717.4	74	—	791.4	22.6	1.435	4′-8½″

FOR HAULING CAPACITY SEE PAGE 290.

1
S. O. Co.
S. O. Co.

BUILT BY

BROOKS LOCOMOTIVE WORKS

DUNKIRK, N. Y., U.S.A.

1891

FOR THE STANDARD OIL COMPANY.

CODE WORD, QUORAM. SERIES, 421.

TYPE, 4-COUPLED SWITCHER. CLASS, 17 E.

WITH 8-WHEELED TENDER, SLOPING BACK, TANK CAPACITY 2500 U. S. GALLONS AND 4 TONS FUEL.

CYLINDERS			WHEELS								BOILER		FIRE BOX		
TYPE	DIA.	STROKE	TENDER NO.	TENDER DIA.	TRAILING NO.	TRAILING DIA.	COUPLED DRIVERS NO.	COUPLED DRIVERS DIA.	LEADING NO.	LEADING DIA.	TYPE	DIA.	TYPE	LENGTH	WIDTH
Simple	17″	24″	8	33″	—	—	4	50″	—	—	Straight	54″	Deep	72″	34″

FLUES			WHEEL BASE				AVERAGE WEIGHT IN WORKING ORDER, POUNDS				
NO.	DIA.	LENGTH	DRIVING	RIGID	ENGINE	ENGINE AND TENDER	TENDER	TRAILING WHEELS	DRIVERS	LEADING WHEELS	TOTAL ENGINE
186	2″	11′-1$\frac{1}{16}$″	7′-0″	7′-0″	7′-0″	34′-3″	62000	—	78000	—	78000

BOILER PRESSURE	FUEL	HEATING SURFACE, SQ. FT.				GRATE AREA	GAUGE OF TRACK	
POUNDS PER SQ. INCH ABOVE ATMOSPHERE	KIND	FLUES	FIRE BOX	ARCH PIPES	TOTAL	SQUARE FEET	METRES	FEET INCHES
165	Bituminous Coal	1071	102	—	1173	16.3	1.435	4′-8½″

FOR HAULING CAPACITY SEE PAGE 290.

C. S. Co.

BUILT BY

BROOKS LOCOMOTIVE WORKS

DUNKIRK, N. Y., U.S.A.

1893

FOR THE CARNEGIE STEEL COMPANY.

CODE WORD, QUOTA. SERIES, 490.

TYPE, 4-WHEELED SWITCHER. CLASS, 16 E.

WITH 8-WHEELED TENDER, SLOPING BACK TANK, CAPACITY 2500 U. S. GALLONS AND 4 TONS FUEL.

CYLINDERS			WHEELS								BOILER		FIRE BOX		
TYPE	DIA.	STROKE	TENDER NO.	TENDER DIA.	TRAILING NO.	TRAILING DIA.	COUPLED DRIVERS NO.	COUPLED DRIVERS DIA.	LEADING NO.	LEADING DIA.	TYPE	DIA.	TYPE	LENGTH	WIDTH
Simple	16″	24″	8	30″	—	—	4	50″	—	—	Rad. Stay, Straight Top	52″	Deep	66″	$34\frac{1}{2}$″

FLUES			WHEEL BASE				AVERAGE WEIGHT IN WORKING ORDER, POUNDS				
NO.	DIA.	LENGTH	DRIVING	RIGID	ENGINE	ENGINE AND TENDER	TENDER	TRAILING WHEELS	DRIVERS	LEADING WHEELS	TOTAL ENGINE
164	2″	11′-1″	7′-0″	7′-0″	7′-0″	35′-6″	60000	—	72500	—	72500

BOILER PRESSURE	FUEL	HEATING SURFACE, SQ. FT.				GRATE AREA	GAUGE OF TRACK	
POUNDS PER SQ. INCH ABOVE ATMOSPHERE	KIND	FLUES	FIRE BOX	ARCH PIPES	TOTAL	SQUARE FEET	METRES	FEET INCHES
150	Bituminous Coal	956	95	—	1051	15.2	1.435	$4'\text{-}8\frac{1}{2}''$

FOR HAULING CAPACITY SEE PAGE 290.

THE AMERICAN WIRE CO.
THE A. W. CO.
BROOKS

BUILT BY

BROOKS LOCOMOTIVE WORKS

DUNKIRK, N. Y., U.S.A.

1890

FOR THE AMERICAN WIRE COMPANY.

CODE WORD, QUOTANT. SERIES, 381.

TYPE, 4-WHEELED SWITCHER. CLASS, 16 E.

WITH 8-WHEELED TENDER, SLOPING BACK, TANK CAPACITY 2500 U. S. GALLONS AND 4 TONS FUEL.

CYLINDERS			WHEELS								BOILER		FIRE BOX		
			TENDER		TRAILING		COUPLED DRIVERS		LEADING						
TYPE	DIA.	STROKE	NO.	DIA.	NO.	DIA.	NO.	DIA.	NO.	DIA.	TYPE	DIA.	TYPE	LENGTH	WIDTH
Simple	16″	22″	8	—	—	—	4	50″	—	—	Straight	46″	Deep	48″	34½″

FLUES			WHEEL BASE				AVERAGE WEIGHT IN WORKING ORDER, POUNDS				
NO.	DIA.	LENGTH	DRIVING	RIGID	ENGINE	ENGINE AND TENDER	TENDER	TRAILING WHEELS	DRIVERS	LEADING WHEELS	TOTAL ENGINE
126	2″	10′-11″	7′-0″	7′-0″	7′-0″	23′-10″	62000	—	58200	—	58200

BOILER PRESSURE	FUEL	HEATING SURFACE, SQ. FT.				GRATE AREA	GAUGE OF TRACK	
POUNDS PER SQ. INCH ABOVE ATMOSPHERE	KIND	FLUES	FIRE BOX	ARCH PIPES	TOTAL	SQUARE FEET	METRES	FEET INCHES
150	Bituminous Coal	715	63	—	778	11.1	1.435	4′-8½″

FOR HAULING CAPACITY SEE PAGE 290.

TONAWANDA IRON & STEEL CO.
RAINBOW
BROOKS

BUILT BY

BROOKS LOCOMOTIVE WORKS

DUNKIRK, N. Y., U.S.A.

1895

FOR THE TONAWANDA IRON & STEEL COMPANY.

CODE WORD, QUOTH. SERIES, 564.

TYPE, 4-WHEELED SADDLE TANK SWITCHER. CLASS, 18 E. T.

TANK CAPACITY 900 U. S. GALLONS AND $1\frac{3}{4}$ TONS FUEL.

CYLINDERS			WHEELS								BOILER		FIRE BOX		
			TENDER		TRAILING		COUPLED DRIVERS		LEADING						
TYPE	DIA.	STROKE	NO.	DIA.	NO.	DIA.	NO.	DIA.	NO.	DIA.	TYPE	DIA.	TYPE	LENGTH	WIDTH
Simple	16″	24″	—	—	—	—	4	48″	—	—	Crown Bar, Straight Top	48″	Deep	48″	35″

FLUES			WHEEL BASE				AVERAGE WEIGHT IN WORKING ORDER, POUNDS				
NO.	DIA.	LENGTH	DRIVING	RIGID	ENGINE	ENGINE AND TENDER	TENDER	TRAILING WHEELS	DRIVERS	LEADING WHEELS	TOTAL ENGINE
126	2″	$10'\text{-}10\frac{1}{16}''$	7′-0″	7′-0″	7′-0″	—	—	—	76000	—	76000

BOILER PRESSURE	FUEL	HEATING SURFACE, SQ. FT.				GRATE AREA	GAUGE OF TRACK	
POUNDS PER SQ. INCH ABOVE ATMOSPHERE	KIND	FLUES	FIRE BOX	ARCH PIPES	TOTAL	SQUARE FEET	METRES	FEET INCHES
165	Bituminous Coal	711	67	—	778	11.3	1.435	$4'\text{-}8\frac{1}{2}''$

FOR HAULING CAPACITY SEE PAGE 290.

THE CARNEGIE STEEL CO.
LIMITED
DUQUESNE STEEL
WORKS.
BROOKS

BUILT BY

BROOKS LOCOMOTIVE WORKS

DUNKIRK, N. Y., U.S.A.

1895

FOR THE CARNEGIE STEEL COMPANY.

CODE WORD, QUOTIDIAN. SERIES, 543.

TYPE, 4-WHEELED SADDLE TANK SWITCHER. CLASS, 16 E. T.

TANK CAPACITY 900 U. S. GALLONS AND $1\frac{3}{4}$ TONS FUEL.

CYLINDERS			WHEELS								BOILER		FIRE BOX		
TYPE	DIA.	STROKE	TENDER		TRAILING		COUPLED DRIVERS		LEADING		TYPE	DIA.	TYPE	LENGTH	WIDTH
			NO.	DIA.	NO.	DIA.	NO.	DIA.	NO.	DIA.					
Simple	16″	24″	—	—	—	—	4	48″	—	—	Crown Bar, Straight Top	48″	Deep	48″	$34\frac{1}{2}$″

FLUES			WHEEL BASE				AVERAGE WEIGHT IN WORKING ORDER, POUNDS				
NO.	DIA.	LENGTH	DRIVING	RIGID	ENGINE	ENGINE AND TENDER	TENDER	TRAILING WHEELS	DRIVERS	LEADING WHEELS	TOTAL ENGINE
126	2″	10′-10″	7′-0″	7′-0″	7′-0″	—	—	—	76000	—	76000

BOILER PRESSURE	FUEL	HEATING SURFACE, SQ. FT.				GRATE AREA	GAUGE OF TRACK	
POUNDS PER SQ. INCH ABOVE ATMOSPHERE	KIND	FLUES	FIRE BOX	ARCH PIPES	TOTAL	SQUARE FEET	METRES	FEET INCHES
165	Bituminous Coal	711	67	—	778	11.1	1.435	$4'\text{-}8\frac{1}{2}''$

FOR HAULING CAPACITY SEE PAGE 290.

CHICAGO
&
SOUTH BEND R. R.
STUDEBAKER
3
BROOKS

BUILT BY

BROOKS LOCOMOTIVE WORKS

DUNKIRK, N. Y., U.S.A.

1892

FOR THE STUDEBAKER BROS M'F'G COMPANY.

CODE WORD, QUOTIENT. SERIES, 451.

TYPE, 4-WHEELED SADDLE TANK SWITCHER. CLASS, 14 E. T.

TANK CAPACITY 700 U. S. GALLONS AND 1 TON FUEL.

CYLINDERS			WHEELS								BOILER		FIRE BOX		
TYPE	DIA.	STROKE	TENDER NO.	TENDER DIA.	TRAILING NO.	TRAILING DIA.	COUPLED DRIVERS NO.	COUPLED DRIVERS DIA.	LEADING NO.	LEADING DIA.	TYPE	DIA.	TYPE	LENGTH	WIDTH
Simple	14″	22″	—	—	—	—	4	$42\frac{1}{2}$″	—	—	Crown Bar, Straight	44″	Deep	42″	35″

FLUES			WHEEL BASE				AVERAGE WEIGHT IN WORKING ORDER, POUNDS				
NO.	DIA.	LENGTH	DRIVING	RIGID	ENGINE	ENGINE AND TENDER	TENDER	TRAILING WHEELS	DRIVERS	LEADING WHEELS	TOTAL ENGINE
150	2″	10′-10″	7′-0″	7′-0″	7′-0″	—	—	—	60000	—	60000

BOILER PRESSURE	FUEL	HEATING SURFACE, SQ. FT.				GRATE AREA	GAUGE OF TRACK	
POUNDS PER SQ. INCH ABOVE ATMOSPHERE	KIND	FLUES	FIRE BOX	ARCH PIPES	TOTAL	SQUARE FEET	METRES	FEET INCHES
120	Bituminous Coal	596	64	—	660	9.7	1.435	4′-$8\frac{1}{2}$″

FOR HAULING CAPACITY SEE PAGE 290.

No.1

BUILT BY

BROOKS LOCOMOTIVE WORKS

DUNKIRK, N. Y., U.S.A.

1897

FOR THE JEFFERSON & CLEARFIELD COAL & IRON COMPANY.

CODE WORD, QUOTIX. SERIES, 598.

TYPE, 4-WHEELED SADDLE TANK SWITCHER. CLASS, 8 E. T.

TANK CAPACITY 200 U. S. GALLONS AND ½ TON FUEL.

CYLINDERS			WHEELS								BOILER		FIRE BOX		
			TENDER		TRAILING		COUPLED DRIVERS		LEADING						
TYPE	DIA.	STROKE	NO.	DIA.	NO.	DIA.	NO.	DIA.	NO.	DIA.	TYPE	DIA.	TYPE	LENGTH	WIDTH
Simple	8″	12″	—	—	—	—	4	30″	—	—	Direct Stay Straight Top	26″	Deep	30½″	38″

FLUES			WHEEL BASE				AVERAGE WEIGHT IN WORKING ORDER, POUNDS				
NO.	DIA.	LENGTH	DRIVING	RIGID	ENGINE	ENGINE AND TENDER	TENDER	TRAILING WHEELS	DRIVERS	LEADING WHEELS	TOTAL ENGINE
50	1½″	7′-2⅞″	4′-8″	4′-8″	4′-8″	—	—	—	23000	—	23000

BOILER PRESSURE	FUEL	HEATING SURFACE, SQ. FT.				GRATE AREA	GAUGE OF TRACK	
POUNDS PER SQ. INCH ABOVE ATMOSPHERE	KIND	FLUES	FIRE BOX	ARCH PIPES	TOTAL	SQUARE FEET	METRES	FEET INCHES
180	Bituminous Coal	141	28	—	169	7.5	1.435	4′-8½″

FOR HAULING CAPACITY SEE PAGE 290.

BUILT BY

BROOKS LOCOMOTIVE WORKS

DUNKIRK, N. Y., U.S.A.

1893

FOR THE CHICAGO & NORTHERN PACIFIC RAILROAD.

CODE WORD, QUOTOON. SERIES, 487.

TYPE, 6-COUPLED DOUBLE ENDER TANK ENGINE. CLASS, 18 B. R. X.

REAR TANK, CAPACITY 2600 U. S. GALLONS AND 4½ TONS FUEL.

CYLINDERS			WHEELS								BOILER		FIRE BOX		
			TENDER		TRAILING		COUPLED DRIVERS		LEADING						
TYPE	DIA.	STROKE	NO.	DIA.	NO.	DIA.	NO.	DIA.	NO.	DIA.	TYPE	DIA.	TYPE	LENGTH	WIDTH
Simple	18″	24″	—	—	6	30″	6	63″	2	30″	Crown Bar, Wagon Top	58″	Long, Sloping	102″	33″

FLUES			WHEEL BASE				AVERAGE WEIGHT IN WORKING ORDER, POUNDS				
NO.	DIA.	LENGTH	DRIVING	RIGID	ENGINE	ENGINE AND TENDER	TENDER	TRAILING WHEELS	DRIVERS	LEADING WHEELS	TOTAL ENGINE
250	2″	11′-1″	15′-0″	15′-0″	35′-9″	——	——	48000	102000	16000	166000

BOILER PRESSURE	FUEL	HEATING SURFACE, SQ. FT.				GRATE AREA	GAUGE OF TRACK	
POUNDS PER SQ. INCH ABOVE ATMOSPHERE	KIND	FLUES	FIRE BOX	ARCH PIPES	TOTAL	SQUARE FEET	METRES	FEET INCHES
180	Bituminous Coal	1453	144	23	1620	22.6	1.435	4′-8½″

FOR HAULING CAPACITY SEE PAGE 290.

JOSEPH E. GAY
ATLANTIC MINING Co.

BUILT BY

BROOKS LOCOMOTIVE WORKS

DUNKIRK, N. Y., U.S.A.

1890

FOR THE ATLANTIC MINING COMPANY.

CODE WORD, QUOTUM. SERIES, 394.

TYPE, 4-COUPLED, "FORNEY," TANK ENGINE. CLASS, 16 E. Q. x.

REAR TANK, CAPACITY 1120 U. S. GALLONS AND 3 TONS FUEL.

CYLINDERS			WHEELS								BOILER		FIRE BOX		
TYPE	DIA.	STROKE	TENDER		TRAILING		COUPLED DRIVERS		LEADING		TYPE	DIA.	TYPE	LENGTH	WIDTH
			NO.	DIA.	NO.	DIA.	NO.	DIA.	NO.	DIA.					
Simple	16″	24″	—	—	4	30″	4	50″	—	—	Straight	52″	Deep	72″	$34\frac{1}{2}$″

FLUES			WHEEL BASE				AVERAGE WEIGHT IN WORKING ORDER, POUNDS				
NO.	DIA.	LENGTH	DRIVING	RIGID	ENGINE	ENGINE AND TENDER	TENDER	TRAILING WHEELS	DRIVERS	LEADING WHEELS	TOTAL ENGINE
156	2″	11′-$1\frac{1}{16}$″	6′-6″	6′-6″	22′-0″	—	—	22000	68800	—	90800

BOILER PRESSURE	FUEL	HEATING SURFACE, SQ. FT.				GRATE AREA	GAUGE OF TRACK		
POUNDS PER SQ. INCH ABOVE ATMOSPHERE	KIND	FLUES	FIRE BOX	ARCH PIPES	TOTAL	SQUARE FEET	METRES	FEET	INCHES
165	Bituminous Coal	899	91	—	990	16.3	1.244	4′-1″	

FOR HAULING CAPACITY SEE PAGE 290.

20
20
C. & N. P. R. R.
20
BROOKS

BUILT BY

BROOKS LOCOMOTIVE WORKS

DUNKIRK, N. Y., U.S.A.

1890

FOR THE CHICAGO & NORTHERN PACIFIC RAILROAD.

CODE WORD, QUOTUOR.

TYPE, 4-COUPLED, DOUBLE ENDER, TANK ENGINE.

SIDE TANKS, CAPACITY 1600 U. S. GALLONS AND 3 TONS FUEL.

SERIES, 395.

CLASS, 15 A. Q. Y.

CYLINDERS			WHEELS								BOILER		FIRE BOX		
TYPE	DIA.	STROKE	TENDER NO.	TENDER DIA.	TRAILING NO.	TRAILING DIA.	COUPLED DRIVERS NO.	COUPLED DRIVERS DIA.	LEADING NO.	LEADING DIA.	TYPE	DIA.	TYPE	LENGTH	WIDTH
Simple	15″	22″	—	—	4	30	4	57″	4	30″	Crown Bar, Wagon Top	46″	Long, Sloping	84″	34″

FLUES			WHEEL BASE				AVERAGE WEIGHT IN WORKING ORDER, POUNDS				
NO.	DIA.	LENGTH	DRIVING	RIGID	ENGINE	ENGINE AND TENDER	TENDER	TRAILING WHEELS	DRIVERS	LEADING WHEELS	TOTAL ENGINE
140	2″	9′-0″	7′-0″	7′-0″	28′-6″	—	—	21000	56000	23000	100000

BOILER PRESSURE	FUEL	HEATING SURFACE, SQ. FT.				GRATE AREA	GAUGE OF TRACK	
POUNDS PER SQ. INCH ABOVE ATMOSPHERE	KIND	FLUES	FIRE BOX	ARCH PIPES	TOTAL	SQUARE FEET	METRES	FEET INCHES
165	Coke or Coal	654	112	—	766	19.6	1.435	4′-8½″

FOR HAULING CAPACITY SEE PAGE 290.

1
CHIHUAHUA AL PACIFICO
1

BUILT BY

BROOKS LOCOMOTIVE WORKS

DUNKIRK, N. Y., U. S. A.

1898

FOR THE CHIHUAHUA & PACIFIC RAILROAD.

CODE WORD, YABYAN. SERIES, 659.

TYPE, 8-WHEELED PASSENGER. CLASS, 18 A.

WITH 8-WHEELED TENDER TANK CAPACITY 4000 U. S. GALLONS AND 8 TONS FUEL.

CYLINDERS			WHEELS								BOILER		FIRE BOX		
TYPE	DIA.	STROKE	TENDER		TRAILING		COUPLED DRIVERS		LEADING		TYPE	DIA.	TYPE	LENGTH	WIDTH
			NO.	DIA.	NO.	DIA.	NO.	DIA.	NO.	DIA.					
Simple	18″	24″	8	33″	—	—	4	62″	4	30″	Rad. Stay, Wagon Top	56″	Long, Sloping	97″	33″

FLUES			WHEEL BASE				AVERAGE WEIGHT IN WORKING ORDER, POUNDS				
NO.	DIA.	LENGTH	DRIVING	RIGID	ENGINE	ENGINE AND TENDER	TENDER	TRAILING WHEELS	DRIVERS	LEADING WHEELS	TOTAL ENGINE
225	2″	11′-7$\frac{1}{8}$″	8′-0″	8′-0″	22′-9″	48′-6″	80000	—	68500	37000	105500

BOILER PRESSURE	FUEL	HEATING SURFACE, SQ. FT.				GRATE AREA	GAUGE OF TRACK	
POUNDS PER SQ. INCH ABOVE ATMOSPHERE	KIND	FLUES	FIRE BOX	ARCH PIPES	TOTAL	SQUARE FEET	METRES	FEET INCHES
180	Oak or Mesquite	1356	134	—	1490	21.8	1.435	4′-8$\frac{1}{2}$″

FOR HAULING CAPACITY SEE PAGE 290.

176
IMPERIAL GOVERNMENT RAILWAYS.

BUILT BY

BROOKS LOCOMOTIVE WORKS

DUNKIRK, N. Y., U.S.A.

1897

FOR THE IMPERIAL GOVERNMENT RAILWAYS,

JAPAN.

CODE WORD, YACCA. SERIES, 626.

TYPE, 8-WHEELED PASSENGER. CLASS, 15 A.

WITH 6-WHEELED TENDER TANK CAPACITY 2400 U. S. GALLONS AND $3\frac{1}{2}$ TONS FUEL.

CYLINDERS			WHEELS								BOILER		FIRE BOX		
TYPE	DIA.	STROKE	TENDER		TRAILING		COUPLED DRIVERS		LEADING		TYPE	DIA.	TYPE	LENGTH	WIDTH
			NO.	DIA.	NO.	DIA.	NO.	DIA.	NO.	DIA.					
Simple	15″	22″	6	$35\frac{1}{2}$″	—	—	4	54″	4	$27\frac{1}{2}$″	Rad. Stay, Straight Top	54″	Long, Wide, Sloping	78″	$29\frac{1}{2}$″

FLUES			WHEEL BASE				AVERAGE WEIGHT IN WORKING ORDER, POUNDS				
NO.	DIA.	LENGTH	DRIVING	RIGID	ENGINE	ENGINE AND TENDER	TENDER	TRAILING WHEELS	DRIVERS	LEADING WHEELS	TOTAL ENGINE
210	$1\frac{3}{4}$″	9′-$7\frac{1}{16}$″	7′-0″	7′-0″	19′-4″	38′-$10\frac{1}{2}$″	52000	—	50400	24100	74500

BOILER PRESSURE	FUEL	HEATING SURFACE, SQ. FT.				GRATE AREA	GAUGE OF TRACK	
POUNDS PER SQ. INCH ABOVE ATMOSPHERE	KIND	FLUES	FIRE BOX	ARCH PIPES	TOTAL	SQUARE FEET	METRES	FEET INCHES
160	Bituminous Coal, Japanese	915	89.9	—	1004.9	15.2	1.067	3′-6″

FOR HAULING CAPACITY SEE PAGE 290.

2
2
MATEHUALA
2
FERRO CARRIL
VANEGAS, CEDRAL Y RIO VERDE

BUILT BY

BROOKS LOCOMOTIVE WORKS

DUNKIRK, N. Y., U.S.A.

1890

FOR THE VANEGAS, CEDRAL & RIO VERDE RAILROAD OF MEXICO.

CODE WORD, YACHT. SERIES, 366.

TYPE, 8-WHEELED PASSENGER. CLASS, 15 A.

WITH 8-WHEELED TENDER TANK CAPACITY 2400 U. S. GALLONS AND 5 TONS FUEL.

CYLINDERS			WHEELS								BOILER		FIRE BOX		
			TENDER		TRAILING		COUPLED DRIVERS		LEADING						
TYPE	DIA.	STROKE	NO.	DIA.	NO.	DIA.	NO.	DIA.	NO.	DIA.	TYPE	DIA.	TYPE	LENGTH	WIDTH
Simple	15″	20″	8	28″	—	—	4	50″	4	28″	Crown Bar, Wagon Top	48″	Long, Wide, Sloping	84″	24″

FLUES			WHEEL BASE				AVERAGE WEIGHT IN WORKING ORDER, POUNDS				
NO.	DIA.	LENGTH	DRIVING	RIGID	ENGINE	ENGINE AND TENDER	TENDER	TRAILING WHEELS	DRIVERS	LEADING WHEELS	TOTAL ENGINE
154	2″	9′-0″	7′-0″	7′-0″	18′-2″	41′-0″	55000	—	48000	17000	65000

BOILER PRESSURE	FUEL	HEATING SURFACE, SQ. FT.				GRATE AREA	GAUGE OF TRACK	
POUNDS PER SQ. INCH ABOVE ATMOSPHERE	KIND	FLUES	FIRE BOX	ARCH TUBES	TOTAL	SQUARE FEET	METRES	FEET INCHES
150	Bituminous Coal	718	79	—	797	13.5	.915	3′-0″

FOR HAULING CAPACITY SEE PAGE 290.

E. F. C. B.

BUILT BY

BROOKS LOCOMOTIVE WORKS

DUNKIRK, N. Y., U.S.A.

1895

FOR THE CENTRAL RAILWAY OF BRAZIL.

CODE WORD, YAFFLE. SERIES, 536.

TYPE, 8-WHEELED PASSENGER. CLASS, 14 A.

WITH 8-WHEELED TENDER TANK CAPACITY 2400 U. S. GALLONS AND 5 TONS FUEL.

CYLINDERS			WHEELS								BOILER		FIRE BOX		
TYPE	DIA.	STROKE	TENDER NO.	TENDER DIA.	TRAILING NO.	TRAILING DIA.	COUPLED DRIVERS NO.	COUPLED DRIVERS DIA.	LEADING NO.	LEADING DIA.	TYPE	DIA.	TYPE	LENGTH	WIDTH
Simple	14″	18″	8	27½″	—	—	4	46″	4	25½″	Improved Belpaire	50¼″	Long, Wide, Sloping	84″	27½″

FLUES			WHEEL BASE				AVERAGE WEIGHT IN WORKING ORDER, POUNDS				
NO.	DIA.	LENGTH	DRIVING	RIGID	ENGINE	ENGINE AND TENDER	TENDER	TRAILING WHEELS	DRIVERS	LEADING WHEELS	TOTAL ENGINE
155	2″	9′-0⅜″	7′-0″	7′-0″	18′-2″	42′-0″	58000	——	50000	24000	74000

BOILER PRESSURE	FUEL	HEATING SURFACE, SQ. FT.				GRATE AREA	GAUGE OF TRACK	
POUNDS PER SQ. INCH ABOVE ATMOSPHERE	KIND	FLUES	FIRE BOX	ARCH PIPES	TOTAL	SQUARE FEET	METRES	FEET INCHES
165	Cardiff Coal	727	100	——	827	15.4	1.000	3′-3⅜″

FOR HAULING CAPACITY SEE PAGE 290.

9
9
HANKAKU RY. Co

BUILT BY

BROOKS LOCOMOTIVE WORKS

DUNKIRK, N. Y., U.S.A.

1898

FOR THE HANKAKU RAILWAY COMPANY OF JAPAN.

CODE WORD, YAGER. SERIES, 665.

TYPE, 8-WHEELED PASSENGER. CLASS, 14 A.

WITH 6-WHEELED TENDER TANK CAPACITY 2400 U. S. GALLONS AND 5 TONS FUEL.

CYLINDERS			WHEELS								BOILER		FIRE BOX		
TYPE	DIA.	STROKE	TENDER		TRAILING		COUPLED DRIVERS		LEADING		TYPE	DIA.	TYPE	LENGTH	WIDTH
			NO.	DIA.	NO.	DIA.	NO.	DIA.	NO.	DIA.					
Simple	14″	24″	6	33½″	—	—	4	60″	4	27½″	Rad. Stay, Wagon Top	48″	Long, Wide, Sloping	70″	29½″

FLUES			WHEEL BASE				AVERAGE WEIGHT IN WORKING ORDER, POUNDS				
NO.	DIA.	LENGTH	DRIVING	RIGID	ENGINE	ENGINE AND TENDER	TENDER	TRAILING WHEELS	DRIVERS	LEADING WHEELS	TOTAL ENGINE
192	1¾″	9′-0″	7′-0″	7′-0″	18′-8″	37′-6″	45000	——	47000	21000	68000

BOILER PRESSURE	FUEL	HEATING SURFACE, SQ. FT.				GRATE AREA	GAUGE OF TRACK	
POUNDS PER SQ. INCH ABOVE ATMOSPHERE	KIND	FLUES	FIRE BOX	ARCH PIPES	TOTAL	SQUARE FEET	METRES	FEET INCHES
160	Bituminous Coal	785	76	——	861	14.0	1.067	3′-6″

FOR HAULING CAPACITY SEE PAGE 290.

C.M.
43
43

BUILT BY

BROOKS LOCOMOTIVE WORKS

DUNKIRK, N. Y., U.S.A.

1899

FOR THE MEXICAN CENTRAL RAILWAY.

CODE WORD, YAKIN.

TYPE, MOGUL FREIGHT.

WITH 8-WHEELED TENDER

SERIES, 676.

CLASS, 20 B.

TANK CAPACITY 4500 U. S. GALLONS AND $8\frac{1}{2}$ TONS FUEL.

CYLINDERS			WHEELS								BOILER		FIRE BOX		
			TENDER		TRAILING		COUPLED DRIVERS		LEADING						
TYPE	DIA.	STROKE	NO.	DIA.	NO.	DIA.	NO.	DIA.	NO.	DIA.	TYPE	DIA.	TYPE	LENGTH	WIDTH
Simple	20″	26″	8	$34\frac{1}{2}$″	—	—	6	55″	2	$28\frac{1}{2}$″	Improved Belpaire	70″	Long, Wide	97″	$38\frac{1}{2}$″

FLUES			WHEEL BASE				AVERAGE WEIGHT IN WORKING ORDER, POUNDS				
NO.	DIA.	LENGTH	DRIVING	RIGID	ENGINE	ENGINE AND TENDER	TENDER	TRAILING WHEELS	DRIVERS	LEADING WHEELS	TOTAL ENGINE
320	2″	11′-$7\frac{1}{8}$″	10′-0″	10′-0″	18′-1″	46′-$4\frac{1}{4}$″	91300	——	132000	24300	156300

BOILER PRESSURE	FUEL	HEATING SURFACE, SQ. FT.				GRATE AREA	GAUGE OF TRACK	
POUNDS PER SQ. INCH ABOVE ATMOSPHERE	KIND	FLUES	FIRE BOX	ARCH PIPES	TOTAL	SQUARE FEET	METRES	FEET INCHES
180	Bituminous Coal	1923	165	——	2088	24.6	1.435	4′-$8\frac{1}{2}$″

FOR HAULING CAPACITY SEE PAGE 290.

3
3
KANSEI T.K.

BUILT BY

BROOKS LOCOMOTIVE WORKS

DUNKIRK, N. Y., U.S.A.

1897

FOR THE KANSEI RAILWAY

OF JAPAN.

CODE WORD, YAKSHA. SERIES, 612.

TYPE, MOGUL FREIGHT. CLASS, 16 B.

WITH 8-WHEELED TENDER TANK CAPACITY 2700 U. S. GALLONS AND $5\frac{1}{2}$ TONS FUEL.

CYLINDERS			WHEELS								BOILER		FIRE BOX		
TYPE	DIA.	STROKE	TENDER NO.	TENDER DIA.	TRAILING NO.	TRAILING DIA.	COUPLED DRIVERS NO.	COUPLED DRIVERS DIA.	LEADING NO.	LEADING DIA.	TYPE	DIA.	TYPE	LENGTH	WIDTH
Simple	16″	22″	8	$27\frac{1}{2}$″	—	—	6	48″	2	$27\frac{1}{2}$″	Rad. Stay, Straight Top	56″	Long, Wide	84″	29″

FLUES			WHEEL BASE				AVERAGE WEIGHT IN WORKING ORDER, POUNDS				
NO.	DIA.	LENGTH	DRIVING	RIGID	ENGINE	ENGINE AND TENDER	TENDER	TRAILING WHEELS	DRIVERS	LEADING WHEELS	TOTAL ENGINE
202	2″	9′-4″	10′-4″	10′-4″	17′-4″	38′-0″	58000	—	12880	70000	82880

BOILER PRESSURE	FUEL	HEATING SURFACE, SQ. FT.				GRATE AREA	GAUGE OF TRACK	
POUNDS PER SQ. INCH ABOVE ATMOSPHERE	KIND	FLUES	FIRE BOX	ARCH PIPES	TOTAL	SQUARE FEET	METRES	FEET INCHES
165	Bituminous Coal	978.8	95.2	—	1074	16.4	1.067	3′-6″

FOR HAULING CAPACITY SEE PAGE 290.

COATEPEC
2
F. C. J. y C.

BUILT BY

BROOKS LOCOMOTIVE WORKS

DUNKIRK, N. Y., U.S.A.

1897

FOR THE JALAPA & CORDOVA RAILWAY COMPANY OF MEXICO.

CODE WORD, YAKSTERN. SERIES, 623.

TYPE, MOGUL FREIGHT. CLASS, 14 B.

WITH 8-WHEELED TENDER TANK CAPACITY 1700 U. S. GALLONS AND 1½ TONS FUEL.

CYLINDERS			WHEELS								BOILER		FIRE BOX		
			TENDER		TRAILING		COUPLED DRIVERS		LEADING						
TYPE	DIA.	STROKE	NO.	DIA.	NO.	DIA.	NO.	DIA.	NO.	DIA.	TYPE	DIA.	TYPE	LENGTH	WIDTH
Simple	14″	20″	8	28″	—	—	6	42″	2	26″	Rad. Stay, Straight Top	52″	Long, Wide	84″	24″

FLUES			WHEEL BASE				AVERAGE WEIGHT IN WORKING ORDER, POUNDS				
NO.	DIA.	LENGTH	DRIVING	RIGID	ENGINE	ENGINE AND TENDER	TENDER	TRAILING WHEELS	DRIVERS	LEADING WHEELS	TOTAL ENGINE
148	2″	8′-2″	10′-4″	10′-4″	16′-10″	40′-3″	50000	—	56000	7800	63800

BOILER PRESSURE	FUEL	HEATING SURFACE, SQ. FT.				GRATE AREA	GAUGE OF TRACK	
POUNDS PER SQ. INCH ABOVE ATMOSPHERE	KIND	FLUES	FIRE BOX	ARCH PIPES	TOTAL	SQUARE FEET	METRES	FEET INCHES
135	Wood	635	83	—	718	13.5	.915	3′-0″

FOR HAULING CAPACITY SEE PAGE 290.

Lovisa-Westjärvi Järnvägsbyggnad
5

BUILT BY

BROOKS LOCOMOTIVE WORKS

DUNKIRK, N. Y., U.S.A.

1899

FOR THE LOVISA-WESIJARVI RAILWAY OF FINLAND.

CODE WORD, YAKTAM. SERIES, 691.

TYPE, MOGUL FREIGHT. CLASS, $12\frac{1}{2}$ B.

WITH 8-WHEELED TENDER TANK CAPACITY 2500 U. S. GALLONS AND 6 TONS FUEL.

CYLINDERS			WHEELS								BOILER		FIRE BOX		
TYPE	DIA.	STROKE	TENDER		TRAILING		COUPLED DRIVERS		LEADING		TYPE	DIA.	TYPE	LENGTH	WIDTH
			NO.	DIA.	NO.	DIA.	NO.	DIA.	NO.	DIA.					
Simple Piston Valve	$12\frac{1}{2}''$	18″	8	$24\frac{1}{2}''$	—	—	6	37″	2	$24\frac{1}{2}''$	Rad. Stay, Straight Top	45″	Long, Wide	91″	19″

FLUES			WHEEL BASE				AVERAGE WEIGHT IN WORKING ORDER, POUNDS				
NO.	DIA.	LENGTH	DRIVING	RIGID	ENGINE	ENGINE AND TENDER	TENDER	TRAILING WHEELS	DRIVERS	LEADING WHEELS	TOTAL ENGINE
120	2″	8′-2″	10′-0″	10′-0″	16′-0″	40′-0″	46297	—	43000	7717	50717

BOILER PRESSURE	FUEL	HEATING SURFACE, SQ. FT.				GRATE AREA	GAUGE OF TRACK	
POUNDS PER SQ. INCH ABOVE ATMOSPHERE	KIND	FLUES	FIRE BOX	ARCH PIPES	TOTAL	SQUARE FEET	METRES	FEET INCHES
150	Coal or Wood	507	78	—	585	12.2	0.75	$2'\text{-}5\frac{1}{2}''$

FOR HAULING CAPACITY SEE PAGE 290.

C.M.
199
199

BUILT BY

BROOKS LOCOMOTIVE WORKS

DUNKIRK, N. Y., U.S.A.

1897

FOR THE MEXICAN CENTRAL RAILWAY.

CODE WORD, YAMMA. SERIES, 618.

TYPE, CONSOLIDATION FREIGHT. CLASS, 21 C.

WITH 8-WHEELED TENDER TANK CAPACITY 4500 U. S. GALLONS AND $8\frac{1}{2}$ TONS FUEL.

CYLINDERS			WHEELS								BOILER		FIRE BOX		
TYPE	DIA.	STROKE	TENDER NO.	TENDER DIA.	TRAILING NO.	TRAILING DIA.	COUPLED DRIVERS NO.	COUPLED DRIVERS DIA.	LEADING NO.	LEADING DIA.	TYPE	DIA.	TYPE	LENGTH	WIDTH
Simple	21″	26″	8	$34\frac{1}{2}$″	—	—	8	57″	2	$28\frac{1}{2}$″	Improved Belpaire	74″	Long, Wide	120″	$37\frac{3}{4}$″

FLUES			WHEEL BASE				AVERAGE WEIGHT IN WORKING ORDER, POUNDS				
NO.	DIA.	LENGTH	DRIVING	RIGID	ENGINE	ENGINE AND TENDER	TENDER	TRAILING WHEELS	DRIVERS	LEADING WHEELS	TOTAL ENGINE
374	2″	11′-$1\frac{5}{16}$″	15′-0″	15′-0″	23′-5″	50′-$9\frac{1}{4}$″	90000	—	160000	20000	180000

BOILER PRESSURE	FUEL	HEATING SURFACE, SQ. FT.				GRATE AREA	GAUGE OF TRACK	
POUNDS PER SQ. INCH ABOVE ATMOSPHERE	KIND	FLUES	FIRE BOX	ARCH PIPES	TOTAL	SQUARE FEET	METRES	FEET INCHES
180	Bituminous Coal	2140	204	—	2344	31.45	1.435	4′-$8\frac{1}{2}$″

FOR HAULING CAPACITY SEE PAGE 290.

30
CHIHUAHUA AL PACIFICO
30
30

BUILT BY

BROOKS LOCOMOTIVE WORKS

DUNKIRK, N. Y., U.S.A.

1898

FOR THE CHIHUAHUA & PACIFIC RAILROAD OF MEXICO.

CODE WORD, YAMPO. SERIES, 660.

TYPE, CONSOLIDATION FREIGHT. CLASS, 18 C.

WITH 8-WHEELED TENDER TANK CAPACITY 4000 U. S. GALLONS AND 10 TONS FUEL.

CYLINDERS			WHEELS								BOILER		FIRE BOX		
			TENDER		TRAILING		COUPLED DRIVERS		LEADING						
TYPE	DIA.	STROKE	NO.	DIA.	NO.	DIA.	NO.	DIA.	NO.	DIA.	TYPE	DIA.	TYPE	LENGTH	WIDTH
Simple	18″	26″	8	33″	—	—	8	50″	2	30″	Rad. Stay, Wagon Top	58″	Long	108″	33″

FLUES			WHEEL BASE				AVERAGE WEIGHT IN WORKING ORDER, POUNDS				
NO.	DIA.	LENGTH	DRIVING	RIGID	ENGINE	ENGINE AND TENDER	TENDER	TRAILING WHEELS	DRIVERS	LEADING WHEELS	TOTAL ENGINE
232	2″	13′-10″	14′-6″	14′-6″	22′-0″	47′-0″	80000	——	116000	14000	130000

BOILER PRESSURE	FUEL	HEATING SURFACE, SQ. FT.				GRATE AREA	GAUGE OF TRACK	
POUNDS PER SQ. INCH ABOVE ATMOSPHERE	KIND	FLUES	FIRE BOX	ARCH PIPES	TOTAL	SQUARE FEET	METRES	FEET INCHES
180	Oak or Mesquite	1657	150	——	1807	24.3	1.435	4′-8½″

FOR HAULING CAPACITY SEE PAGE 290.

A.R.R.&L.Co.
1

BUILT BY

BROOKS LOCOMOTIVE WORKS

DUNKIRK, N. Y., U.S.A.

1898

FOR THE AMERICAN RAILROAD & LUMBER COMPANY OF MEXICO.

CODE WORD, YAPOCK. SERIES, 644.

TYPE, CONSOLIDATION FREIGHT. CLASS, 17 C.

WITH 8-WHEELED TENDER TANK CAPACITY 3000 U. S. GALLONS AND 1½ TONS FUEL.

CYLINDERS			WHEELS								BOILER		FIRE BOX		
			TENDER		TRAILING		COUPLED DRIVERS		LEADING						
TYPE	DIA.	STROKE	NO.	DIA.	NO.	DIA.	NO.	DIA.	NO.	DIA.	TYPE	DIA	TYPE	LENGTH	WIDTH
Simple	17″	20″	8	30″	—	—	8	44″	2	28″	Improved Belpaire	60″	Long, Wide	108″	24″

FLUES			WHEEL BASE				AVERAGE WEIGHT IN WORKING ORDER, POUNDS				
NO.	DIA.	LENGTH	DRIVING	RIGID	ENGINE	ENGINE AND TENDER	TENDER	TRAILING WHEELS	DRIVERS	LEADING WHEELS	TOTAL ENGINE
254	2″	10′-1⅛″	12′-2″	12′-2″	20′-0″	44′-11″	69000	—	93700	10500	104200

BOILER PRESSURE	FUEL	HEATING SURFACE, SQ. FT.				GRATE AREA	GAUGE OF TRACK	
POUNDS PER SQ. INCH ABOVE ATMOSPHERE	KIND	FLUES	FIRE BOX	ARCH PIPES	TOTAL	SQUARE FEET	METRES	FEET INCHES
190	Wood	1331	127	—	1458	17.4	.915	3′-0″

FOR HAULING CAPACITY SEE PAGE 290.

3
Lovisa-Wesijärvi Järnvägsbyggnad

BUILT BY

BROOKS LOCOMOTIVE WORKS

DUNKIRK, N. Y., U.S.A.

1899

FOR THE LOVISA-WESIJARVI RAILWAY OF FINLAND.

CODE WORD, YAPON. SERIES, 690.

TYPE, CONSOLIDATION FREIGHT. CLASS, 14 C.

WITH 8-WHEELED TENDER TANK CAPACITY 2500 U. S. GALLONS AND 6 TONS FUEL.

CYLINDERS			WHEELS								BOILER		FIRE BOX	
TYPE	DIA.	STROKE	TENDER		TRAILING		COUPLED DRIVERS		LEADING		TYPE	DIA.	TYPE	LENGTH WIDTH
			NO.	DIA.	NO.	DIA.	NO.	DIA.	NO.	DIA.				
Simple Piston Valve	14″	18″	8	$24\frac{1}{2}$″	—	—	8	37″	2	$24\frac{1}{2}$″	Rad. Stay, Straight Top	48″	Long, Wide	110″ 20″

FLUES			WHEEL BASE				AVERAGE WEIGHT IN WORKING ORDER, POUNDS				
NO.	DIA.	LENGTH	DRIVING	RIGID	ENGINE	ENGINE AND TENDER	TENDER	TRAILING WHEELS	DRIVERS	LEADING WHEELS	TOTAL ENGINE
147	2″	8′-$2\frac{1}{16}$″	11′-0″	11′-0″	17′-0″	39′-$1\frac{5}{8}$″	46297	—	52919	7716	60635

BOILER PRESSURE	FUEL	HEATING SURFACE, SQ. FT.				GRATE AREA	GAUGE OF TRACK	
POUNDS PER SQ. INCH ABOVE ATMOSPHERE	KIND	FLUES	FIRE BOX	ARCH PIPES	TOTAL	SQUARE FEET	METRES	FEET INCHES
150	Wood or Coal	621	100	—	721	14.5	0.75	2′-$5\frac{1}{2}$″

FOR HAULING CAPACITY SEE PAGE 290.

C.M
207
207

BUILT BY

BROOKS LOCOMOTIVE WORKS

DUNKIRK, N. Y., U.S.A.

1897

FOR THE MEXICAN CENTRAL RAILWAY.

CODE WORD, YAPWAH. SERIES, 605.

TYPE, CONSOLIDATION FREIGHT, DOUBLE ENDER. CLASS, 21 C. P.

WITH 8-WHEELED TENDER TANK CAPACITY 4500 U. S. GALLONS AND 8½ TONS FUEL.

CYLINDERS			WHEELS								BOILER		FIRE BOX		
			TENDER		TRAILING		COUPLED DRIVERS		LEADING						
TYPE	DIA.	STROKE	NO.	DIA.	NO.	DIA.	NO.	DIA.	NO.	DIA.	TYPE	DIA.	TYPE	LENGTH	WIDTH
Simple	21″	26″	8	$35\frac{1}{2}$″	2	$28\frac{1}{2}$″	8	49″	2	$28\frac{1}{2}$″	Improved Belpaire	78″	Long, Wide	120″	$37\frac{3}{4}$″

FLUES			WHEEL BASE				AVERAGE WEIGHT IN WORKING ORDER, POUNDS				
NO.	DIA.	LENGTH	DRIVING	RIGID	ENGINE	ENGINE AND TENDER	TENDER	TRAILING WHEELS	DRIVERS	LEADING WHEELS	TOTAL ENGINE
412	2″	$12'\text{-}1\frac{5}{16}''$	13′-0″	13′-0″	28′-2″	52′-2″	90000	24800	145200	23450	193450

BOILER PRESSURE	FUEL	HEATING SURFACE, SQ. FT.				GRATE AREA	GAUGE OF TRACK	
POUNDS PER SQ. INCH ABOVE ATMOSPHERE	KIND	FLUES	FIRE BOX	ARCH PIPES	TOTAL	SQUARE FEET	METRES	FEET INCHES
180	Bituminous Coal	2585	218	—	2803	31.45	1.435	$4'\text{-}8\frac{1}{2}''$

FOR HAULING CAPACITY SEE PAGE 290.

C.M.
173
173
173

BUILT BY

BROOKS LOCOMOTIVE WORKS

DUNKIRK, N. Y., U.S.A.

1897

FOR THE MEXICAN CENTRAL RAILWAY.

CODE WORD, YARRAN. SERIES, 602.

TYPE, 10-WHEELED PASSENGER. CLASS, 20 D.

WITH 8-WHEELED TENDER TANK CAPACITY 4500 U. S. GALLONS AND $8\frac{1}{2}$ TONS FUEL.

CYLINDERS			WHEELS								BOILER		FIRE BOX		
			TENDER		TRAILING		COUPLED DRIVERS		LEADING						
TYPE	DIA.	STROKE	NO.	DIA.	NO.	DIA.	NO.	DIA.	NO.	DIA.	TYPE	DIA	TYPE	LENGTH	WIDTH
Simple	20″	24″	8	$34\frac{1}{2}$″	—	—	6	60″	4	$34\frac{1}{2}$″	Improved Belpaire	$62\frac{1}{2}$″	Long	$120\frac{13}{16}$″	32″

FLUES			WHEEL BASE				AVERAGE WEIGHT IN WORKING ORDER, POUNDS				
NO.	DIA.	LENGTH	DRIVING	RIGID	ENGINE	ENGINE AND TENDER	TENDER	TRAILING WHEELS	DRIVERS	LEADING WHEELS	TOTAL ENGINE
268	2″	13′-$2\frac{9}{16}$″	11′-0″	11′-0″	23′-4″	51′-4″	85000	—	111000	36500	147500

BOILER PRESSURE	FUEL	HEATING SURFACE, SQ. FT.				GRATE AREA	GAUGE OF TRACK	
POUNDS PER SQ. INCH ABOVE ATMOSPHERE	KIND	FLUES	FIRE BOX	ARCH PIPES	TOTAL	SQUARE FEET	METRES	FEET INCHES
180	Bituminous Coal	1843.8	187.7	—	2031.5	26.1	1.435	4′-$8\frac{1}{2}$″

FOR HAULING CAPACITY SEE PAGE 290.

M. C. Y. P.
7

BUILT BY

BROOKS LOCOMOTIVE WORKS

DUNKIRK, N. Y., U.S.A.

1898

FOR THE MEXICO CUERNAVACA & PACIFIC RAILWAY.

CODE WORD, YARROW. SERIES, 643.

TYPE, 10-WHEELED FREIGHT. CLASS, 20 D.

WITH 8-WHEELED TENDER TANK CAPACITY 4500 U. S. GALLONS AND 8½ TON FUEL.

CYLINDERS			WHEELS								BOILER		FIRE BOX		
			TENDER		TRAILING		COUPLED DRIVERS		LEADING						
TYPE	DIA.	STROKE	NO.	DIA.	NO.	DIA.	NO.	DIA.	NO.	DIA.	TYPE	DIA.	TYPE	LENGTH	WIDTH
Simple	20″	24″	8	$34\frac{1}{2}$″	—	—	6	56″	4	$28\frac{1}{2}$″	Belpaire	$62\frac{1}{2}$″	Long	$120\frac{13}{16}$″	32″

FLUES			WHEEL BASE				AVERAGE WEIGHT IN WORKING ORDER, POUNDS				
NO.	DIA.	LENGTH	DRIVING	RIGID	ENGINE	ENGINE AND TENDER	TENDER	TRAILING WHEELS	DRIVERS	LEADING WHEELS	TOTAL ENGINE
268	2″	13′-$2\frac{9}{16}$″	11′-0″	11′-0″	23′-4″	51′-4″	85000	——	108850	34850	143700

BOILER PRESSURE	FUEL	HEATING SURFACE, SQ. FT.				GRATE AREA	GAUGE OF TRACK	
POUNDS PER SQ. INCH ABOVE ATMOSPHERE	KIND	FLUES	FIRE BOX	ARCH PIPES	TOTAL	SQUARE FEET	METRES	FEET INCHES
180	Wood or Coal	1843.8	187.7	——	2031.5	26.1	1.435	4′-$8\frac{1}{2}$″

FOR HAULING CAPACITY SEE PAGE 290.

230
230
E. F. C. B.

BUILT BY

BROOKS LOCOMOTIVE WORKS

DUNKIRK, N. Y., U.S.A.

1894

FOR THE CENTRAL RAILWAY OF BRAZIL.

CODE WORD, YELDREN. SERIES, 530.

TYPE, 12-WHEELED FREIGHT. CLASS, 21 F.

WITH 8-WHEELED TENDER

TANK CAPACITY 4000 U. S. GALLONS AND 8½ TONS FUEL.

CYLINDERS			WHEELS								BOILER		FIRE BOX		
TYPE	DIA.	STROKE	TENDER		TRAILING		COUPLED DRIVERS		LEADING		TYPE	DIA.	TYPE	LENGTH	WIDTH
			NO.	DIA.	NO.	DIA.	NO.	DIA.	NO.	DIA.					
Simple	21″	26″	8	30″	—	—	8	54″	4	28″	Improved Belpaire	68″	Long	114″	38½″

FLUES			WHEEL BASE				AVERAGE WEIGHT IN WORKING ORDER, POUNDS				
NO.	DIA.	LENGTH	DRIVING	RIGID	ENGINE	ENGINE AND TENDER	TENDER	TRAILING WHEELS	DRIVERS	LEADING WHEELS	TOTAL ENGINE
248	2¼″	13′-10½″	15′-6″	15′-6″	25′-3″	52′-6¾″	82000	—	142000	28000	170000

BOILER PRESSURE	FUEL	HEATING SURFACE, SQ. FT.				GRATE AREA	GAUGE OF TRACK	
POUNDS PER SQ. INCH ABOVE ATMOSPHERE	KIND	FLUES	FIRE BOX	ARCH PIPES	TOTAL	SQUARE FEET	METRES	FEET INCHES
180	Bituminous Coal	1991	209	—	2200	29.3	1.60	5′-3″

FOR HAULING CAPACITY SEE PAGE 290.

2
THE CANADIAN COPPER CO.
H.P. McINTOSH
2
2

BUILT BY

BROOKS LOCOMOTIVE WORKS

DUNKIRK, N. Y., U.S.A.

1895

FOR THE CANADIAN COPPER COMPANY.

CODE WORD, YEOMAN. SERIES, 566.

TYPE, 6-WHEELED SWITCHER. CLASS, 17 H.

WITH 8-WHEELED TENDER, SLOPING BACK TANK, CAPACITY 2500 U. S. GALLONS AND 4 TONS FUEL.

CYLINDERS			WHEELS								BOILER		FIRE BOX		
TYPE	DIA.	STROKE	TENDER		TRAILING		COUPLED DRIVERS		LEADING		TYPE	DIA.	TYPE	LENGTH	WIDTH
			NO.	DIA.	NO.	DIA.	NO.	DIA.	NO.	DIA.					
Simple	17″	24″	8	30″	—	—	6	50″	—	—	Crown Bar, Wagon Top	50¼″	Long	84″	34″

FLUES			WHEEL BASE				AVERAGE WEIGHT IN WORKING ORDER, POUNDS				
NO.	DIA.	LENGTH	DRIVING	RIGID	ENGINE	ENGINE AND TENDER	TENDER	TRAILING WHEELS	DRIVERS	LEADING WHEELS	TOTAL ENGINE
156	2″	9′-7″	10′-0″	10′-0″	10′-0″	36′-0″	62000	—	80000	—	80000

BOILER PRESSURE	FUEL	HEATING SURFACE, SQ. FT.				GRATE AREA	GAUGE OF TRACK	
POUNDS PER SQ. INCH ABOVE ATMOSPHERE	KIND	FLUES	FIRE BOX	ARCH PIPES	TOTAL	SQUARE FEET	METRES	FEET INCHES
150	Bituminous Coal	770	94	—	864	18.6	1.435	4′-8½″

FOR HAULING CAPACITY SEE PAGE 290.

1
TRANSVAAL
AND
DELAGOA BAY COLLIERIES.
BROOKS

BUILT BY

BROOKS LOCOMOTIVE WORKS

DUNKIRK, N. Y., U.S.A.

1896

FOR THE TRANSVAAL & DELAGOA BAY COLLIERIES OF SOUTH AFRICA.

CODE WORD, YESTEL. SERIES, 593.

TYPE, 4-WHEELED SADDLE TANK ENGINE. CLASS, 13 E. T.

TANK CAPACITY 600 U. S. GALLONS AND 1 TON FUEL.

CYLINDERS			WHEELS								BOILER		FIRE BOX		
			TENDER		TRAILING		COUPLED DRIVERS		LEADING						
TYPE	DIA.	STROKE	NO.	DIA.	NO.	DIA.	NO.	DIA.	NO.	DIA.	TYPE	DIA.	TYPE	LENGTH	WIDTH
Simple	13″	18″	—	—	—	—	4	42″	—	—	Rad. Stay, Straight Top	40″	Deep	42″	28″

FLUES			WHEEL BASE			AVERAGE WEIGHT IN WORKING ORDER, POUNDS					
NO.	DIA.	LENGTH	DRIVING	RIGID	ENGINE	ENGINE AND TENDER	TENDER	TRAILING WHEELS	DRIVERS	LEADING WHEELS	TOTAL ENGINE
96	2″	9′-0″	5′-8″	5′-8″	5′-8″	—	—	—	42000	—	42000

BOILER PRESSURE	FUEL	HEATING SURFACE, SQ. FT.				GRATE AREA	GAUGE OF TRACK	
POUNDS PER SQ. INCH ABOVE ATMOSPHERE	KIND	FLUES	FIRE BOX	ARCH PIPES	TOTAL	SQUARE FEET	METRES	FEET INCHES
150	Bituminous Coal	448	49″	—	497	7.8	1.067	3′-6″

FOR HAULING CAPACITY SEE PAGE 290.

E. F. C. B.
200

BUILT BY

BROOKS LOCOMOTIVE WORKS

DUNKIRK, N. Y., U.S.A.

1894

FOR THE CENTRAL RAILWAY OF BRAZIL.

CODE WORD, YOCKEL. SERIES, 533.

TYPE, 6-COUPLED DOUBLE ENDER TANK ENGINE. CLASS, 18 B. R. x.

REAR TANK, CAPACITY 2400 U. S. GALLONS AND $3\frac{1}{2}$ TONS FUEL.

CYLINDERS			WHEELS								BOILER		FIRE BOX		
TYPE	DIA.	STROKE	TENDER NO.	TENDER DIA.	TRAILING NO.	TRAILING DIA.	COUPLED DRIVERS NO.	COUPLED DRIVERS DIA.	LEADING NO.	LEADING DIA.	TYPE	DIA.	TYPE	LENGTH	WIDTH
Simple	18″	24″	—	—	6	$29\frac{1}{2}$″	6	62″	2	$29\frac{1}{2}$	Crown Bar, Wagon Top	58″	Sloping	96″	$38\frac{1}{2}$″

FLUES			WHEEL BASE				AVERAGE WEIGHT IN WORKING ORDER, POUNDS				
NO.	DIA.	LENGTH	DRIVING	RIGID	ENGINE	ENGINE AND TENDER	TENDER	TRAILING WHEELS	DRIVERS	LEADING WHEELS	TOTAL ENGINE
252	2″	11′-$1\frac{3}{8}$″	14′-0″	14′-0″	34′-0″	—	—	50000	110000	16000	176000

BOILER PRESSURE	FUEL	HEATING SURFACE, SQ. FT.				GRATE AREA	GAUGE OF TRACK	
POUNDS PER SQ. INCH ABOVE ATMOSPHERE	KIND	FLUES	FIRE BOX	ARCH PIPES	TOTAL	SQUARE FEET	METRES	FEET INCHES
180	Bituminous Coal	1456	156	—	1612	24.6	1.60	5′-3″

FOR HAULING CAPACITY SEE PAGE 290.

N. W. T. K.
4
2710

BUILT BY

BROOKS LOCOMOTIVE WORKS

DUNKIRK, N. Y., U.S.A.

1896

FOR THE NANWA RAILWAY OF JAPAN.

CODE WORD, YODLER. SERIES, 588.

TYPE, 6-COUPLED DOUBLE ENDER TANK ENGINE. CLASS, 15 B. P. Y.

SIDE TANKS, CAPACITY 1200 U. S. GALLONS AND 1½ TONS FUEL.

CYLINDERS			WHEELS								BOILER		FIRE BOX		
TYPE	DIA.	STROKE	TENDER		TRAILING		COUPLED DRIVERS		LEADING		TYPE	DIA.	TYPE	LENGTH	WIDTH
			NO.	DIA.	NO.	DIA.	NO.	DIA.	NO.	DIA.					
Simple	15″	22″	—	—	2	26″	6	48″	2	26″	Rad. Stay, Straight Top	54″	Long, Wide, Sloping	78″	29″

FLUES			WHEEL BASE				AVERAGE WEIGHT IN WORKING ORDER, POUNDS				
NO.	DIA.	LENGTH	DRIVING	RIGID	ENGINE	ENGINE AND TENDER	TENDER	TRAILING WHEELS	DRIVERS	LEADING WHEELS	TOTAL ENGINE
210	1¾″	9′-4″	10′-4″	10′-4″	23′-8″	——	——	9000	74000	11000	94000

BOILER PRESSURE	FUEL	HEATING SURFACE, SQ. FT.				GRATE AREA	GAUGE OF TRACK	
POUNDS PER SQ. INCH ABOVE ATMOSPHERE	KIND	FLUES	FIRE BOX	ARCH PIPES	TOTAL	SQUARE FEET	METRES	FEET INCHES
150	Bituminous Coal	894.6	87.2	——	981.8	15.2	1.067	3′-6″

FOR HAULING CAPACITY SEE PAGE 290.

6
HANKAKU RY. CO.
6

BUILT BY
BROOKS LOCOMOTIVE WORKS
DUNKIRK, N. Y., U.S.A.
1898
FOR THE HANKAKU RAILWAY
OF JAPAN.

CODE WORD, YODMAT. SERIES, 666.

TYPE, 6-COUPLED DOUBLE ENDER TANK ENGINE. CLASS, 15 B. P. Y.

SIDE TANKS, CAPACITY 1320 U. S. GALLONS AND 2 TONS FUEL.

CYLINDERS			WHEELS								BOILER		FIRE BOX		
TYPE	DIA.	STROKE	TENDER		TRAILING		COUPLED DRIVERS		LEADING		TYPE	DIA.	TYPE	LENGTH	WIDTH
			NO.	DIA.	NO.	DIA.	NO.	DIA.	NO.	DIA.					
Simple	15″	22″	—	—	2	$27\frac{1}{2}$″	6	52″	2	$27\frac{1}{2}$″	Rad. Stay, Straight Top	54″	Long, Wide, Sloping	78″	$29\frac{1}{2}$″

FLUES			WHEEL BASE					AVERAGE WEIGHT IN WORKING ORDER, POUNDS			
NO.	DIA.	LENGTH	DRIVING	RIGID	ENGINE	ENGINE AND TENDER	TENDER	TRAILING WHEELS	DRIVERS	LEADING WHEELS	TOTAL ENGINE
210	$1\frac{3}{4}$″	9′-$4\frac{1}{16}$″	10′-4″	10′-4″	23′-8″	——	——	11000	74000	10000	95000

BOILER PRESSURE	FUEL	HEATING SURFACE, SQ. FT.				GRATE AREA	GAUGE OF TRACK	
POUNDS PER SQ. INCH ABOVE ATMOSPHERE	KIND	FLUES	FIRE BOX	ARCH PIPES	TOTAL	SQUARE FEET	METRES	FEET INCHES
160	Bituminous Coal	890	84.0	——	974	15.6	1.067	3′-6″

FOR HAULING CAPACITY SEE PAGE 290.

KŌYA T.K.
2

BUILT BY

BROOKS LOCOMOTIVE WORKS

DUNKIRK, N. Y., U.S.A.

1897

FOR THE KŌYA RAILWAY COMPANY
OF JAPAN.

CODE WORD, YODSTAR. SERIES, **600.**

TYPE, 6-COUPLED DOUBLE ENDER TANK ENGINE. CLASS, 15 B. P. Y.

SIDE TANKS, CAPACITY 1560 U. S. GALLONS AND 1½ TONS FUEL.

CYLINDERS			WHEELS								BOILER		FIRE BOX		
TYPE	DIA.	STROKE	TENDER		TRAILING		COUPLED DRIVERS		LEADING		TYPE	DIA.	TYPE	LENGTH	WIDTH
			NO.	DIA.	NO.	DIA.	NO.	DIA.	NO.	DIA.					
Simple	15″	22″	—	—	2	26″	6	50″	2	26″	Rad. Stay, Straight Top	51″	Long, Wide, Sloping	75″	$29\frac{1}{2}$″

FLUES			WHEEL BASE			AVERAGE WEIGHT IN WORKING ORDER, POUNDS					
NO.	DIA.	LENGTH	DRIVING	RIGID	ENGINE	ENGINE AND TENDER	TENDER	TRAILING WHEELS	DRIVERS	LEADING WHEELS	TOTAL ENGINE
216	$1\frac{5}{8}$″	9′-$6\frac{1}{16}$″	10′-4″	10′-4″	24′-4″	——	——	11000	70000	11000	92000

BOILER PRESSURE	FUEL	HEATING SURFACE, SQ. FT.				GRATE AREA	GAUGE OF TRACK	
POUNDS PER SQ. INCH ABOVE ATMOSPHERE	KIND	FLUES	FIRE BOX	ARCH PIPES	TOTAL	SQUARE FEET	METRES	FEET INCHES
150	Bituminous Coal	862	78	——	940	14.8	1.067	3′-6″

FOR HAULING CAPACITY SEE PAGE 290.

KOBU T.K.
2

BUILT BY

BROOKS LOCOMOTIVE WORKS

DUNKIRK, N. Y., U.S.A.

1897

FOR THE KOBU RAILWAY OF JAPAN.

CODE WORD, YOGAN. SERIES, 622.

TYPE, 6-COUPLED DOUBLE ENDER TANK ENGINE. CLASS, 14 B. P. Y.

SIDE TANKS, CAPACITY 1440 U. S. GALLONS AND 1½ TONS FUEL.

CYLINDERS			WHEELS								BOILER		FIRE BOX		
			TENDER		TRAILING		COUPLED DRIVERS		LEADING						
TYPE	DIA.	STROKE	NO.	DIA.	NO.	DIA.	NO.	DIA.	NO.	DIA.	TYPE	DIA.	TYPE	LENGTH	WIDTH
Simple	14″	20″	—	—	2	26″	6	48″	2	26″	Rad. Stay, Straight Top	48″	Long, Wide, Sloping	70″	29″

FLUES			WHEEL BASE				AVERAGE WEIGHT IN WORKING ORDER, POUNDS				
NO.	DIA.	LENGTH	DRIVING	RIGID	ENGINE	ENGINE AND TENDER	TENDER	TRAILING WHEELS	DRIVERS	LEADING WHEELS	TOTAL ENGINE
170	$1\frac{3}{4}$″	9′-$1\frac{1}{16}$″	9′-8″	9′-8″	22′-0″	——	——	13000	65000	9000	87000

BOILER PRESSURE	FUEL	HEATING SURFACE, SQ. FT.				GRATE AREA	GAUGE OF TRACK	
POUNDS PER SQ. INCH ABOVE ATMOSPHERE	KIND	FLUES	FIRE BOX	ARCH PIPES	TOTAL	SQUARE FEET	METRES	FEET INCHES
165	Bituminous Coal	693	74	——	767	13.6	1.067	3′-6″

FOR HAULING CAPACITY SEE PAGE 290.

24
KIUSHIU T. K.

BUILT BY

BROOKS LOCOMOTIVE WORKS

DUNKIRK, N. Y., U.S.A.

1898

FOR THE KIUSHIU RAILWAY

OF JAPAN.

CODE WORD, YONDER. SERIES, 630.

TYPE, 6-COUPLED TANK ENGINE. CLASS, 17 B. Y.

SIDE TANKS, CAPACITY 1320 U. S. GALLONS AND $1\frac{1}{2}$ TONS FUEL.

CYLINDERS			WHEELS								BOILER		FIRE BOX		
			TENDER		TRAILING		COUPLED DRIVERS		LEADING						
TYPE	DIA.	STROKE	NO.	DIA.	NO.	DIA.	NO.	DIA.	NO.	DIA.	TYPE	DIA.	TYPE	LENGTH	WIDTH
Simple	17″	22″	—	—	—	—	6	50″	2	30″	Rad. Stay, Straight Top	50″	Long, Wide, Sloping	72″	$29\frac{1}{2}$″

FLUES			WHEEL BASE				AVERAGE WEIGHT IN WORKING ORDER, POUNDS				
NO.	DIA.	LENGTH	DRIVING	RIGID	ENGINE	ENGINE AND TENDER	TENDER	TRAILING WHEELS	DRIVERS	LEADING WHEELS	TOTAL ENGINE
190	$1\frac{3}{4}$″	9′-7″	12′-0″	12′-0″	19′-0″	——	——	——	74000	15600	89600

BOILER PRESSURE	FUEL	HEATING SURFACE, SQ. FT.				GRATE AREA	GAUGE OF TRACK	
POUNDS PER SQ. INCH ABOVE ATMOSPHERE	KIND	FLUES	FIRE BOX	ARCH PIPES	TOTAL	SQUARE FEET	METRES	FEET INCHES
160	Bituminous Coal	827	78.1	——	905.1	14.1	1.067	3′-6″

FOR HAULING CAPACITY SEE PAGE 290.

S. & C. R. R.
SEOUL-CHEMULPO
2
2

BUILT BY

BROOKS LOCOMOTIVE WORKS

DUNKIRK, N. Y., U.S.A.

1897

FOR THE SEOUL-CHEMULPO RAILWAY OF KOREA.

CODE WORD, YONGE. SERIES, 629.

TYPE, 6-COUPLED TANK ENGINE. CLASS, 14 B. Y.

SIDE TANKS, CAPACITY 960 U. S. GALLONS AND 1 TON FUEL.

CYLINDERS			WHEELS								BOILER		FIRE BOX		
			TENDER		TRAILING		COUPLED DRIVERS		LEADING						
TYPE	DIA.	STROKE	NO.	DIA.	NO.	DIA.	NO.	DIA.	NO.	DIA.	TYPE	DIA	TYPE	LENGTH	WIDTH
Simple	14″	22″	—	—	—	—	6	42″	2	28″	Rad. Stay, Straight Top	46″	Deep	54″	35″

FLUES			WHEEL BASE				AVERAGE WEIGHT IN WORKING ORDER, POUNDS				
NO.	DIA.	LENGTH	DRIVING	RIGID	ENGINE	ENGINE AND TENDER	TENDER	TRAILING WHEELS	DRIVERS	LEADING WHEELS	TOTAL ENGINE
122	2″	9′-1″	12′-3″	12′-3″	19′-0″	——	——	——	65000	10000	75000

BOILER PRESSURE	FUEL	HEATING SURFACE, SQ. FT.				GRATE AREA	GAUGE OF TRACK	
POUNDS PER SQ. INCH ABOVE ATMOSPHERE	KIND	FLUES	FIRE BOX	ARCH PIPES	TOTAL	SQUARE FEET	METRES	FEET INCHES
140	Bituminous Coal	575	71.2	——	646.2	12.66	1.435	4′-8½″

FOR HAULING CAPACITY SEE PAGE 290.

3
SEIWA T.K.

BUILT BY

BROOKS LOCOMOTIVE WORKS

DUNKIRK, N. Y., U.S.A.

1897

FOR THE SEIWA RAILWAY OF JAPAN.

CODE WORD, YONKER.

TYPE, 6-WHEELED TANK ENGINE.

SERIES, 625.

CLASS, 15 H. Y.

SIDE TANKS, CAPACITY 1120 U. S. GALLONS AND 1½ TONS FUEL.

CYLINDERS			WHEELS								BOILER		FIRE BOX		
			TENDER		TRAILING		COUPLED DRIVERS		LEADING						
TYPE	DIA.	STROKE	NO.	DIA.	NO.	DIA.	NO.	DIA.	NO.	DIA.	TYPE	DIA.	TYPE	LENGTH	WIDTH
Simple	15″	22″	—	—	—	—	6	48″	—	—	Rad. Stay, Straight Top	50″	Long, Wide, Sloping	72″	29½″

FLUES			WHEEL BASE			AVERAGE WEIGHT IN WORKING ORDER, POUNDS					
NO.	DIA.	LENGTH	DRIVING	RIGID	ENGINE	ENGINE AND TENDER	TENDER	TRAILING WHEELS	DRIVERS	LEADING WHEELS	TOTAL ENGINE
176	1¾″	9′-7″	11′-9″	11′-9″	11′-9″	—	—	—	85000	—	85000

BOILER PRESSURE	FUEL	HEATING SURFACE, SQ. FT.				GRATE AREA	GAUGE OF TRACK	
POUNDS PER SQ. INCH ABOVE ATMOSPHERE	KIND	FLUES	FIRE BOX	ARCH PIPES	TOTAL	SQUARE FEET	METRES	FEET INCHES
140	Bituminous Coal	764	77	—	841	14.1	1.067	3′-6″

FOR HAULING CAPACITY SEE PAGE 290.

SANUKI T.K.
1

BUILT BY
BROOKS LOCOMOTIVE WORKS
DUNKIRK, N. Y., U.S.A.
1897
FOR THE SANUKI RAILWAY
OF JAPAN.

CODE WORD, YOWL. SERIES, 631.

TYPE, 6-WHEELED TANK ENGINE. CLASS, 14 H. Y.

SIDE TANKS, CAPACITY 972 U. S. GALLONS AND 1½ TON FUEL.

CYLINDERS			WHEELS								BOILER		FIRE BOX		
TYPE	DIA.	STROKE	TENDER		TRAILING		COUPLED DRIVERS		LEADING		TYPE	DIA.	TYPE	LENGTH	WIDTH
			NO.	DIA.	NO.	DIA.	NO.	DIA.	NO.	DIA.					
Simple	14″	18″	—	—	—	—	6	36″	—	—	Rad. Stay, Straight Top	45″	Long, Sloping	$60\frac{1}{8}$″	$23\frac{1}{8}$″

FLUES			WHEEL BASE				AVERAGE WEIGHT IN WORKING ORDER, POUNDS					
NO.	DIA.	LENGTH	DRIVING	RIGID	ENGINE	ENGINE AND TENDER	TENDER	TRAILING WHEELS	DRIVERS	LEADING WHEELS	TOTAL ENGINE
124	$1\frac{3}{4}$″	8′-4″	11′-0″	11′-0″	11′-0″	——	——	——	60000	——	60000

BOILER PRESSURE	FUEL	HEATING SURFACE, SQ. FT.				GRATE AREA	GAUGE OF TRACK		
POUNDS PER SQ. INCH ABOVE ATMOSPHERE	KIND	FLUES	FIRE BOX	ARCH PIPES	TOTAL	SQUARE FEET	METRES	FEET	INCHES
150	Bituminous Coal	466	68	——	534	9.5	1.067	3′-6″	

FOR HAULING CAPACITY SEE PAGE 290.

2
2
SUNG-WU RAILWAY

BUILT BY

BROOKS LOCOMOTIVE WORKS

DUNKIRK, N. Y., U.S.A.

1897

FOR THE SUNG-WU RAILWAY OF CHINA.

CODE WORD, YUCCAN. SERIES, 611.

TYPE, 4-COUPLED DOUBLE ENDER TANK ENGINE. CLASS, 17 J. P. Y.

SIDE TANKS, CAPACITY 1360 U. S. GALLONS AND 1¼ TONS FUEL.

CYLINDERS			WHEELS								BOILER		FIRE BOX		
			TENDER		TRAILING		COUPLED DRIVERS		LEADING						
TYPE	DIA.	STROKE	NO.	DIA.	NO.	DIA.	NO.	DIA.	NO.	DIA.	TYPE	DIA.	TYPE	LENGTH	WIDTH
Simple	16.536″	23.62″	—	—	2	42″	4	62.59″	2	42″	Crown Bar, Wagon Top	48″	Long, Sloping	78″	34″

FLUES			WHEEL BASE			AVERAGE WEIGHT IN WORKING ORDER, POUNDS					
NO.	DIA.	LENGTH	DRIVING	RIGID	ENGINE	ENGINE AND TENDER	TENDER	TRAILING WHEELS	DRIVERS	LEADING WHEELS	TOTAL ENGINE
165	2″	11′-1¼″	7′-6″	7′-6″	20′-0″	—	—	24800	59000	29000	112800

BOILER PRESSURE	FUEL	HEATING SURFACE, SQ. FT.				GRATE AREA	GAUGE OF TRACK		
POUNDS PER SQ. INCH ABOVE ATMOSPHERE	KIND	FLUES	FIRE BOX	ARCH PIPES	TOTAL	SQUARE FEET	METRES	FEET	INCHES
162	Bituminous Coal	957	93.82	—	1050.82	17.9	1.435	4′-8½″	

FOR HAULING CAPACITY SEE PAGE 290.

K. W. T. K.
3

BUILT BY

BROOKS LOCOMOTIVE WORKS

DUNKIRK, N. Y., U.S.A.

1897

FOR THE KIWA RAILWAY OF JAPAN.

CODE WORD, YULAN. SERIES, 615.

TYPE, 4-COUPLED DOUBLE ENDER TANK ENGINE. CLASS, 14 J. P. Y.

SIDE AND REAR TANKS, CAPACITY 1200 U. S. GALLONS AND 2 TONS FUEL.

CYLINDERS			WHEELS								BOILER		FIRE BOX		
TYPE	DIA.	STROKE	TENDER		TRAILING		COUPLED DRIVERS		LEADING		TYPE	DIA.	TYPE	LENGTH	WIDTH
			NO.	DIA.	NO.	DIA.	NO.	DIA.	NO.	DIA.					
Simple	14″	20″	—	—	2	37″	4	52″	2	37″	Rad. Stay, Straight Top	42″	Long Sloping	67″	27″

FLUES			WHEEL BASE				AVERAGE WEIGHT IN WORKING ORDER, POUNDS				
NO.	DIA.	LENGTH	DRIVING	RIGID	ENGINE	ENGINE AND TENDER	TENDER	TRAILING WHEELS	DRIVERS	LEADING WHEELS	TOTAL ENGINE
150	$1\frac{3}{4}$″	9′-7″	7′-6″	7′-6″	19′-6″	——	——	15350	43800	18500	77650

BOILER PRESSURE	FUEL	HEATING SURFACE, SQ. FT.				GRATE AREA	GAUGE OF TRACK	
POUNDS PER SQ. INCH ABOVE ATMOSPHERE	KIND	FLUES	FIRE BOX	ARCH PIPES	TOTAL	SQUARE FEET	METRES	FEET INCHES
140	Bituminous Coal	658	64	——	722	12.5	1.067	3′-6″

FOR HAULING CAPACITY SEE PAGE 290.

BISAI T. K.
1

BUILT BY

BROOKS LOCOMOTIVE WORKS

DUNKIRK, N. Y., U.S.A.

1897

FOR THE BISAI RAILWAY

OF JAPAN.

CODE WORD, YUMAS.

TYPE, 4-COUPLED DOUBLE ENDER TANK ENGINE.

SERIES, 614.

CLASS, 12 A. P. Y.

SIDE TANKS, CAPACITY 700 U. S. GALLONS AND ¾ TON FUEL.

CYLINDERS			WHEELS								BOILER		FIRE BOX		
TYPE	DIA.	STROKE	TENDER NO.	TENDER DIA.	TRAILING NO.	TRAILING DIA.	COUPLED DRIVERS NO.	COUPLED DRIVERS DIA.	LEADING NO.	LEADING DIA.	TYPE	DIA.	TYPE	LENGTH	WIDTH
Simple	12″	18″	—	—	2	24″	4	42″	4	24″	Rad. Stay, Straight Top	42″	Long, Sloping	72″	24″

FLUES			WHEEL BASE				AVERAGE WEIGHT IN WORKING ORDER, POUNDS				
NO.	DIA.	LENGTH	DRIVING	RIGID	ENGINE	ENGINE AND TENDER	TENDER	TRAILING WHEELS	DRIVERS	LEADING WHEELS	TOTAL ENGINE
118	$1\frac{3}{4}$″	9′-0″	7′-6″	7′-6″	24′-0″	——	——	8000	36000	14000	58000

BOILER PRESSURE	FUEL	HEATING SURFACE, SQ. FT.				GRATE AREA	GAUGE OF TRACK	
POUNDS PER SQ. INCH ABOVE ATMOSPHERE	KIND	FLUES	FIRE BOX	ARCH PIPES	TOTAL	SQUARE FEET	METRES	FEET INCHES
165	Bituminous Coal	482.7	67.3	——	550	11.6	1.067	3′-6″

FOR HAULING CAPACITY SEE PAGE 290.

ESTRADA DE FERRO
SANTA MARIA MAGDALENA
2
2

BUILT BY

BROOKS LOCOMOTIVE WORKS

DUNKIRK, N. Y., U.S.A.

1891

FOR THE SANTA MARIA MAGDALENA RAILWAY OF BRAZIL.

CODE WORD, YUPAS. SERIES, 437.

TYPE, 4-COUPLED DOUBLE ENDER SADDLE TANK ENGINE. CLASS, 12 J. P. T.

TANK CAPACITY 700 U. S. GALLONS AND 1 TON FUEL.

CYLINDERS			WHEELS								BOILER		FIRE BOX		
TYPE	DIA.	STROKE	TENDER		TRAILING		COUPLED DRIVERS		LEADING		TYPE	DIA.	TYPE	LENGTH	WIDTH
			NO.	DIA.	NO.	DIA.	NO.	DIA.	NO.	DIA.					
Simple	12″	18″	—	—	2	24″	4	42″	2	24″	Straight Top	40″	Deep	60″	24″

FLUES			WHEEL BASE				AVERAGE WEIGHT IN WORKING ORDER, POUNDS				
NO.	DIA.	LENGTH	DRIVING	RIGID	ENGINE	ENGINE AND TENDER	TENDER	TRAILING WHEELS	DRIVERS	LEADING WHEELS	TOTAL ENGINE.
92	2″	9′-0″	5′-8″	5′-8″	20′-0″	—	—	14000	36000	6000	56000

BOILER PRESSURE	FUEL	HEATING SURFACE, SQ. FT.				GRATE AREA	GAUGE OF TRACK		
POUNDS PER SQ. INCH ABOVE ATMOSPHERE	KIND	FLUES	FIRE BOX	ARCH PIPES	TOTAL	SQUARE FEET	METRES	FEET	INCHES
150	Bituminous Coal	430	63	—	493	9.6	1.000	3′-3 3/8″	

FOR HAULING CAPACITY SEE PAGE 290.

N.Y.T.K.
3

BUILT BY

BROOKS LOCOMOTIVE WORKS

DUNKIRK, N. Y., U.S.A.

1897

FOR THE NANYO RAILWAY OF JAPAN.

CODE WORD, YUPONT.

TYPE, 4-WHEELED TANK ENGINE.

SERIES, 613.

CLASS, 8 E. Y.

SIDE TANKS, CAPACITY 360 U. S. GALLONS AND ½ TON FUEL.

CYLINDERS			WHEELS								BOILER		FIRE BOX		
TYPE	DIA.	STROKE	TENDER		TRAILING		COUPLED DRIVERS		LEADING		TYPE	DIA.	TYPE	LENGTH	WIDTH
			NO.	DIA.	NO.	DIA.	NO.	DIA.	NO.	DIA.					
Simple	8″	14″	—	—	—	—	4	30″	—	—	Rad. Stay, Straight Top	30″	Deep	27″	24⅝″

FLUES			WHEEL BASE			AVERAGE WEIGHT IN WORKING ORDER, POUNDS					
NO.	DIA.	LENGTH	DRIVING	RIGID	ENGINE	ENGINE AND TENDER	TENDER	TRAILING WHEELS	DRIVERS	LEADING WHEELS	TOTAL ENGINE
56	1⅝″	8′-0″	4′-6″	4′-6″	4′-6″	—	—	—	23000	—	23000

BOILER PRESSURE	FUEL	HEATING SURFACE, SQ. FT.				GRATE AREA	GAUGE OF TRACK	
POUNDS PER SQ. INCH ABOVE ATMOSPHERE	KIND	FLUES	FIRE BOX	ARCH PIPES	TOTAL	SQUARE FEET	METRES	FEET INCHES
150	Bituminous Coal	212	22.4	—	234.4	4.3	.7628	2′-6″

FOR HAULING CAPACITY SEE PAGE 290.

TABLES OF INFORMATION.

EXPLANATION OF TABLES.

In the formulæ used to calculate the tables found on the succeeding pages, the following symbols are used :

D = Diameter of cylinders in inches.
L = Length of stroke in inches.
w = Diameter of drivers in inches.
P = Boiler pressure.
p = Mean available pressure in cylinders = mean effective pressure less an amount equivalent to the internal friction of the engine.
W = Weight of engine and tender in tons of 2000 pounds.
T = Tractive power in pounds.
H = Hauling capacity = weight of train behind the draw bar in tons of 2000 pounds.
S = Speed in miles per hour.
M = Grade in feet per mile.
C = Curvature of track in degrees.
R_s = Resistance of train in pounds per ton of 2000 pounds, due to speed.
R_m = Resistance of train in pounds per ton of 2000 pounds, due to grade.
R_c = Resistance of train in pounds per ton of 2000 pounds, due to curves.
$R = R_s + R_m + R_c$ = Resistance of train in pounds per ton of 2000 pounds.

Table I.

TRACTIVE POWER OF LOCOMOTIVES.

This table gives the value of T for different values of p; it is calculated from the formula,

$$T = \frac{D^2 \times L}{W} \times p$$

Table II.

NUMBER OF FEET THE PISTON TRAVELS PER ENGINE MILE.

This table is to enable one to find the speed of the piston in feet per minute when the stroke, driving wheel diameter and speed of engine in miles per hour are known. The table is in two parts, being divided by a diagonal line; the upper part gives the piston travel per engine mile as calculated from the stroke and driving wheel diameter, while the lower part gives the piston travel per engine mile as calculated from the piston speed in feet per minute and the speed in miles per hour at which the engine is running.

The use of the table is best explained by means of an example. Let us take a locomotive with 24″ stroke and 62″ drivers, running at a speed of thirty miles per hour. In the upper part of the table on the same line as 24″ in the stroke column, and under 62″ diameter of drivers, is found 1301; now in the lower part of the table on the same line with thirty miles per hour look for the number nearest to 1301, which number, 1300, is to be found over a piston speed of 650 feet per minute. The piston speed of the engine in this example is therefore very close to 650 feet per minute.

Table III.

MEAN AVAILABLE PRESSURES AT DIFFERENT PISTON SPEEDS AND BOILER PRESSURES.

In order to avoid an extra calculation for the internal friction of the engine, the mean available instead of the mean effective pressures at the different piston speeds are given. The mean available pressure is the mean effective pressure, reduced by the amount that would be required to overcome the internal friction of the engine.

Table IV.

NUMBER OF REVOLUTIONS OF DRIVING WHEELS PER MILE.

This table gives the number of revolutions made by driving wheels of different diameters in running a mile.

Table V.

TRAIN RESISTANCE IN POUNDS PER TON.

In this table are given the values of train resistance for different grades and speeds.

The resistances due to speed have been calculated from the formula :

$$R_s = \frac{S}{4} + 2$$

while for the grade resistances the formula

$$R_m = 0.3788\ M$$

has been used.

The values in the table are equal to $R_s + R_m$. On the line with a speed of 0 miles per hour are to be found the resistances due to grade alone, while in the column under 0 grade, the resistances due to speed on a level track are given.

Table VI.

RESISTANCE OF CURVES.

The easiest way to account for the resistance due to curvature of the track is to find the grade that offers the same resistance as the curve in question. The resistance due to curvature is taken at ½ pound per degree of curvature.

Then,

$$R_c = 0.5\ C$$

but,

$$R_m = 0.3788\ M$$

To find the equivalent grade put $R_c = R_m$

or

$$0.3788\ M = 0.5\ C$$

then

$$M = \frac{0.5}{0.3788}\ C = 1.32\ C$$

Therefore, to find the grade equivalent of a curve multiply the curve in degrees by 1.32 and the result will be the equivalent grade in feet per mile. The grade equivalents are given in this table.

TABLE VII.

SPEED IN MILES PER HOUR.

This table gives the speed in miles per hour for various diameters of drivers and different revolutions of same per minute.

HAULING CAPACITY OF LOCOMOTIVES.

To find the hauling capacity of a locomotive, first find the piston speed by means of Table II., then look in Table III. for the mean available pressure corresponding to that piston speed and to the boiler pressure of the engine in question. Then in Table I. find the tractive power corresponding to the diameter of cylinder, stroke, driving wheel diameter and the mean available pressure nearest to the one just found in Table III. After finding the grade equivalent of the curvature in Table VI., add it to the actual grade; then under this sum, and on a line with the speed in miles per hour in Table V., ascertain the total resistance, R. The hauling capacity in tons is then represented by the formula:

$$H = \frac{T}{R} - W$$

that is, the hauling capacity equals the tractive power divided by the resistance per ton, less the weight of engine and tender.

TABLE VIII.

MEAN EFFECTIVE PRESSURE.

This diagram gives the ratio between the mean effective pressure on the piston and the boiler pressure at different piston speeds.

TABLE IX.

MEAN AVAILABLE PRESSURE.

This diagram gives the ratio between the mean available pressure acting on the piston, and the boiler pressure at different piston speeds.

COMPOUND LOCOMOTIVES.—For tables of relative dimensions see pages 22–24.

TABLE I.

TRACTIVE POWER OF LOCOMOTIVES, IN POUNDS, FOR DIFFERENT MEAN EFFECTIVE PRESSURES.

CYLINDERS DIA. STROKE	MEAN EFF. PRES.	DIAMETER OF DRIVERS 28"	30"	32"	34"	36"	38"	40"	42"	44"	46"	48"	50"
8" x 10"	1	22.85	21.33	20.00	18.82	17.78	16.84	16.00	15.24	14.54	13.91	13.33	12.80
	35	800	746	700	659	622	589	560	533	509	487	466	448
	50	1142	1066	1000	941	889	842	800	762	727	695	666	640
	65	1485	1386	1300	1223	1156	1094	1040	990	945	904	866	832
	80	1828	1706	1600	1505	1422	1347	1280	1219	1163	1113	1066	1024
	95	2170	2026	1900	1788	1689	1600	1520	1448	1381	1321	1266	1216
	110	2514	2346	2200	2070	1956	1852	1760	1676	1599	1530	1466	1408
	125	2856	2666	2500	2352	2222	2105	2000	1905	1817	1739	1666	1600
8" x 12"	1	27.42	25.59	24.00	22.58	21.33	20.21	19.20	18.28	17.45	16.69	16.00	15.36
	35	960	896	840	790	746	707	672	640	611	584	560	537
	50	1371	1279	1200	1129	1066	1010	960	914	872	834	800	768
	65	1782	1663	1560	1467	1386	1313	1248	1188	1134	1085	1040	998
	80	2193	2047	1920	1806	1706	1617	1536	1462	1396	1335	1280	1228
	95	2605	2431	2280	2145	2026	1920	1824	1736	1657	1585	1520	1459
	110	3016	2815	2640	2484	2346	2223	2112	2011	1920	1836	1760	1690
	125	3427	3199	3000	2822	2666	2526	2400	2285	2181	2086	2000	1920
8" x 14"	1	32.00	29.86	28.00	26.35	24.89	23.58	22.40	21.33	20.36	19.48	18.66	17.92
	35	1120	1045	980	922	871	825	784	746	712	682	653	627
	50	1600	1493	1400	1317	1244	1179	1120	1066	1018	974	933	896
	65	2080	1941	1820	1712	1618	1533	1456	1386	1323	1266	1213	1165
	80	2560	2388	2240	2108	1991	1886	1792	1706	1628	1558	1493	1433
	95	3040	2836	2660	2503	2364	2240	2128	2026	1934	1850	1772	1702
	110	3520	3285	3080	2898	2738	2594	2464	2346	2240	2143	2052	1971
	125	4000	3732	3500	3294	3111	2947	2800	2666	2545	2435	2332	2240
8" x 16"	1	36.57	34.12	32.00	30.11	28.44	26.94	25.60	24.38	23.27	22.26	21.33	20.48
	35	1280	1194	1120	1054	995	943	896	853	815	779	747	717
	50	1828	1706	1600	1505	1422	1347	1280	1219	1163	1113	1066	1024
	65	2377	2218	2080	1957	1848	1751	1664	1584	1512	1447	1386	1331
	80	2925	2730	2560	2408	2275	2155	2048	1950	1861	1781	1706	1638
	95	3474	3242	3040	2860	2702	2559	2432	2316	2210	2114	2026	1945
	110	4023	3754	3520	3312	3128	2963	2816	2682	2560	2449	2346	2253
	125	4571	4266	4000	3764	3555	3367	3200	3047	2909	2782	2666	2560

TABLE I.—(Continued).

TRACTIVE POWER OF LOCOMOTIVES, IN POUNDS, FOR DIFFERENT MEAN EFFECTIVE PRESSURES.

CYLINDERS	MEAN EFF. PRES.	DIAMETER OF DRIVERS											
DIA. STROKE		28″	30″	32″	34″	36″	38″	40″	42″	44″	46″	48″	50″
9″ x 12″	1	34.71	32.40	30.37	28.58	27.00	25.58	24.30	23.14	22.09	21.13	20.25	19.44
	35	1214	1134	1063	1000	945	895	850	810	773	740	709	680
	50	1735	1620	1518	1429	1350	1279	1215	1157	1104	1056	1012	972
	65	2256	2106	1974	1857	1755	1662	1579	1504	1435	1373	1316	1263
	80	2776	2592	2429	2286	2160	2046	1944	1851	1767	1690	1620	1555
	95	3297	3078	2885	2715	2565	2430	2308	2198	2098	2007	1923	1846
	110	3818	3564	3341	3144	2970	2814	2673	2545	2430	2324	2227	2138
	125	4339	4050	3796	3572	3375	3197	3037	2892	2761	2641	2531	2430
9″ x 14″	1	40.50	37.80	35.44	33.35	31.50	29.84	28.35	27.00	25.77	24.65	23.62	22.68
	35	1417	1323	1240	1167	1102	1044	992	945	902	863	827	794
	50	2025	1890	1772	1667	1575	1492	1417	1350	1288	1232	1181	1134
	65	2632	2457	2303	2168	2047	1939	1842	1755	1675	1602	1535	1474
	80	3240	3024	2835	2668	2520	2387	2268	2160	2061	1972	1889	1814
	95	3847	3591	3366	3168	2992	2835	2693	2565	2448	2341	2244	2154
	110	4455	4158	3898	3669	3465	3282	3118	2970	2835	2711	2598	2495
	125	5061	4725	4430	4169	3937	3730	3544	3375	3221	3081	2952	2835
9″ x 16″	1	46.28	43.20	40.50	38.12	36.00	34.10	32.40	30.86	29.45	28.17	27.00	25.92
	35	1620	1512	1417	1334	1260	1193	1134	1080	1031	986	945	907
	50	2314	2160	2025	1906	1800	1705	1620	1543	1472	1408	1350	1296
	65	3008	2808	2632	2478	2340	2216	2106	2006	1914	1831	1755	1685
	80	3702	3456	3240	3049	2880	2728	2592	2469	2356	2254	2160	2074
	95	4396	4104	3847	3621	3420	3239	3078	2932	2798	2676	2565	2462
	110	5091	4752	4455	4193	3960	3751	3564	3395	3240	3099	2970	2851
	125	5786	5400	5063	4765	4500	4263	4050	3858	3681	3521	3375	3240
9″ x 18″	1	52.07	48.60	45.56	42.88	40.50	38.37	36.45	34.71	33.14	31.70	30.38	29.16
	35	1822	1701	1594	1501	1417	1343	1276	1215	1160	1109	1063	1021
	50	2603	2430	2278	2144	2025	1918	1822	1735	1657	1585	1519	1458
	65	3385	3159	2961	2787	2632	2494	2369	2256	2154	2060	1975	1895
	80	4165	3888	3645	3430	3240	3069	2916	2777	2651	2536	2430	2333
	95	4946	4617	4328	4073	3847	3645	3463	3297	3148	3011	2886	2770
	110	5728	5346	5011	4717	4455	4221	4010	3818	3646	3487	3342	3208
	125	6510	6075	5696	5360	5063	4797	4557	4339	4143	3963	3798	3645

Table I.—(Continued).

TRACTIVE POWER OF LOCOMOTIVES, IN POUNDS, FOR DIFFERENT MEAN EFFECTIVE PRESSURES.

CYLINDERS DIA. STROKE	MEAN EFF. PRES.	DIAMETER OF DRIVERS 28″	30″	32″	34″	36″	38″	40″	42″	44″	46″	48″	50″
10″ x 12″	1	42.86	40.00	37.50	35.30	33.33	31.58	30.00	28.57	27.27	26.09	25.00	24.00
	35	1500	1400	1313	1235	1166	1105	1050	1000	954	913	875	840
	50	2143	2000	1875	1765	1667	1579	1500	1428	1363	1305	1250	1200
	65	2786	2600	2438	2294	2167	2053	1950	1857	1772	1696	1625	1560
	80	3429	3200	3000	2824	2667	2526	2400	2286	2181	2087	2000	1920
	95	4071	3800	3562	3353	3167	3000	2850	2714	2590	2478	2375	2280
	110	4715	4400	4125	3883	3667	3474	3300	3143	3000	2870	2750	2640
	125	5358	5000	4688	4413	4167	3948	3750	3571	3409	3261	3125	3000
10″ x 14″	1	50.00	46.67	43.75	41.18	38.89	36.84	35.00	33.33	31.82	30.44	29.17	28.00
	35	1750	1633	1531	1441	1361	1289	1225	1167	1114	1065	1021	980
	50	2500	2333	2187	2059	1944	1842	1750	1667	1591	1522	1459	1400
	65	3250	3033	2844	2677	2528	2395	2275	2167	2068	1978	1896	1820
	80	4000	3733	3500	3294	3111	2947	2800	2666	2546	2435	2334	2240
	95	4750	4434	4156	3912	3694	3500	3325	3166	3023	2892	2771	2660
	110	5500	5134	4813	4530	4278	4053	3850	3667	3500	3349	3209	3080
	125	6250	5834	5469	5148	4861	4605	4375	4167	3978	3805	3647	3500
10″ x 16″	1	57.15	53.33	50.00	47.06	44.45	42.11	40.00	38.10	36.37	34.78	33.33	32.00
	35	2000	1866	1750	1647	1556	1474	1400	1333	1273	1217	1167	1120
	50	2857	2666	2500	2353	2222	2105	2000	1905	1818	1739	1667	1600
	65	3714	3466	3250	3059	2889	2737	2600	2476	2364	2261	2167	2080
	80	4572	4266	4000	3765	3556	3369	3200	3048	2909	2782	2666	2560
	95	5430	5066	4750	4471	4223	4000	3800	3619	3455	3304	3167	3040
	110	6287	5867	5500	5177	4890	4633	4400	4191	4001	3826	3667	3520
	125	7144	6667	6250	5883	5557	5264	5000	4763	4547	4348	4167	4000
10″ x 18″	1	64.29	60.00	56.25	52.94	50.00	47.37	45.00	42.86	40.91	39.13	37.50	36.00
	35	2250	2100	1969	1853	1750	1658	1575	1500	1432	1370	1313	1260
	50	3214	3000	2812	2647	2500	2368	2250	2143	2045	1956	1875	1800
	65	4178	3900	3656	3441	3250	3079	2925	2786	2659	2543	2438	2340
	80	5143	4800	4500	4235	4000	3790	3600	3429	3273	3130	3000	2880
	95	6107	5700	5344	5029	4750	4500	4275	4072	3886	3717	3562	3420
	110	7072	6600	6188	5824	5500	5211	4950	4715	4501	4305	4126	3960
	125	8037	7500	7032	6618	6250	5922	5625	5358	5114	4892	4688	4500

Table I.—(Continued).

TRACTIVE POWER OF LOCOMOTIVES, IN POUNDS, FOR DIFFERENT MEAN EFFECTIVE PRESSURES.

CYLINDERS DIA. STROKE	MEAN EFF. PRES.	DIAMETER OF DRIVERS 28″	30″	32″	34″	36″	38″	40″	42″	44″	46″	48″	50″
11″ x 14″	1	60.50	56.46	52.91	49.82	47.05	44.58	42.35	40.33	38.50	36.83	35.29	33.88
	35	2117	1976	1853	1743	1646	1560	1482	1411	1347	1289	1235	1186
	50	3025	2823	2647	2491	2352	2229	2117	2016	1925	1841	1764	1694
	65	3932	3669	3441	3238	3058	2897	2752	2621	2502	2394	2294	2202
	80	4840	4516	4235	3985	3764	3566	3387	3226	3080	2946	2823	2710
	95	5747	5363	5029	4732	4469	4235	4023	3831	3657	3498	3352	3218
	110	6655	6210	5824	5480	5176	4904	4658	4436	4235	4051	3882	3727
	125	7563	7057	6618	6228	5882	5572	5294	5041	4813	4604	4411	4235
11″ x 16″	1	69.14	64.53	60.50	56.94	53.78	50.91	48.40	46.09	44.00	42.09	40.33	38.72
	35	2420	2258	2117	1993	1882	1783	1694	1613	1540	1473	1411	1355
	50	3457	3226	3025	2847	2689	2547	2420	2304	2200	2104	2016	1936
	65	4494	4194	3932	3701	3495	3311	3145	2995	2860	2736	2621	2516
	80	5531	5162	4840	4555	4302	4075	3871	3687	3520	3367	3226	3097
	95	6568	6130	5747	5409	5108	4839	4597	4378	4180	3998	3831	3678
	110	7606	7098	6655	6264	5916	5603	5324	5070	4840	4630	4436	4259
	125	8643	8066	7563	7118	6721	6367	6050	5761	5500	5261	5041	4840
11″ x 18″	1	77.78	72.60	68.06	64.06	60.50	57.31	54.45	51.86	49.50	47.35	45.37	43.56
	35	2722	2541	2382	2242	2117	2006	1906	1815	1732	1657	1588	1524
	50	3889	3630	3403	3203	3025	2865	2722	2593	2475	2367	2268	2178
	65	5055	4718	4423	4163	3932	3724	3539	3370	3217	3077	2949	2831
	80	6222	5808	5444	5124	4840	4584	4355	4148	3960	3787	3629	3484
	95	7389	6896	6465	6085	5747	5441	5172	4926	4702	4498	4310	4138
	110	8556	7986	7487	7046	6655	6304	5990	5705	5445	5208	4991	4792
	125	9723	9075	8508	8008	7563	7164	6806	6483	6188	5918	5671	5445
11″ x 20″	1	......	80.66	75.62	71.17	67.22	63.68	60.50	57.62	55.00	52.61	50.42	48.40
	35	......	2823	2646	2491	2352	2228	2117	2016	1925	1841	1764	1694
	50	......	4033	3780	3558	3361	3184	3025	2881	2750	2630	2521	2420
	65	......	5242	4915	4626	4369	4139	3932	3745	3575	3419	3277	3146
	80	......	6452	6049	5693	5377	5094	4840	4609	4400	4208	4033	3872
	95	......	7662	7183	6760	6385	6049	5747	5473	5225	4997	4790	4597
	110	......	8873	8318	7829	7394	7005	6655	6338	6050	5788	5546	5324
	125	......	10080	9452	8896	8402	7960	7563	7203	6875	6577	6302	6050

Table I.—(Continued).

TRACTIVE POWER OF LOCOMOTIVES, IN POUNDS, FOR DIFFERENT MEAN EFFECTIVE PRESSURES.

CYLINDERS Dia. Stroke	Mean Eff. Pres.	DIAMETER OF DRIVERS 30″	32″	34″	36″	38″	40″	42″	44″	46″	48″	50″	52″	54″	56″	58″	60″
12″ x 14″	1	67.20	63.00	59.30	56.00	53.05	50.40	48.00	45.82	43.83	42.00	40.32	......	......	......	......	......
	35	2352	2205	2075	1960	1857	1764	1680	1604	1534	1470	1411	......	......	......	......	......
	50	3330	3150	2965	2800	2652	2520	2400	2291	2191	2100	2016	......	......	......	......	......
	65	4358	4095	3855	3640	3448	3276	3120	2978	2849	2730	2621	......	......	......	......	......
	80	5376	5040	4744	4480	4244	4032	3840	3665	3506	3360	3225	......	......	......	......	......
	95	6384	5985	5634	5320	5040	4788	4560	4353	4164	3990	3830	......	......	......	......	......
	110	7392	6930	6523	6160	5836	5544	5280	5040	4822	4620	4435	......	......	......	......	......
	125	8400	7875	7413	7000	6632	6300	6000	5728	5479	5250	5040	......	......	......	......	......
	140	9408	8820	8303	7840	7428	7056	6720	6415	6137	5880	5645	......	......	......	......	......
12″ x 16″	1	76.80	72.00	67.77	64.00	60.64	57.60	54.86	52.36	50.04	48.00	46.08	44.31	42.67	41.14	......	......
	35	2688	2520	2372	2240	2122	2016	1920	1833	1751	1680	1613	1551	1493	1440	......	......
	50	3840	3600	3388	3200	3032	2880	2743	2618	2502	2400	2304	2215	2133	2057	......	......
	65	4992	4680	4405	4160	3941	3744	3566	3403	3252	3120	2995	2880	2773	2674	......	......
	80	6144	5760	5421	5120	4851	4608	4388	4188	4003	3840	3686	3545	3413	3291	......	......
	95	7296	6840	6438	6080	5760	5472	5211	4974	4754	4560	4377	4209	4054	3908	......	......
	110	8449	7920	7455	7040	6670	6337	6035	5760	5505	5280	5070	4875	4694	4526	......	......
	125	9601	9001	8472	8001	7580	7201	6858	6546	6256	6000	5760	5539	5334	5143	......	......
	140	10750	10080	9488	8961	8490	8064	7681	7331	7006	6720	6452	6204	5974	5760	......	......
12″ x 18″	1	......	81.00	76.24	72.00	68.21	64.80	61.72	58.91	56.35	54.00	51.84	49.85	48.01	46.29	......	......
	35	......	2835	2668	2520	2387	2268	2160	2062	1974	1890	1814	1745	1680	1620	......	......
	50	......	4050	3812	3600	3410	3240	3086	2945	2817	2700	2592	2492	2400	2314	......	......
	65	......	5264	4955	4680	4433	4212	4011	3829	3662	3509	3369	3240	3120	3008	......	......
	80	......	6480	6099	5760	5456	5184	4937	4712	4508	4320	4147	3988	3840	3703	......	......
	95	......	7695	7242	6840	6480	6156	5863	5596	5353	5130	4924	4735	4560	4397	......	......
	110	......	8910	8386	7920	7504	7128	6790	6480	6199	5940	5702	5484	5280	5092	......	......
	125	......	10120	9530	9000	8527	8100	7715	7364	7044	6750	6480	6231	6000	5786	......	......
	140	......	11340	10670	10080	9550	9072	8641	8248	7889	7560	7258	6980	6720	6481	......	......
12″ x 20″	1	......	90.00	84.71	80.00	75.79	72.00	68.57	65.46	62.61	60.00	57.60	55.39	53.34	51.43	49.65	48.00
	35	......	3150	2964	2800	2652	2520	2400	2291	2191	2100	2016	1938	1867	1800	1737	1680
	50	......	4500	4235	4000	3789	3600	3428	3273	3130	3000	2880	2769	2667	2571	2482	2400
	65	......	5850	5506	5200	4926	4680	4456	4255	4069	3900	3743	3600	3467	3343	3227	3120
	80	......	7200	6776	6400	6063	5760	5485	5236	5008	4800	4607	4431	4267	4114	3972	3840
	95	......	8550	8047	7600	7200	6840	6514	6218	5948	5700	5472	5262	5067	4885	4716	4560
	110	......	9900	9318	8800	8337	7920	7543	7201	6887	6600	6336	6093	5867	5657	5462	5280
	125	......	11250	10590	10000	9474	9000	8571	8183	7827	7500	7200	6924	6667	6429	6206	6000
	140	......	12600	11860	11200	10610	10080	9600	9165	8765	8400	8064	7755	7467	7200	6951	6720

Table I.—(Continued).

TRACTIVE POWER OF LOCOMOTIVES, IN POUNDS, FOR DIFFERENT MEAN EFFECTIVE PRESSURES.

CYLINDERS Dia. Stroke	Mean Eff. Pres.	DIAMETER OF DRIVERS 30″	32″	34″	36″	38″	40″	42″	44″	46″	48″	50″	52″	54″	56″	58″	60″	62″	64″	66″
13″ x 16″	1	90.13	84.50	79.52	75.11	71.16	67.60	64.38	61.45	58.78	56.33	54.08	52.00	50.07	48.28	46.62	45.07	.....	.....	.....
	35	3154	2957	2783	2628	2490	2366	2253	2150	2057	1971	1893	1820	1752	1690	1631	1577	.....	.....	.....
	50	4506	4225	3976	3755	3558	3380	3219	3072	2938	2816	2704	2600	2503	2414	2331	2253	.....	.....	.....
	65	5858	5492	5168	4882	4625	4394	4184	3994	3820	3661	3515	3380	3254	3138	3030	2929	.....	.....	.....
	80	7210	6760	6361	6008	5692	5408	5150	4916	4702	4506	4326	4160	4005	3862	3729	3605	.....	.....	.....
	95	8562	8027	7554	7135	6760	6422	6116	5837	5584	5351	5137	4940	4756	4586	4428	4281	.....	.....	.....
	110	9914	9295	8747	8262	7828	7436	7082	6760	6466	6196	5949	5720	5508	5311	5128	4958	.....	.....	.....
	125	11260	10560	9940	9389	8895	8450	8048	7681	7348	7041	6760	6500	6259	6035	5828	5634	.....	.....	.....
	140	12620	11830	11130	10510	9962	9464	9014	8603	8229	7886	7571	7280	7010	6760	6527	6310	.....	.....	.....
13″ x 18″	1	.....	95.06	89.47	84.50	80.05	76.05	72.43	69.14	66.13	63.38	60.84	58.50	56.34	54.32	52.45	50.70	.....	.....	.....
	35	.....	3327	3132	2957	2801	2661	2535	2420	2314	2218	2129	2047	1972	1901	1835	1774	.....	.....	.....
	50	.....	4755	4476	4225	4002	3802	3621	3457	3306	3169	3042	2925	2817	2716	2622	2535	.....	.....	.....
	65	.....	6178	5815	5492	5203	4943	4707	4494	4298	4119	3954	3802	3662	3530	3409	3295	.....	.....	.....
	80	.....	7604	7157	6760	6404	6084	5794	5531	5290	5070	4867	4680	4507	4345	4196	4056	.....	.....	.....
	95	.....	9030	8499	8027	7604	7224	6880	6568	6282	6021	5779	5557	5352	5160	4982	4816	.....	.....	.....
	110	.....	10450	9842	9295	8806	8366	7968	7606	7275	6972	6693	6435	6198	5975	5770	5577	.....	.....	.....
	125	.....	11880	11180	10560	10000	9506	9054	8643	8267	7923	7605	7313	7043	6790	6557	6338	.....	.....	.....
	140	.....	13310	12520	11830	11200	10640	10140	9680	9259	8873	8518	8190	7887	7605	7343	7098	.....	.....	.....
13″ x 20″	1	.....	105.62	99.41	93.89	88.94	84.50	80.48	76.82	73.48	70.42	67.60	65.00	62.59	60.36	58.28	56.33	.....	.....	.....
	35	.....	3697	3479	3286	3113	2957	2816	2688	2572	2464	2366	2275	2190	2112	2040	1971	.....	.....	.....
	50	.....	5281	4970	4694	4447	4225	4024	3841	3674	3521	3380	3250	3129	3018	2914	2816	.....	.....	.....
	65	.....	6866	6461	6103	5781	5492	5231	4993	4776	4577	4394	4225	4068	3923	3788	3661	.....	.....	.....
	80	.....	8451	7953	7511	7115	6760	6438	6145	5878	5633	5408	5200	5007	4828	4662	4506	.....	.....	.....
	95	.....	10030	9444	8919	8449	8027	7645	7298	6980	6690	6422	6175	5946	5734	5536	5351	.....	.....	.....
	110	.....	11620	10930	10330	9784	9295	8853	8450	8083	7746	7436	7150	6885	6640	6411	6196	.....	.....	.....
	125	.....	13200	12420	11730	11120	10560	10060	9603	9185	8803	8450	8125	7824	7545	7285	7041	.....	.....	.....
	140	.....	14790	13920	13140	12450	11830	11260	10750	10280	9859	9464	9100	8763	8450	8160	7886	.....	.....	.....
13″ x 22″	1	.....	.....	.....	103.29	97.85	92.96	88.53	84.50	80.83	77.47	74.36	71.51	68.86	66.40	61.11	61.97	59.97	58.10	56.34
	35	.....	.....	.....	3615	3425	3253	3098	2957	2829	2711	2602	2503	2410	2324	2244	2169	2099	2033	1972
	50	.....	.....	.....	5164	1892	4648	4426	4225	4041	3873	3718	3575	3443	3320	3205	3098	2998	2905	2817
	65	.....	.....	.....	6714	6360	6042	5754	5492	5253	5035	4833	4648	4476	4316	4167	4028	3898	3776	3662
	80	.....	.....	.....	8263	7827	7436	7082	6760	6466	6197	5948	5721	5508	5312	5128	4957	4797	4648	4507
	95	.....	.....	.....	9812	9295	8831	8410	8027	7678	7359	7064	6793	6541	6308	6090	5887	5697	5519	5352
	110	.....	.....	.....	11360	10760	10220	9739	9295	8891	8522	8180	7866	7575	7305	7052	6817	6597	6391	6198
	125	.....	.....	.....	12910	12230	11620	11060	10560	10100	9684	9295	8939	8608	8300	8014	7746	7497	7263	7043
	140	.....	.....	.....	14460	13700	13010	12390	11830	11310	10840	10410	10010	9641	9296	8976	8676	8396	8134	7887
	155	.....	.....	.....	16010	15160	14410	13720	13090	12530	12010	11520	11080	10670	10290	9937	9606	9296	9006	8733

TABLE I.—(Continued).

TRACTIVE POWER OF LOCOMOTIVES, IN POUNDS, FOR DIFFERENT MEAN EFFECTIVE PRESSURES.

CYLINDERS DIA. STROKE	MEAN EFF. PRES.	DIAMETER OF DRIVERS 34″	36″	38″	40″	42″	44″	46″	48″	50″	52″	54″	56″	58″	60″	62″	64″	66″
14″ x 18″	1	103.76	98.00	92.84	88.20	84.00	80.19	76.70	73.50	70.56	67.84	65.34	63.00	60.83	58.80	56.91	55.12	53.46
	35	3632	3430	3249	3087	2940	2806	2684	2572	2469	2374	2287	2205	2129	2058	1992	1929	1871
	50	5188	4900	4612	4410	4200	4009	3835	3675	3528	3392	3267	3150	3041	2940	2845	2756	2673
	65	6744	6370	6034	5733	5460	5212	4985	4777	4586	4409	4247	4095	3954	3822	3699	3583	3475
	80	8300	7840	7427	7056	6720	6415	6136	5880	5645	5427	5227	5040	4866	4704	4552	4409	4276
	95	9848	9310	8820	8378	7980	7618	7286	6982	6703	6444	6207	5985	5778	5586	5406	5236	5078
	110	11410	10780	10210	9703	9240	8821	8437	8086	7762	7462	7188	6930	6691	6468	6260	6064	5881
	125	12970	12250	11600	11020	10500	10020	9588	9188	8820	8480	8168	7875	7604	7350	7114	6890	6683
	140	14520	13720	13000	12350	11760	11220	10740	10290	9878	9498	9148	8820	8516	8232	7968	7717	7484
	155	16080	15190	14390	13670	13020	12430	11890	11390	10930	10510	10130	9765	9429	9115	8821	8544	8286
14″ x 20″	1	115.29	108.89	103.15	98.00	93.33	89.09	85.22	81.67	78.40	75.39	72.60	70.00	67.59	65.33	63.23	61.25	59.39
	35	4035	3811	3610	3430	3266	3118	2982	2858	2744	2638	2541	2450	2365	2286	2213	2143	2078
	50	5764	5444	5158	4900	4666	4454	4261	4083	3920	3769	3630	3500	3379	3266	3161	3062	2969
	65	7494	7077	6705	6370	6066	5790	5539	5308	5096	4900	4718	4550	4393	4246	4110	3981	3860
	80	9223	8710	8252	7840	7466	7127	6817	6533	6272	6031	5808	5600	5407	5226	5058	4900	4751
	95	10950	10340	9800	9310	8866	8463	8096	7758	7448	7162	6897	6650	6421	6206	6007	5818	5642
	110	12680	11980	11350	10780	10260	9800	9374	8984	8624	8293	7986	7700	7435	7187	6956	6738	6534
	125	14410	13610	12890	12250	11660	11130	10650	10210	9800	9424	9075	8750	8449	8167	7904	7656	7424
	140	16140	15240	14440	13720	13060	12470	11930	11430	10970	10550	10160	9800	9463	9147	8852	8575	8315
	155	17870	16870	15990	15190	14460	13810	13210	12660	12150	11680	11250	10850	10470	10130	9801	9494	9206
14″ x 22″	1	......	119.78	113.47	107.79	102.67	98.01	93.74	89.84	86.24	82.92	79.85	77.00	74.34	71.87	69.55	67.38	65.33
	35	......	4192	3971	3772	3593	3430	3281	3144	3018	2902	2794	2695	2602	2515	2434	2358	2286
	50	......	5989	5673	5390	5134	4900	4687	1492	4312	4146	3992	3850	3717	3593	3477	3369	3266
	65	......	7785	7375	7006	6673	6371	6093	5839	5605	5390	5190	5004	4832	4671	4520	4379	4246
	80	......	9582	9078	8623	8214	7840	7499	7187	6899	6633	6388	6160	5947	5750	5564	5390	5226
	95	......	11380	10780	10240	9754	9310	8905	8535	8192	7877	7585	7314	7062	6827	6607	6401	6206
	110	......	13170	12480	11850	11290	10780	10310	9883	9487	9122	8784	8470	8178	7906	7651	7412	7187
	125	......	14970	14180	13470	12830	12250	11720	11230	10780	10360	9982	9625	9293	8984	8694	8423	8167
	140	......	16770	15880	15090	14370	13720	13120	12580	12070	11610	11180	10780	10410	10060	9737	9433	9147
	155	......	18560	17590	16700	15910	15190	14530	13920	13360	12850	12370	11930	11520	11140	10780	10430	10120
14″ x 24″	1	......	......	123.80	117.60	112.00	106.90	102.28	98.01	94.08	90.47	87.12	84.00	81.11	78.40	75.88	73.51	71.28
	35	......	......	4333	4116	3920	3741	3579	3430	3293	3166	3049	2940	2839	2744	2655	2573	2495
	50	......	......	6190	5881	5600	5345	5113	4900	4704	4523	4356	4200	4055	3920	3794	3675	3564
	65	......	......	8047	7644	7280	6949	6647	6371	6115	5880	5663	5460	5272	5096	4932	4778	4633
	80	......	......	9904	9408	8960	8553	8181	7840	7526	7237	6969	6720	6488	6272	6070	5880	5702
	95	......	......	11760	11170	10640	10150	9715	9310	8937	8594	8276	7980	7705	7448	7208	6983	6772
	110	......	......	13620	12940	12320	11760	11250	10780	10350	9952	9584	9240	8922	8624	8347	8086	7841
	125	......	......	15470	14700	14000	13360	12780	12250	11760	11310	10890	10500	10140	9800	9485	9190	8910
	140	......	......	17330	16460	15680	14970	14320	13720	13171	12660	12190	11760	11350	10970	11620	10290	9979
	155	......	......	19190	18230	17360	16570	15850	15190	14580	14020	13500	13020	12570	12150	11760	11390	11050

Table I.—(Continued).

TRACTIVE POWER OF LOCOMOTIVES, IN POUNDS, FOR DIFFERENT MEAN EFFECTIVE PRESSURES.

CYLINDERS DIA. STROKE	MEAN EFF. PRES.	DIAMETER OF DRIVERS 34″	36″	38″	40″	42″	44″	46″	48″	50″	52″	54″	56″	58″	60″	62″	64″	66″	68″	70″
15″ x 18″	1	119.10	112.50	106.58	101.25	96.42	92.04	88.04	84.37	81.00	77.88	75.00	72.32	69.83	67.50	65.32	63.28	61.36	......	......
	35	4169	3938	3730	3543	3375	3221	3081	2953	2835	2726	2625	2531	2444	2362	2286	2215	2147	......	......
	50	5955	5625	5329	5062	4821	4602	4402	4218	4050	3894	3750	3616	3492	3375	3266	3164	3068	......	......
	65	7742	7313	6928	6581	6267	5982	5723	5484	5264	5062	4875	4700	4539	4387	4245	4113	3988	......	......
	80	9529	9000	8526	8100	7712	7363	7043	6749	6480	6230	6000	5785	5586	5400	5225	5062	4908	......	......
	95	11310	10690	10120	9618	9160	8744	8364	8015	7695	7398	7125	6870	6634	6412	6205	6012	5829	......	......
	110	13100	12370	11720	11140	10600	10120	9685	9282	8910	8567	8250	7955	7682	7425	7186	6961	6750	......	......
	125	14890	14060	13320	12650	12050	11500	11000	10540	10120	9735	9375	9040	8729	8438	8165	7910	7670	......	......
	140	16670	15750	14920	14170	13500	12880	12320	11810	11340	10900	10500	10120	9777	9450	9146	8860	8590	......	......
	155	18460	17440	16520	15690	14940	14260	13640	13070	12550	12070	11620	11210	10820	10460	10120	9809	9511	......	......
15″ x 20″	1	132.34	125.00	118.40	112.50	107.14	102.28	97.83	93.75	90.00	86.54	83.33	80.36	77.59	75.00	72.59	70.31	68.18	......	......
	35	4632	4375	4144	3938	3750	3579	3424	3281	3150	3028	2916	2812	2715	2625	2540	2461	2386	......	......
	50	6618	6250	5920	5625	5358	5114	4891	4687	4500	4327	4166	4018	3879	3750	3629	3515	3409	......	......
	65	8603	8125	7697	7313	6965	6647	6359	6094	5850	5624	5416	5223	5043	4875	4718	4570	4431	......	......
	80	10580	10000	9473	9000	8572	8182	7826	7500	7200	6923	6666	6428	6207	6000	5807	5624	5454	......	......
	95	12570	11870	11250	10690	10180	9716	9293	8906	8550	8221	7916	7634	7370	7125	6896	6679	6477	......	......
	110	14560	13750	13020	12370	11780	11250	10760	10310	9900	9520	9167	8840	8535	8250	7985	7735	7500	......	......
	125	16540	15620	14800	14060	13390	12780	12230	11720	11250	10820	10110	10040	9700	9375	9074	8790	8523	......	......
	140	18530	17500	16570	15750	15000	14320	13690	13120	12600	12110	11660	11250	10860	10500	10160	9844	9545	......	......
	155	20510	19370	18350	17440	16610	15850	15160	14530	13950	13410	12910	12450	12020	11620	11250	10900	10570	......	......
15″ x 22″	1	......	137.50	130.25	123.73	117.84	112.50	107.60	103.11	99.00	95.19	91.67	88.39	85.34	82.50	79.84	77.34	75.00	......	......
	35	......	4812	4559	4331	4125	3938	3766	3609	3465	3331	3208	3093	2987	2887	2794	2707	2625	......	......
	50	......	6875	6513	6187	5893	5625	5380	5156	4950	4759	4583	4419	4267	4125	3992	3867	3750	......	......
	65	......	8938	8467	8044	7660	7313	6994	6703	6435	6187	5958	5745	5546	5362	5189	5027	4875	......	......
	80	......	11000	10420	9900	9428	9000	8608	8249	7920	7615	7333	7071	6827	6600	6387	6187	6000	......	......
	95	......	13060	12370	11750	11190	10690	10220	9796	9404	9043	8708	8397	8107	7837	7585	7347	7125	......	......
	110	......	15120	14330	13610	12960	12370	11830	11340	10890	10470	10080	9724	9387	9076	8783	8508	8250	......	......
	125	......	17190	16280	15470	14730	14060	13450	12890	12374	11900	11460	11050	10660	10310	9980	9668	9375	......	......
	140	......	19250	18240	17320	16500	15750	15060	14430	13860	13320	12830	12370	11950	11550	11180	10830	10500	......	......
	155	......	21310	20190	19180	18270	17440	16680	15980	15345	14750	14210	13700	13230	12790	12370	11990	11620	......	......
15″ x 24″	1	......	......	142.10	135.00	128.57	122.72	117.39	112.50	108.00	103.83	100.00	96.42	93.10	90.00	87.10	84.37	81.81	79.41	77.14
	35	......	......	4973	4725	4500	4296	4108	3938	3780	3634	3500	3375	3258	3150	3048	2953	2863	2779	2700
	50	......	......	7105	6750	6429	6137	5869	5625	5400	5192	5000	4821	4655	4500	4355	4218	4090	3970	3857
	65	......	......	9236	8775	8357	7978	7630	7313	7020	6749	6500	6267	6052	5850	5661	5484	5317	5162	5014
	80	......	......	11370	10800	10280	9818	9391	9000	8640	8307	8000	7712	7448	7200	6968	6749	6544	6353	6171
	95	......	......	13500	12820	12210	11660	11150	10690	10260	9864	9500	9160	8844	8550	8274	8015	7772	7544	7328
	110	......	......	15630	14850	14140	13500	12910	12370	11880	11420	11000	10600	10240	9900	9582	9281	9000	8736	8486
	125	......	......	17760	16870	16070	15340	14670	14060	13500	12980	12500	12050	11640	11250	10890	10540	10220	9926	9643
	140	......	......	19890	18900	18000	17180	16430	15750	15120	14540	14000	13500	13030	12600	12190	11810	11450	11120	10800
	155	......	......	22020	20920	19930	19020	18190	17440	16740	16090	15500	14940	14430	13950	13500	13070	12680	12310	11950

Table I.—(Continued).

TRACTIVE POWER OF LOCOMOTIVES, IN POUNDS, FOR DIFFERENT MEAN EFFECTIVE PRESSURES.

Cylinders Dia. Stroke	Mean Eff. Pres.	Diameter of Drivers 36″	38″	40″	42″	44″	46″	48″	50″	52″	54″	56″	58″	60″	62″	64″	66″	68″	70″
16″ x 20″	1	142.20	134.72	128.00	121.90	116.34	111.30	106.67	102.40	98.46	94.82	91.43	88.27	85.33	82.58	80.00	77.57	75.30	73.14
	35	4977	4715	4480	4266	4072	3896	3733	3584	3446	3318	3200	3089	2986	2890	2800	2715	2635	2560
	50	7110	6737	6400	6095	5817	5565	5333	5120	4923	4741	4571	4413	4266	4129	4000	3878	3765	3657
	65	9243	8757	8320	7924	7563	7235	6933	6655	6400	6163	5943	5737	5546	5367	5200	5042	4894	4754
	80	11370	10780	10240	9752	9308	8904	8533	8192	7876	7585	7314	7062	6826	6606	6400	6205	6024	5851
	95	13510	12800	12160	11580	11050	10570	10130	9728	9353	9007	8685	8385	8106	7845	7600	7369	7153	6948
	110	15640	14820	14080	13410	12800	12240	11730	11260	10830	10430	10060	9711	9386	9085	8800	8533	8283	8046
	125	17770	16840	16000	15240	14540	13910	13330	12800	12310	11850	11430	11030	10660	10320	10000	9697	9412	9143
	140	19910	18860	17920	17070	16290	15580	14930	14330	13780	13270	12800	12360	11940	11560	11200	10860	10540	10240
	155	22040	20880	19840	18890	18030	17250	16530	15870	15260	14690	14170	13680	13220	12800	12400	12020	11670	11340
	170	24170	22900	21760	20720	19780	18920	18130	17410	16740	16120	15540	15000	14500	14040	13600	13180	12800	12430
16″ x 22″	1	......	148.20	140.80	134.10	128.00	122.42	117.32	112.62	108.31	104.29	100.58	97.10	93.86	90.84	88.00	85.33	82.82	80.45
	35	......	5187	4928	4697	4480	4285	4107	3942	3792	3650	3520	3398	3285	3179	3080	2986	2898	2815
	50	......	7410	7040	6705	6400	6122	5867	5632	5416	5214	5028	4855	4693	4542	4400	4266	4141	4022
	65	......	9633	9152	8717	8320	7958	7627	7321	7040	6779	6537	6311	6101	5904	5720	5546	5383	5229
	80	......	11850	11260	10730	10240	9795	9387	9011	8665	8343	8045	7768	7509	7267	7040	6826	6625	6436
	95	......	14080	13370	12740	12160	11630	11140	10700	10290	9907	9554	9224	8917	8630	8360	8106	7867	7642
	110	......	16300	15490	14750	14080	13470	12910	12330	11910	11470	11060	10680	10320	9992	9680	9386	9110	8850
	125	......	18520	17600	16760	16000	15300	14670	14080	13540	13030	12570	12140	11730	11350	11000	10660	10350	10050
	140	......	20750	19710	18770	17920	17140	16430	15770	15160	14600	14080	13590	13140	12720	12320	11940	11590	11260
	155	......	22970	21820	20780	19840	18980	18190	17460	16790	16160	15590	15050	14550	14080	13640	13220	12830	12470
	170	......	25190	23940	22800	21760	20810	19950	19150	18410	17730	17090	16500	15950	15440	14960	14500	14080	13670
16″ x 24″	1	......	......	153.60	146.29	139.62	133.56	128.00	122.88	118.15	113.78	109.71	105.92	102.40	99.10	96.00	93.09	90.36	87.77
	35	......	......	5376	5120	4887	4675	4480	4301	4135	3982	3840	3708	3584	3468	3360	3258	3162	3072
	50	......	......	7680	7314	6982	6678	6400	6144	5908	5688	5486	5297	5120	4955	4800	4654	4518	4388
	65	......	......	9984	9509	9077	8682	8320	7986	7680	7395	7132	6886	6655	6442	6240	6051	5873	5705
	80	......	......	12290	11700	11170	10680	10240	9830	9453	9102	8777	8475	8192	7928	7680	7447	7228	7021
	95	......	......	14590	13890	13260	12690	12160	11670	11220	10810	10420	10060	9728	9414	9120	8843	8584	8338
	110	......	......	16890	16090	15360	14690	14080	13520	13000	12510	12070	11650	11260	10900	10560	10240	9940	9656
	125	......	......	19200	18280	17450	16690	16000	15360	14770	14220	13710	13240	12800	12390	12000	11630	11290	10970
	140	......	......	21500	20480	19550	18700	17920	17200	16540	15930	15360	14830	14330	13870	13440	13030	12650	12290
	155	......	......	23810	22670	21640	20700	19840	19040	18310	17630	17010	16420	15870	15360	14880	14430	14000	13600
	170	......	......	26110	24870	23740	22700	21760	20890	20090	19340	18650	18010	17410	16850	16320	15820	15360	14920
16″ x 26″	1	......	......	......	158.47	151.28	144.70	138.67	133.11	128.00	123.26	118.85	114.76	110.92	107.35	104.00	100.85	97.89	95.09
	35	......	......	......	5547	5294	5064	4853	4659	4480	4314	4160	4016	3883	3757	3640	3530	3426	3328
	50	......	......	......	7924	7564	7235	6933	6656	6400	6163	5943	5738	5547	5368	5200	5042	4894	4754
	65	......	......	......	10300	9833	9405	9013	8653	8320	8012	7726	7459	7211	6978	6760	6555	6363	6180
	80	......	......	......	12670	12100	11570	11090	10650	10240	9860	9508	9180	8875	8588	8320	8068	7831	7607
	95	......	......	......	15059	14370	13740	13170	12640	12160	11710	11290	10900	10540	10200	9880	9580	9299	9033
	110	......	......	......	17430	16640	15920	15250	14640	14080	13560	13070	12620	12200	11810	11440	11090	10770	10460
	125	......	......	......	19810	18910	18090	17330	16640	16000	15410	14860	14340	13870	13420	13000	12600	12230	11880
	140	......	......	......	22180	21180	20260	19410	18640	17920	17250	16640	16060	15530	15030	14560	14120	13700	13310
	155	......	......	......	24560	23440	22430	21490	20630	19840	19100	18420	17790	17190	16640	16120	15630	15170	14740
	170	......	......	......	26940	25710	24600	23570	22630	21760	20950	20200	19510	18860	18250	17680	17140	16640	16160

Table I.—(Continued).

TRACTIVE POWER OF LOCOMOTIVES, IN POUNDS, FOR DIFFERENT MEAN EFFECTIVE PRESSURES.

CYLINDERS DIA. STROKE	MEAN EFF. PRES.	DIAMETER OF DRIVERS 38″	40″	42″	44″	46″	48″	50″	52″	54″	56″	58″	60″	62″	64″	66″	68″	70″	72″	74″	76″
17″ x 20″	1	152.10	144.50	137.61	131.38	125.65	120.41	115.60	111.16	107.02	103.20	99.65	96.34	93.22	90.32	87.57	85.00	82.57	......	......	......
	50	7605	7225	6881	6568	6283	6021	5780	5558	5352	5160	4982	4817	4661	4516	4378	4250	4128	......	......	......
	65	9887	9393	8945	8540	8168	7827	7514	7226	6957	6708	6477	6261	6059	5870	5692	5525	5367	......	......	......
	80	12170	11560	11010	10510	10050	9631	9248	8893	8563	8256	7972	7707	7457	7225	7005	6800	6605	......	......	......
	95	14450	13730	13070	12480	11930	11440	10980	10560	10170	9805	9466	9152	8856	8580	8319	8075	7844	......	......	......
	110	16730	15890	15140	14450	13820	13240	12720	12230	11770	11350	10960	10600	10250	9935	9633	9350	9083	......	......	......
	125	19010	18060	17200	16420	15710	15050	14450	13890	13380	12900	12450	12040	11650	11290	10940	10620	10320	......	......	......
	140	21290	20230	19270	18390	17590	16860	16180	15560	14980	14450	13950	13490	13050	12640	12260	11900	11560	......	......	......
	155	23570	22400	21330	20360	19480	18660	17920	17230	16590	16000	15440	14930	14450	14000	13570	13170	12800	......	......	......
	170	25860	24560	23390	22330	21360	20470	19650	18900	18190	17540	16940	16370	15850	15350	14880	14450	14030	......	......	......
	185	28140	26730	25460	24300	23250	22280	21390	20560	19800	19090	18430	17820	17250	16710	16200	15720	15270	......	......	......
17″ x 22″	1	......	158.94	151.38	144.50	138.21	132.45	127.16	122.28	117.72	113.52	109.61	105.97	102.52	99.34	96.34	93.50	90.83	......	......	......
	50	......	7948	7569	7225	6911	6623	6358	6114	5887	5677	5481	5298	5127	4967	4817	4675	4541	......	......	......
	65	......	10330	9840	9393	8985	8610	8265	7947	7653	7380	7126	6888	6664	6457	6262	6077	5903	......	......	......
	80	......	12710	12110	11560	11060	10590	10170	9781	9420	9083	8770	8477	8202	7947	7707	7480	7266	......	......	......
	95	......	15100	14380	13730	13130	12580	12080	11610	11180	10780	10410	10070	9741	9437	9152	8882	8629	......	......	......
	110	......	17480	16650	15890	15200	14570	13990	13450	12950	12490	12060	11660	11280	10930	10590	10280	9991	......	......	......
	125	......	19870	18920	18060	17280	16560	15890	15280	14720	14190	13760	13250	12820	12420	12040	11690	11350	......	......	......
	140	......	22250	21190	20230	19350	18540	17800	17120	16480	15890	15350	14830	14350	13910	13490	13090	12710	......	......	......
	155	......	24640	23460	22400	21420	20530	19710	18950	18250	17600	16990	16420	15890	15400	14930	14490	14080	......	......	......
	170	......	27020	25730	24560	23500	22520	21620	20780	20010	19300	18630	18010	17430	16890	16380	15890	15440	......	......	......
	185	......	29400	28000	26730	25570	24500	23520	22620	21780	21000	20280	19600	18970	18380	17820	17300	16800	......	......	......
17″ x 24″	1	......	......	165.12	157.62	150.78	144.50	138.71	133.38	128.43	123.84	119.59	115.60	111.87	108.38	105.09	102.00	99.08	96.33	93.73	91.26
	50	......	......	8257	7882	7539	7225	6936	6669	6422	6193	5979	5780	5594	5419	5255	5100	4954	4816	4686	4563
	65	......	......	10730	10240	9800	9393	9017	8670	8348	8051	7773	7514	7272	7044	6831	6630	6440	6261	6092	5932
	80	......	......	13210	12610	12060	11560	11090	10670	10270	9908	9567	9248	8950	8670	8407	8160	7926	7706	7498	7300
	95	......	......	15690	14970	14320	13730	13180	12670	12200	11760	11360	10980	10630	10290	9983	9690	9412	9151	8904	8670
	110	......	......	18170	17340	16580	15890	15260	14670	14130	13620	13150	12720	12300	11920	11560	11220	10900	10590	10310	10040
	125	......	......	20640	19700	18850	18060	17340	16670	16050	15480	14950	14450	13980	13550	13130	12750	12380	12040	11710	11410
	140	......	......	23120	22070	21110	20230	19420	18670	17980	17340	16740	16180	15660	15170	14710	14280	13870	13480	13120	12770
	155	......	......	25600	24430	23370	22400	21500	20670	19910	19200	18530	17920	17340	16800	16290	15810	15360	14930	14530	14140
	170	......	......	28070	26800	25630	24560	23580	22670	21830	21050	20330	19650	19020	18420	17860	17340	16840	16370	15930	15510
	185	......	......	30550	29160	27890	26730	25660	24670	23760	22910	22120	21390	20700	20050	19440	18870	18330	17820	17340	16880

Table I.—(Continued).

TRACTIVE POWER OF LOCOMOTIVES, IN POUNDS, FOR DIFFERENT MEAN EFFECTIVE PRESSURES.

CYLINDERS Dia. Stroke	Mean Eff. Pres.	DIAMETER OF DRIVERS 44″	46″	48″	50″	52″	54″	56″	58″	60″	62″	64″	66″	68″	70″	72″	74″	76″	78″
17″ x 26″	1	170.77	163.34	156.52	150.28	144.50	139.13	134.18	129.54	125.22	121.19	117.40	113.84	110.50	107.32	104.36	101.53	98.87	......
	50	8539	8168	7827	7514	7225	6957	6709	6478	6262	6060	5870	5692	5525	5367	5218	5077	4943	......
	65	11100	10620	10170	9768	9393	9045	8721	8421	8141	7877	7632	7400	7183	6977	6784	6600	6427	......
	80	13660	13070	12520	12020	11560	11130	10730	10360	10020	9695	9392	9108	8840	8587	8349	8123	7909	......
	95	16220	15520	14870	14270	13730	13220	12740	12310	11900	11510	11150	10810	10500	10200	9914	9646	9392	......
	110	18780	17970	17220	16530	15890	15300	14760	14250	13780	13330	12910	12520	12150	11810	11480	11170	10870	......
	125	21350	20420	19570	18780	18060	17390	16770	16190	15650	15150	14670	14230	13810	13420	13040	12690	12360	......
	140	23910	22870	21920	21040	20230	19480	18780	18140	17530	16960	16440	15940	15470	15030	14610	14210	13840	......
	155	26470	25320	24260	23290	22400	21570	20800	20080	19410	18780	18200	17640	17130	16630	16180	15740	15320	......
	170	29030	27770	26610	25540	24560	23650	22810	22020	21290	20600	19960	19350	18780	18250	17740	17260	16810	......
	185	31590	30220	28960	27800	26730	25740	24820	23970	23170	22420	21720	21060	20440	19860	19310	18780	18290	......
17″ x 28″	1	......	175.90	168.58	161.82	155.60	149.82	144.50	139.50	134.86	130.50	126.42	122.60	119.00	115.60	112.39	109.34	106.47	103.72
	65	......	11430	10960	10520	10110	9740	9393	9068	8766	8483	8218	7970	7735	7514	7305	7108	6920	6743
	80	......	14070	13480	12940	12450	11990	11560	11160	10790	10440	10110	9808	9520	9248	8991	8748	8517	8299
	95	......	16710	16010	15370	14780	14230	13730	13250	12810	12400	12010	11650	11300	10980	10670	10390	10110	9855
	110	......	19350	18540	17800	17120	16480	15890	15340	14830	14350	13910	13490	13090	12720	12360	12030	11710	11410
	125	......	21990	21070	20230	19450	18730	18060	17440	16860	16310	15800	15320	14870	14450	14050	13670	13310	12970
	140	......	24630	23600	22660	21780	20980	20230	19530	18880	18270	17700	17160	16660	16180	15730	15310	14900	14520
	155	......	27270	26130	25080	24120	23220	22400	21620	20900	20230	19600	19000	18440	17920	17420	16950	16500	16080
	170	......	29900	28660	27511	26450	25470	24560	23710	22920	22180	21490	20840	20230	19650	19100	18590	18100	17630
	185	......	32540	31180	29940	28790	27720	26730	25810	24950	24140	23390	22680	22010	21390	20790	20230	19700	19190
	200	......	35180	33710	32360	31120	29970	28900	27900	26970	26100	25280	24520	23800	23120	22480	21870	21290	20740
17″ x 30″	1	......	......	180.62	173.40	166.72	160.56	154.80	149.49	144.50	139.82	135.48	131.35	127.50	123.84	120.41	117.15	114.09	111.14
	65	......	......	11740	11270	10840	10430	10060	9717	9393	9090	8805	8538	8288	8051	7827	7615	7415	7225
	80	......	......	14450	13870	13340	12840	12380	11960	11560	11180	10840	10510	10200	9908	9634	9372	9127	8892
	95	......	......	17160	16470	15840	15250	14700	14200	13730	13280	12870	12480	12110	11760	11440	11130	10840	10560
	110	......	......	19870	19070	18340	17660	17030	16440	15890	15380	14900	14450	14020	13620	13240	12890	12550	12230
	125	......	......	22580	21670	20840	20070	19350	18680	18060	17480	16930	16420	15940	15480	15050	14640	14260	13890
	140	......	......	25290	24280	23340	22480	21670	20930	20230	19580	18970	18390	17850	17340	16860	16400	15970	15560
	155	......	......	28000	26880	25840	24880	23990	23170	22400	21670	21000	20360	19760	19200	18660	18160	17680	17230
	170	......	......	30710	29480	28340	27290	26320	25410	24560	23770	23030	22330	21670	21050	20470	19920	19390	18890
	185	......	......	33420	32080	30840	29700	28640	27650	26730	25870	25060	24300	23580	22910	22280	21670	21100	20560
	200	......	......	36120	34680	33340	32110	30960	29900	28900	27960	27090	26270	25500	24770	24080	23430	22820	22230

Table I.—(Continued).

TRACTIVE POWER OF LOCOMOTIVES, IN POUNDS, FOR DIFFERENT MEAN EFFECTIVE PRESSURES.

Cylinders Dia. Stroke	Mean Eff. Pres.	Diameter of Drivers 40″	42″	44″	46″	48″	50″	52″	54″	56″	58″	60″	62″	64″	66″	68″	70″	72″	74″	76″
18″ x 22″	1	178.20	169.71	162.00	154.95	148.50	142.55	137.08	132.00	127.28	122.90	118.80	114.97	111.38	108.00	104.82	101.83	99.00	96.33	......
	65	11580	11030	10530	10070	9653	9266	8909	8580	8272	7988	7722	7472	7240	7020	6814	6619	6435	6261	......
	80	14250	13580	12960	12390	11880	11400	10960	10560	10180	9832	9501	9197	8910	8640	8386	8146	7920	7706	......
	95	16930	16120	15390	14720	14110	13540	12020	12540	12090	11670	11280	10920	10580	10260	9960	9674	9404	9151	......
	110	19600	18670	17820	17040	16330	15680	15080	14520	14000	13520	13070	12640	12250	11880	11530	11200	10890	10590	......
	125	22270	21210	20250	19370	18560	17820	17130	16500	15910	15350	14850	14370	13920	13500	13100	12730	12370	12040	......
	140	24950	23760	22680	21690	20790	19960	19190	18480	17820	17200	16630	16090	15590	15120	14680	14250	13860	13480	......
	155	27620	26310	25110	24020	23020	22090	21240	20460	19730	19050	18410	17820	17260	16740	16250	15780	15340	14930	......
	170	30290	28850	27540	26340	25240	24230	23300	22440	21630	20890	20190	19540	18930	18360	17820	17310	16830	16370	......
	185	32960	31400	29970	28670	27470	26370	25360	24420	23540	22730	21980	21270	20600	19980	19390	18840	18310	17820	......
	200	35640	33940	32400	30990	29700	28510	27410	26400	25150	24580	23760	22990	22270	21600	20960	20360	19800	19260	......
	215	38310	36490	34830	33310	31930	30650	29470	28380	27360	26420	25540	24720	23940	23220	22540	21890	21280	20710	......
	230	40990	39040	37260	35640	34160	32780	31520	30360	29270	28260	27320	26440	25610	24840	24110	23420	22770	22150	......
18″ x 24″	1	......	185.12	176.71	169.03	162.00	155.51	149.52	144.00	138.85	134.07	129.59	125.41	121.50	117.81	114.35	111.08	108.00	105.08	......
	65	......	12030	11480	10990	10530	10110	9720	9360	9026	8714	8423	8152	7897	7658	7433	7220	7020	6830	......
	80	......	14810	14130	13520	12960	12440	11960	11520	11110	10720	10360	10030	9720	9425	9148	8886	8640	8406	......
	95	......	17580	16790	16060	15390	14770	14200	13680	13190	12730	12310	11910	11540	11190	10860	10550	10260	9982	......
	110	......	20360	19440	18590	17820	17110	16450	15840	15270	14750	14250	13790	13360	12960	12580	12220	11880	11560	......
	125	......	23140	22090	21130	20250	19440	18690	18000	17360	16760	16200	15680	15190	14730	14290	13880	13500	13130	......
	140	......	25920	24740	23660	22680	21770	20930	20160	19440	18770	18140	17560	17010	16490	16010	15550	15120	14710	......
	155	......	28690	27390	26200	25110	24110	23180	22320	21520	20780	20080	19440	18830	18260	17720	17220	16740	16290	......
	170	......	31470	30040	28730	27540	26440	25420	24480	23600	22790	22030	21320	20650	20030	19440	18880	18360	17860	......
	185	......	34250	32690	31270	29970	28770	27660	26640	25690	24800	23970	23200	22480	21790	21150	20550	19980	19440	......
	200	......	37020	35340	33800	32400	31100	29900	28800	27770	26810	25920	25080	24300	23560	22870	22210	21600	21010	......
	215	......	39800	37990	36340	34830	33440	32150	30960	29850	28820	27860	26960	26120	25330	24580	23880	23220	22590	......
	230	......	42580	40650	38880	37260	35770	34390	33120	31940	30830	29800	28850	27940	27100	26300	25550	24840	24170	......
18″ x 26″	1	......	......	191.45	183.12	175.50	168.48	162.00	156.00	150.41	145.22	140.39	135.87	131.61	127.62	123.88	120.33	117.00	113.83	110.83
	65	......	......	12440	11900	11410	10950	10530	10140	9777	9440	9126	8831	8555	8296	8052	7822	7606	7388	7205
	80	......	......	15310	14650	14040	13470	12960	12480	12030	11620	11230	10870	10530	10210	9910	9627	9360	9107	8867
	95	......	......	18190	17390	16670	16000	15390	14820	14290	13790	13330	12900	12500	12120	11770	11430	11110	10810	10530
	110	......	......	21060	20140	19310	18530	17820	17160	16540	15980	15440	14940	14480	14040	13630	13210	12870	12520	12190
	125	......	......	23930	22890	21940	21060	20250	19500	18800	18150	17550	16980	16450	15950	15480	15040	14620	14230	13850
	140	......	......	26800	25640	24570	23580	22680	21840	21060	20330	19650	19020	18430	17870	17340	16850	16380	15940	15520
	155	......	......	29670	28380	27200	26110	25110	24180	23310	22510	21760	21060	20400	19780	19200	18650	18130	17640	17180
	170	......	......	32550	31130	29830	28640	27540	26520	25570	24690	23870	23100	22370	21700	21060	20460	19890	19350	18840
	185	......	......	35420	33880	32470	31160	29970	28860	27830	26870	25970	25130	24350	23610	22920	22260	21640	21060	20500
	200	......	......	38290	36620	35100	33690	32400	31200	30080	29040	28080	27170	26320	25520	24770	24060	23400	22760	22160
	215	......	......	41160	39370	37730	36220	34830	33540	32340	31220	30180	29210	28300	27440	26630	25870	25160	24470	23830
	230	......	......	44030	42120	40370	38750	37260	35880	34600	33400	32290	31250	30270	29350	28490	27680	26910	26180	25490

Table I.—(Continued).

TRACTIVE POWER OF LOCOMOTIVES, IN POUNDS, FOR DIFFERENT MEAN EFFECTIVE PRESSURES.

Cylinders Dia. Stroke	Mean Eff. Pres.	46″	48″	50″	52″	54″	56″	58″	60″	62″	64″	66″	68″	70″	72″	74″	76″	78″	80″	82″	84″
		Diameter of Drivers																			
18″ x 28″	1	197.20	189.00	181.42	174.46	168.00	162.00	156.40	151.20	146.31	141.73	137.44	133.40	129.60	126.00	122.59	119.46	......	......	......	......
	65	12820	12280	11790	11340	10920	10530	10170	9828	9511	9213	8934	8672	8424	8190	7969	7765	......	......	......	......
	80	15770	15120	14510	13950	13440	12960	12510	12090	11700	11340	10990	10670	10370	10080	9807	9557	......	......	......	......
	95	18730	17950	17230	16570	15960	15390	14860	14360	13900	13460	13050	12670	12310	11970	11640	11350	......	......	......	......
	110	21690	20790	19960	19190	18480	17820	17200	16630	16100	15590	15120	14670	14260	13860	13480	13140	......	......	......	......
	125	24650	23620	22680	21810	21000	20250	19550	18900	18290	17720	17180	16670	16200	15750	15320	14930	......	......	......	......
	140	27610	26460	25400	24420	23520	22680	21900	21170	20480	19840	19240	18689	18140	17640	17160	16720	......	......	......	......
	155	30570	29290	28120	27040	26040	25110	24240	23430	22680	21970	21309	20680	20090	19530	19000	18510	......	......	......	......
	170	33520	32130	30840	29660	28560	27540	26590	25700	24870	24090	23360	22680	22030	21420	20840	20310	......	......	......	......
	185	36480	34960	33560	32270	31080	29970	28930	27970	27070	26220	25430	24680	23970	23310	22680	22100	......	......	......	......
	200	39440	37800	36280	34890	33600	32400	31280	30240	29260	28340	27490	26680	25920	25200	24520	23890	......	......	......	......
	215	42400	40630	39010	37510	36120	34830	33630	32510	31460	30470	29550	28680	27860	27090	26360	25680	......	......	......	......
	230	45360	43470	41730	40130	38640	37260	35970	34770	33650	32600	31610	30680	29810	28980	28200	27470	......	......	......	......
18″ x 30″	1	......	202.50	194.40	186.90	180.00	173.56	167.57	162.00	156.78	151.88	147.27	142.93	138.84	135.00	131.33	127.90	124.60	121.50	118.52	115.70
	65	......	13160	12630	12150	11700	11280	10890	10530	10190	9872	9573	9291	9026	8775	8537	8314	8100	7897	7705	7521
	80	......	16200	15550	14950	14400	13880	13400	12960	12540	12150	11780	11430	11100	10800	10500	10230	9968	9720	9483	9256
	95	......	19240	18460	17750	17100	16480	15920	15390	14890	14430	13990	13580	13190	12820	12470	12150	11830	11540	11260	10990
	110	......	22270	21380	20560	19800	19090	18430	17820	17240	16700	16200	15720	15270	14850	14450	14070	13700	13360	13040	12730
	125	......	25310	24300	23360	22500	21690	20950	20250	19600	18980	18410	17870	17350	16870	16420	15990	15570	15190	14820	14460
	140	......	28350	27210	26170	25200	24300	23460	22680	21950	21260	20620	20010	19440	18900	18390	17900	17440	17010	16590	16200
	155	......	31380	30130	28970	27900	26900	25970	25110	24300	23540	22820	22150	21520	20920	20360	19820	19310	18830	18370	17930
	170	......	34420	33050	31770	30600	29500	28480	27540	26650	25820	25030	24300	23600	22950	22330	21740	21180	20650	20150	19670
	185	......	37460	35960	34570	33300	32110	31000	29970	29000	28090	27240	26440	25690	24970	24300	23660	23050	22480	21930	21400
	200	......	40500	38880	37380	36000	34710	33510	32400	31350	30370	29450	28580	27770	27000	26260	25580	24920	24300	23700	23140
	215	......	43530	41800	40180	38700	37310	36030	34830	33700	32650	31660	30730	29850	29020	28240	27500	26790	26120	25480	24870
	230	......	46570	44710	42990	41400	39920	38540	37260	36000	34930	33870	32870	31940	31050	30210	29420	28660	27940	27260	26610
18″ x 32″	1	......	......	207.33	199.33	191.99	185.11	178.72	172.79	167.20	162.00	157.07	152.45	148.10	143.98	140.09	136.40	132.90	129.60	126.42	123.41
	65	......	......	13470	12960	12480	12030	11620	11230	10870	10530	10210	9910	9627	9358	9106	8866	8639	8424	8218	8022
	80	......	......	16580	15940	15360	14810	14300	13820	13370	12960	12560	12190	11850	11520	11200	10910	10630	10370	10110	9873
	95	......	......	19690	18940	18240	17580	16980	16410	15880	15390	14920	14480	14070	13670	13310	12960	12620	12310	12010	11720
	110	......	......	22810	21930	21120	20360	19660	19010	18390	17820	17280	16770	16290	15840	15410	15000	14620	14260	13910	13570
	125	......	......	25920	24920	24000	23140	22340	21600	20900	20250	19630	19060	18510	17990	17510	17050	16610	16200	15800	15430
	140	......	......	29030	27910	26880	25920	25020	24190	23410	22680	21990	21340	20730	20150	19610	19090	18600	18140	17700	17280
	155	......	......	32140	30900	29760	28690	27700	26780	25910	25110	24340	23630	22960	22310	21710	21140	20600	20090	19590	19130
	170	......	......	35250	33890	32630	31470	30380	29370	28420	27540	26700	25910	25180	24470	23810	23190	22590	22030	21490	20980
	185	......	......	38360	36880	35520	34250	33060	31960	30930	29970	29060	28200	27400	26630	25910	25230	24590	23970	23390	22830
	200	......	......	41470	39860	38400	37020	35740	34560	33440	32400	31410	30490	29620	28790	28020	27280	26580	25920	25280	24680
	215	......	......	44580	42860	41270	39800	38420	37150	35950	34830	33770	32780	31840	30950	30120	29320	28570	27860	27180	26530
	230	......	......	47690	45850	44150	42580	41100	39740	38450	37260	36130	35060	34060	33110	32220	31370	30570	29810	29080	28390

Table I.—(Continued).

TRACTIVE POWER OF LOCOMOTIVES, IN POUNDS, FOR DIFFERENT MEAN EFFECTIVE PRESSURES.

CYLINDERS DIA. STROKE	MEAN EFF. PRES.	44″	46″	48″	50″	52″	54″	56″	58″	60″	62″	64″	66″	68″	70″	72″	74″	76″	78″	80″	82″	84″
		DIAMETER OF DRIVERS																				
19″ x 24″	1	196.90	188.33	180.50	173.28	166.60	160.44	154.70	149.37	144.39	139.73	135.38	131.27	127.41	123.77	120.32	117.08	114.00	111.08	108.30	105.64	103.12
	65	12800	12240	11731	11260	10830	10430	10050	9710	9384	9084	8799	8533	8282	8045	7822	7610	7410	7220	7040	6867	6701
	80	15750	15060	14440	13860	13330	12830	12370	11950	11550	11180	10830	10500	10190	9901	9627	9365	9120	8886	8664	8452	8250
	95	18700	17890	17147	16460	15830	15240	14690	14190	13710	13270	12860	12470	12100	11750	11430	11120	10830	10550	10290	10049	9798
	110	21660	20720	19857	19060	18330	17650	17020	16430	15880	15370	14890	14440	14020	13610	13240	12880	12540	12220	11910	11620	11340
	125	24610	23540	22563	21660	20830	20060	19340	18670	18050	17470	16920	16410	15930	15470	15040	14630	14250	13880	13540	13200	12890
	140	27570	26370	25270	24260	23320	22460	21660	20910	20210	19560	18950	18380	17840	17330	16850	16390	15960	15550	15162	14790	14440
	155	30520	29190	27979	26860	25820	24870	23980	23150	22380	21660	20980	20350	19750	19180	18650	18150	17670	17220	16790	16370	15980
	170	33470	32020	30686	29460	28320	27280	26300	25390	24540	23760	23010	22310	21660	21040	20160	19900	19380	18880	18410	17960	17530
	195	36430	34840	33393	32060	30820	29680	28620	27630	26710	25850	25040	24280	23570	22900	22260	21660	21090	20550	20040	19540	19080
	200	39380	37660	36100	34650	33320	32090	30940	29870	28880	27940	27070	26250	25480	24750	24060	23410	22800	22210	21660	21130	20620
	215	42330	40490	38808	37250	35820	34490	33260	32110	31040	30040	29100	28220	27390	26610	25870	25170	24510	23880	23280	22710	22170
	230	45290	43320	41520	39850	38320	36900	35580	34350	33200	32140	31130	30190	29300	28470	27680	26930	26220	25550	24910	24300	23720
19″ x 26″	1	......	204.05	195.53	187.71	180.50	173.81	167.60	161.82	156.42	151.38	146.66	142.21	138.03	134.08	130.36	126.83	123.50	120.32	117.32	114.47	111.73
	65	......	13260	12710	12200	11730	11300	10890	10520	10170	9840	9533	9244	8973	8715	8474	8214	8028	7822	7627	7140	7264
	80	......	16320	15640	15010	14440	13900	13410	12940	12510	12110	11730	11370	11040	10720	10430	10150	9880	9627	9387	9157	8940
	95	......	19380	18570	17830	17140	16510	15920	15370	14860	14380	13930	13510	13110	12730	12380	12050	11730	11430	11140	10870	10610
	110	......	22450	21510	20650	19850	19120	18440	17800	17210	16650	16130	15640	15180	14750	14340	13950	13580	13240	12910	12590	12290
	125	......	25510	24440	23460	22560	21730	20950	20230	19550	18920	18330	17780	17250	16760	16290	15850	15440	15040	14670	14310	13970
	140	......	28570	27380	26280	25270	24330	23460	22660	21900	21190	20530	19910	19330	18770	18250	17760	17290	16850	16430	16020	15640
	155	......	31630	30310	29100	27980	26940	25980	25080	24250	23460	22730	22040	21400	20780	20200	19660	19140	18650	18190	17740	17320
	170	......	34690	33240	31910	30680	29550	28490	27510	26590	25730	24930	24180	23470	22790	22160	21560	20990	20450	19950	19460	18990
	185	......	37750	36170	34730	33390	32160	31000	29940	28940	28000	27130	26310	25540	24800	24120	23460	22850	22260	21710	21170	20670
	200	......	40810	39100	37540	36100	34760	33520	32360	31280	30270	29330	28440	27600	26810	26070	25360	24700	24060	23460	22890	22340
	215	......	43870	42040	40360	38810	37370	36030	34790	33630	32540	31530	30570	29630	28820	28030	27270	26550	25870	25220	24610	24020
	230	......	46930	44970	43180	41520	39980	38550	37220	35980	34810	33730	32710	31750	30830	29980	29170	28110	27680	26990	26320	25700
19″ x 28″	1	......	......	210.57	202.13	194.37	187.17	180.50	174.26	168.46	163.01	157.91	153.13	148.62	144.39	140.39	136.59	132.99	129.60	126.33	123.26	120.32
	65	......	......	13690	13140	12630	12160	11730	11320	10950	10590	10260	9951	9662	9384	9126	8878	8644	8424	8212	8012	7822
	80	......	......	16840	16170	15550	14970	14440	13940	13470	13040	12630	12250	11890	11550	11230	10920	10640	10370	10110	9860	9627
	95	......	......	20000	19200	18460	17780	17140	16550	16000	15480	15000	14550	14120	13710	13337	12970	12630	12310	12000	11710	11430
	110	......	......	23160	22230	21380	20590	19850	19170	18530	17930	17370	16840	16350	15880	15440	15020	14630	14260	13900	13560	13240
	125	......	......	26320	25270	24290	23400	22560	21780	21060	20380	19740	19140	18580	18050	17550	17070	16620	16200	15790	15410	15040
	140	......	......	29480	28300	27210	26200	25270	24390	23580	22820	22110	21440	20810	20210	19650	19120	18620	18140	17690	17250	16850
	155	......	......	32640	31330	30120	29010	27980	27010	26110	25270	24480	23730	23040	22380	21760	21170	20610	20090	19580	19100	18650
	170	......	......	35800	34360	33040	31820	30680	29620	28640	27710	26850	26030	25270	24540	23870	23220	22610	22030	21480	20950	20460
	185	......	......	38950	37390	35960	34630	33390	32240	31160	30160	29210	28330	27490	26710	25970	25270	24600	23970	23370	22800	22260
	200	......	......	42110	40420	38870	37430	36100	34850	33690	32600	31580	30620	29720	28880	28080	27320	26600	25920	25260	24650	24060
	215	......	......	45270	43460	41780	40240	38810	37470	36220	35050	33950	32920	31950	31040	30180	29360	28590	27860	27160	26500	25870
	230	......	......	48430	46490	44700	43050	41520	40080	38750	37490	36320	35220	34180	33200	32290	31410	30590	29810	29060	28350	27680

TABLE I.—(Continued).

TRACTIVE POWER OF LOCOMOTIVES, IN POUNDS, FOR DIFFERENT MEAN EFFECTIVE PRESSURES.

CYLINDERS	MEAN	DIAMETER OF DRIVERS																	
DIA. STROKE	EFF. PRES.	50″	52″	54″	56″	58″	60″	62″	64″	66″	68″	70″	72″	74″	76″	78″	80″	82″	84″
19″ x 30″	1	216.60	208.28	200.58	193.40	186.72	180.50	174.69	169.22	164.09	159.28	154.70	150.41	146.34	142.50	138.84	135.38	132.08	128.92
	65	14080	13540	13040	12570	12140	11730	11350	11000	10660	10350	10050	9777	9513	9263	9026	8799	8585	8380
	80	17330	16660	16040	15470	14940	14440	13970	13540	13120	12740	12370	12030	11710	11400	11110	10830	10560	10310
	95	20570	19780	19050	18370	17740	17140	16590	16070	15590	15130	14690	14290	13900	13540	13190	12860	12540	12250
	110	23830	22910	22060	21270	20540	19850	19210	18610	18050	17520	17020	16540	16100	15670	15270	14890	14530	14180
	125	27070	26030	25070	24170	23340	22560	21830	21150	20510	19910	19340	18800	18290	17810	17360	16920	16510	16110
	140	30320	29160	28080	27070	26140	25270	24450	23690	22970	22300	21660	21060	20490	19950	19440	18950	18490	18050
	155	33570	32280	31080	29970	28940	27980	27080	26230	25430	24690	23980	23310	22680	22090	21520	20980	20470	19980
	170	36820	35400	34090	32870	31740	30680	29690	28770	27890	27070	26300	25570	24880	24220	23600	23010	22450	21920
	185	40070	38530	37100	35780	34540	33390	32320	31310	30350	29460	28620	27830	27070	26360	25690	25040	24430	23850
	200	43320	41650	40010	39680	37340	36100	34940	33840	32820	31850	30940	30080	29270	28500	27770	27070	26410	25780
	215	46570	44780	43120	41580	40150	38810	37560	36380	35280	34240	33260	32340	31460	30640	29850	29100	28390	27720
	230	49820	47900	46130	44480	42950	41520	40180	38920	37740	36630	35580	34600	33660	32770	31940	31130	30380	29650
19″ x 32″	1	......	222.18	213.98	206.30	199.20	192.56	186.33	180.50	175.03	169.90	165.04	160.44	156.10	152.00	148.10	144.40	140.88	137.52
	65	......	14440	13910	13410	12950	12510	12110	11730	11380	11040	10730	10430	10150	9880	9620	9384	9157	9840
	80	......	17770	17120	16500	15930	15400	14900	14440	14000	13590	13200	12830	12490	12160	11850	11550	11270	11000
	95	......	21100	20320	19600	18920	18290	17700	17140	16630	16140	15680	15240	14830	14440	14070	13710	13380	13060
	110	......	24440	23530	22690	21910	21180	20500	19850	19250	18690	18160	17650	17170	16720	16290	15880	15500	15130
	125	......	27770	26740	25790	24900	24070	23290	22560	21880	21240	20630	20060	19510	19000	18510	18050	17610	17190
	140	......	31100	29950	28880	27890	26960	26090	25270	24500	23790	23110	22460	21850	21280	20730	20210	19720	19250
	155	......	34440	33160	31980	30870	29840	28880	27980	27130	26330	25580	24870	24200	23560	22960	22380	21830	21320
	170	......	37770	36370	35070	33860	32730	31680	30680	29750	28880	28060	27280	26540	25840	25180	24540	23950	23380
	185	......	41100	39580	38170	36850	35620	34470	33390	32380	31430	30530	29680	28880	28120	27400	26710	26060	25440
	200	......	44430	42390	41260	39840	38510	37260	36100	35000	33980	33010	32090	31220	30400	29620	28880	28170	27500
	215	......	47770	46000	44350	42830	41400	40060	38810	37630	36530	35480	34490	33560	32680	31840	31040	30290	29570
	230	......	51100	49210	47450	45820	44290	42850	41520	40260	39070	37960	36900	35900	34960	34060	33200	32400	31630
19″ x 34″	1	......	......	227.32	219.20	211.64	204 60	198.00	191.80	185.99	180.50	175.36	170.49	165.88	161.51	157.38	153.43	149.70	146.12
	65	......	......	14770	14250	13750	13300	12870	12460	12090	11730	11400	11080	10780	10500	10230	9974	9731	9499
	80	......	......	18180	17530	16930	16370	15840	15340	14880	14440	14030	13640	13270	12920	12590	12270	11970	11690
	95	......	......	21590	20820	20100	19430	18810	18220	17670	17140	16660	16190	15760	15340	14950	14570	14220	13880
	110	......	......	25010	24110	23280	22510	21780	21100	20469	19850	19290	18750	18250	17770	17310	16880	16460	16070
	125	......	......	28420	27400	26450	25570	24750	23970	23250	22560	21920	21310	20730	20190	19670	19180	18710	18270
	140	......	......	31820	30690	29630	28640	27720	26850	26040	25270	24550	23870	23220	22610	22030	21480	20960	20460
	155	......	......	35230	33970	32800	31710	30690	29730	28830	27980	27180	26420	25710	25030	24390	23780	23200	22650
	170	......	......	38650	37260	35980	34780	33660	32600	31620	30680	29810	28980	28200	27460	26750	26080	25450	24840
	185	......	......	42060	40550	39150	37850	36630	35480	34410	33390	32440	31540	30690	29880	29110	28380	27690	27030
	200	......	......	45460	43840	42330	40920	39600	38360	37200	36100	35070	34100	33170	32300	31470	30680	29940	29220
	215	......	......	48870	47130	45500	43980	42570	41230	39990	38810	37700	36650	35660	34720	33830	32980	32180	31410
	230	......	......	52280	50420	48680	47050	45540	44110	42780	41520	40330	39210	38150	37150	36200	35290	34430	33600

Table I.—(Continued).

TRACTIVE POWER OF LOCOMOTIVES, IN POUNDS, FOR DIFFERENT MEAN EFFECTIVE PRESSURES.

CYLINDERS Dia. Stroke	Mean Eff. Pres.	DIAMETER OF DRIVERS 44″	46″	48″	50″	52″	54″	56″	58″	60″	62″	64″	66″	68″	70″	72″	74″	76″	78″	80″	82″	84″	
20″ x 24″	1	218.18	208.69	200.00	192.00	184.60	177.78	171.41	165.50	160.00	151.84	150.00	145.45	141.18	137.14	133.33	129.72	126.32	123.08	120.00	117.08	114.29	......
	65	14180	13560	13000	12480	12000	11550	11140	10760	10400	10060	9750	9454	9176	8914	8667	8432	8212	8000	7800	7610	7428	......
	80	17450	16690	16000	15360	14770	14220	13710	13240	12800	12390	12000	11630	11290	10970	10670	10380	10100	9846	9600	9360	9143	......
	95	20720	19820	19000	18240	17530	16890	16280	15720	15200	14710	14250	13820	13410	13030	12670	12320	12000	11690	11400	11120	10850	......
	110	24000	22950	22000	21120	20310	19550	18860	18200	17600	17030	16500	16000	15530	15090	14670	14270	13890	13540	13200	12880	12570	......
	125	27270	26080	25000	24000	23070	22220	21430	20690	20000	19360	18750	18180	17650	17140	16670	16220	15790	15380	15000	14630	14280	......
	140	30540	29210	28000	26880	25840	24890	24000	23170	22400	21680	21000	20360	19760	19200	18670	18160	17680	17230	16800	16390	16000	......
	155	33820	32340	31000	29760	28610	27550	26570	25650	24800	24000	23250	22540	21880	21260	20670	20110	19580	19070	18600	18150	17710	......
	170	37090	35470	34000	32640	31380	30220	29140	28130	27200	26320	25500	24720	24000	23310	22670	22050	21470	20920	20400	19900	19430	......
	185	40360	38600	37000	35520	34150	32890	31710	30620	29600	28650	27750	26910	26120	25370	24670	24000	23370	22770	22200	21660	21140	......
	200	43630	41730	40000	38400	36920	35550	34280	33100	32000	30970	30000	29090	28230	27430	26670	25940	25260	24610	24000	23410	22850	......
	215	46910	44860	43000	41280	39690	38220	36850	35580	34400	33290	32250	31270	30350	29490	28670	27890	27160	26460	25800	25170	24570	......
	230	50180	47990	46000	44160	42460	40890	39420	38070	36800	35610	34500	33450	32470	31540	30670	29840	29050	28300	27600	26930	26280	......
20″ x 26″	1	......	226.09	216.67	208.00	200.00	192.60	185.71	179.31	173.33	167.73	162.50	157.58	152.95	148.57	144.44	140.53	136.85	133.33	130.00	126.83	123.81	......
	65	......	14690	14080	13520	13000	12520	12070	11650	11260	10900	10560	10240	9942	9657	9389	9136	8895	8667	8450	8214	8049	......
	80	......	18080	17330	16640	16000	15410	14850	14340	13860	13420	13000	12600	12230	11880	11550	11240	10950	10670	10400	10150	9905	......
	95	......	21470	20580	19760	19000	18290	17640	17030	16460	15930	15430	14970	14530	14110	13720	13350	13000	12670	12350	12050	11760	......
	110	......	24870	23830	22880	22000	21180	20430	19720	19060	18450	17870	17330	16820	16340	15890	15460	15050	14670	14300	13950	13620	......
	125	......	28260	27080	26000	25000	24070	23210	22410	21669	20960	20310	19690	19120	18570	18050	17570	17110	16670	16250	15850	15480	......
	140	......	31650	30330	29120	28000	26960	26000	25100	24260	23480	22750	22060	21410	20800	20220	19670	19160	18670	18200	17760	17330	......
	155	......	35040	33580	32240	31000	29850	28790	27790	26860	26000	25180	24420	23700	23030	22390	21780	21210	20670	20150	19660	19190	......
	170	......	38430	36830	35360	34000	32740	31570	30480	29460	28510	27620	26790	26000	25250	24550	23890	23260	22670	22100	21560	21050	......
	185	......	41820	40080	38480	37000	35630	34360	33170	32060	31030	30060	29150	28290	27480	26720	26000	25320	24670	24050	23460	22910	......
	200	......	45220	43330	41600	40000	38520	37140	35860	34660	33540	32500	31510	30590	29710	28890	28100	27370	26670	26000	25360	24760	......
	215	......	48610	46580	44720	43000	41400	39930	38550	37260	36060	34930	33880	32880	31940	31050	30210	29420	28670	27950	27270	26620	......
	230	......	52000	49830	47840	46000	44300	42720	41240	39860	38580	37370	36240	35170	34170	33220	32320	31470	30670	29900	29170	28480	......
20″ x 28″	1	......	......	233.34	224.00	215.38	207.40	200.00	193.10	186.67	180.66	175.00	169.70	164.71	160.00	155.56	151.36	147.38	143.60	140.00	136.59	133.33	......
	65	......	......	15170	14560	14000	13480	13000	12550	12130	11740	11370	11030	10710	10400	10110	9838	9580	9334	9100	8878	8667	......
	80	......	......	18670	17920	17230	16590	16000	15450	14930	14450	14000	13570	13170	12800	12440	12110	11790	11480	11200	10920	10670	......
	95	......	......	22170	21280	20460	19700	19000	18340	17730	17160	16620	16120	15640	15200	14770	14380	14000	13640	13300	12970	12670	......
	110	......	......	25670	24640	23690	22810	22000	21240	20530	19870	19250	18670	18120	17600	17110	16650	16210	15790	15400	15020	14670	......
	125	......	......	29170	28000	26920	25920	25000	24140	23330	22580	21870	21210	20590	20000	19440	18920	18420	17950	17500	17070	16670	......
	140	......	......	32670	31360	30150	29030	28000	27030	26130	25290	24500	23760	23060	22400	21780	21190	20630	20100	19600	19120	18670	......
	155	......	......	36170	34720	33380	32150	31000	29930	28930	28000	27120	26300	25530	24800	24110	23460	22840	22260	21700	21170	20670	......
	170	......	......	39670	38080	36610	35260	34000	32820	31730	30710	29750	28850	28000	27200	26440	25730	25050	24410	23800	23220	22670	......
	185	......	......	43170	41440	39840	38370	37000	35720	34530	33420	32370	31400	30470	29600	28780	28000	27260	26560	25900	25270	24670	......
	200	......	......	46670	44800	43070	41480	40000	38620	37330	36130	35000	33940	32940	32000	31110	30270	29470	28720	28000	27320	26670	......
	215	......	......	50170	48160	46300	44590	43000	41510	40130	38840	37620	36490	35410	34400	33440	32540	31680	30870	30100	29360	28670	......
	230	......	......	53670	51520	49530	47700	46000	44410	42930	41550	40250	39030	37880	36800	35780	34810	33900	33020	32200	31410	30670	......

Table I.—(Continued).

TRACTIVE POWER OF LOCOMOTIVES, IN POUNDS, FOR DIFFERENT MEAN EFFECTIVE PRESSURES.

Cylinders Dia. Stroke	Mean Eff. Pres.	Diameter of Drivers 50″	52″	54″	56″	58″	60″	62″	64″	66″	68″	70″	72″	74″	76″	78″	80″	82″	84″
20″ x 30″	1	240.00	230.78	222.23	214.30	206.90	200.00	193.56	187.50	181.82	176.49	171.43	166.67	162.17	157.91	153.85	150.00	146.34	142.86
	65	15600	15000	14440	13930	13450	13000	12580	12180	11820	11470	11140	10830	10540	10260	10000	9750	9513	9286
	80	19200	18460	17770	17140	16550	16000	15480	15000	14540	14120	13710	13330	12970	12630	12300	12000	11710	11430
	95	22800	21920	21110	20360	19650	19000	18380	17810	17270	16760	16280	15830	15400	15000	14610	14250	13900	13570
	110	26400	25380	24440	23570	22760	22000	21290	20620	20000	19410	18860	18330	17840	17370	16920	16500	16100	15710
	125	30000	28850	27780	26790	25860	25000	24190	23430	22730	22060	21430	20830	20270	19740	19230	18750	18290	17850
	140	33600	32310	31110	30000	28960	28000	27100	26250	25450	24700	24000	23330	22700	22110	21540	21000	20490	20000
	155	37200	35770	34450	33210	32070	31000	30000	29060	28180	27350	26570	25830	25130	24480	23850	23250	22680	22140
	170	40800	39230	37780	36430	35170	34000	32900	31870	30910	30000	29140	28330	27570	26850	26150	25500	24880	24280
	185	44400	42690	41110	39640	38280	37000	35810	34680	33640	32650	31710	30830	30000	29210	28460	27750	27070	26430
	200	48000	46150	44440	42860	41380	40000	38710	37500	36360	35300	34280	33330	32430	31580	30770	30000	29270	28570
	215	51600	49610	47780	46070	44480	43000	41610	40310	39090	37940	36860	35830	34860	33950	33080	32250	31460	30710
	230	55200	53080	51110	49280	47590	46000	44510	43120	41820	40590	39430	38330	37300	36320	35380	34500	33660	32850
20″ x 32″	1	......	246.16	237.04	228.58	220.69	213.33	206.45	200.00	193.94	188.24	182.87	177.78	172.99	168.42	164.10	160.00	156.10	152.38
	65	......	16000	15410	14850	14340	13860	13420	13000	12600	12230	11880	11550	11240	10950	10660	10400	10150	9904
	80	......	19690	18960	18280	17650	17060	16510	16000	15510	15060	14630	14220	13840	13470	13130	12800	12490	12190
	95	......	23380	22520	21710	20960	20260	19610	19000	18420	17880	17370	16890	16430	16000	15590	15200	14830	14470
	110	......	27080	26070	25140	24270	23460	22710	22000	21330	20710	20120	19550	19030	18530	18050	17600	17170	16760
	125	......	30770	29630	28570	27580	26660	25800	25000	24240	23530	22860	22220	21620	21050	20510	20000	19510	19050
	140	......	34460	33180	32000	30890	29860	28900	28000	27150	26350	25600	24890	24220	23580	22970	22400	21850	21330
	155	......	38150	36740	35430	34210	33060	32000	31000	30060	29180	28340	27550	26810	26100	25430	24800	24200	23610
	170	......	41840	40300	38850	37510	36260	35090	34000	32970	32000	31080	30220	29400	28630	27890	27200	26540	25900
	185	......	45540	43850	42280	40830	39460	38190	37000	35880	34820	33830	32890	32000	31160	30360	29600	28880	28190
	200	......	49230	47410	45710	44140	42660	41290	40000	38790	37650	36570	35550	34600	33680	32820	32000	31220	30470
	215	......	52920	50960	49140	47440	45860	44380	43000	41690	40470	39310	38220	37190	36210	35280	34400	33560	32760
	230	......	56620	54520	52570	50760	49060	47480	46000	44610	43300	42060	40890	39780	38740	37740	36800	35900	35040
20″ x 34″	1	......	......	251.88	242.87	234.49	226.66	219.36	212.51	206.07	200.00	194.29	188.90	183.79	178.96	174.37	170.00	165.85	161.90
	65	......	......	16370	15780	15240	14730	14260	13810	13390	13000	12630	12280	11940	11630	11330	11050	10780	10520
	80	......	......	20150	19430	18760	18130	17550	17000	16480	16000	15540	15110	14700	14310	13950	13600	13270	12950
	95	......	......	23930	23070	22270	21530	20840	20190	19570	19000	18450	17940	17460	17000	16560	16150	15750	15380
	110	......	......	27710	26710	25790	24930	24130	23380	22670	22000	21370	20780	20220	19680	19180	18700	18240	17810
	125	......	......	31480	30360	29310	28330	27420	26560	25760	25000	24280	23610	22970	22370	21790	21250	20730	20240
	140	......	......	35260	34000	32830	31730	30710	29750	28850	28000	27200	26440	25730	25050	24410	23800	23220	22670
	155	......	......	39040	37640	36340	35130	34000	32940	31940	31000	30110	29280	28480	27740	27030	26350	25710	25090
	170	......	......	42820	41280	39860	38530	37290	36130	35030	34000	33020	32110	31240	30420	29640	28900	28190	27520
	185	......	......	46600	44930	43380	41930	40580	39320	38120	37000	35940	34940	34000	33100	32260	31450	30680	29950
	200	......	......	50370	48570	46900	45330	43870	42500	41210	40000	38860	37780	36760	35790	34870	34000	33170	32380
	215	......	......	54150	52210	50410	48730	47160	45690	44300	43000	41770	40610	39510	38470	37490	36550	35660	34810
	230	......	......	57930	55860	53930	52130	50450	48880	47390	46000	44680	43450	42270	41160	40100	39100	38150	37230

Table I.—(Continued).

TRACTIVE POWER OF LOCOMOTIVES, IN POUNDS, FOR DIFFERENT MEAN EFFECTIVE PRESSURES.

CYLINDERS DIA. STROKE	MEAN EFF. PRES.	DIAMETER OF DRIVERS 48″	50″	52″	54″	56″	58″	60″	62″	64″	66″	68″	70″	72″	74″	76″	78″	80″	82″	84″
21″ x 26″	1	238.87	229.32	220.50	212.33	204.75	197.69	191.10	184.92	179.16	173.72	168.62	163.80	159.25	154.94	150.87	147.00	143.32	139.82	136.50
	65	15520	14900	14330	13800	13310	12850	12420	12020	11640	11290	10960	10650	10350	10070	9807	9555	9317	9090	8872
	80	19110	18340	17640	16980	16380	15810	15280	14790	14330	13900	13490	13100	12740	12390	12070	11760	11460	11180	10920
	95	22690	21780	20950	20170	19450	18780	18150	17560	17020	16500	16020	15560	15130	14720	14330	13960	13610	13280	12960
	110	26270	25230	24250	23360	22520	21740	21020	20340	19710	19110	18550	18020	17520	17040	16590	16170	15760	15380	15010
	125	29860	28670	27560	26540	25590	24710	23880	23110	22390	21720	21080	20470	19910	19370	18860	18370	17920	17480	17060
	140	33440	32110	30870	29730	28660	27670	26750	25890	25080	24320	23610	22930	22290	21690	21120	20580	20070	19580	19110
	155	37020	35550	34180	32910	31740	30640	29620	28660	27770	26930	26140	25390	24680	24020	23380	22780	22210	21670	21160
	170	40600	38980	37480	36100	34800	33600	32480	31430	30450	29530	28670	27840	27070	26340	25650	24990	24360	23770	23200
	185	44190	42420	40790	39280	37880	36570	35350	34210	33140	32140	31200	30300	29460	28660	27910	27190	26510	25870	25250
	200	47770	45860	44100	42460	40950	39530	38220	36980	35830	34740	33730	32760	31850	30990	30170	29400	28660	27960	27300
	215	51350	49300	47410	45650	44020	42500	41080	39760	38510	37350	36250	35210	34240	33310	32430	31600	30810	30060	29340
	230	54930	52740	50720	48840	47090	45470	43950	42530	41200	39960	38780	37670	36630	35640	34700	33810	32960	32160	31390
21″ x 28″	1	......	246.96	237.47	228.67	220.50	212.90	205.80	199.17	192.94	187.08	181.60	176.40	171.50	166.87	162.47	158.30	154.35	158.58	147.00
	65	......	16050	15430	14860	14330	13840	13370	12940	12540	12160	11800	11460	11150	10840	10560	10290	10030	10310	9555
	80	......	19750	18990	18290	17640	17030	16460	15930	15430	14960	14530	14110	13720	13350	13000	12660	12350	12680	11760
	95	......	23460	22560	21720	20950	20220	19550	18920	18330	17770	17250	16760	16290	15850	15430	15040	14660	15060	13960
	110	......	27160	26120	25150	24250	23420	22640	21910	21220	20580	19970	19400	18860	18360	17870	17410	16980	17440	16170
	125	......	30870	29680	28580	27560	26610	25720	24890	24120	23380	22700	22050	21440	20860	20310	19790	19290	19820	18370
	140	......	34570	33240	32010	30870	29800	28810	27880	27010	26190	25420	24700	24010	23360	22750	22160	21610	22220	20580
	155	......	38280	36810	35440	34180	33000	31900	30870	29900	28990	28150	27340	26580	25860	25180	24530	23920	24580	22780
	170	......	41980	40370	38870	37480	36190	34980	33860	32800	31800	30870	29990	29150	28370	27620	26910	26240	26950	24990
	185	......	45690	43930	42300	40790	39380	38070	36840	35690	34610	33590	32630	31730	30870	30060	29280	28550	29330	27190
	200	......	49390	47490	45730	44100	42580	41160	39830	38590	37410	36320	35280	34300	33370	32490	31660	30870	31710	29400
	215	......	53100	51050	49160	47410	45770	44240	42820	41480	40220	39040	37920	36870	35880	34930	34030	33180	34090	31600
	230	......	56800	54620	52590	50720	48970	47330	45810	44370	43030	41760	40570	39440	38380	37370	36410	35500	36470	33810
21″ x 30″	1	......	......	254.44	245.00	236.26	228.10	220.50	213.40	206.72	200.45	194.58	189.00	183.75	178.78	174.08	169.61	165.37	161.34	157.50
	65	......	......	16540	15920	15350	14820	14330	13870	13440	13030	12650	12280	11940	11620	11310	11020	10750	10480	10240
	80	......	......	20350	19600	18900	18250	17640	17070	16540	16030	15560	15120	14700	14300	13920	13570	13230	12910	12600
	95	......	......	24170	23270	22440	21670	20950	20270	19640	19040	18480	17950	17450	16980	16530	16110	15710	15330	14960
	110	......	......	27990	26950	25990	25090	24250	23470	22740	22050	21400	20790	20210	19660	19150	18660	18190	17750	17320
	125	......	......	31800	30620	29530	28510	27560	26670	25840	25050	24320	23620	22970	22340	21760	21200	20670	20170	19690
	140	......	......	35620	34300	33070	31930	30870	29870	28940	28060	27240	26460	25720	25030	24370	23750	23150	22590	22050
	155	......	......	39440	37970	36620	35350	34180	33070	32040	31070	30160	29290	28480	27710	26980	26290	25630	25010	24410
	170	......	......	43250	41650	40160	38770	37480	36280	35140	34070	33080	32130	31230	30390	29590	28830	28110	27430	26770
	185	......	......	47070	45320	43700	42200	40790	39480	38240	37080	36000	34960	33990	33070	32200	31380	30590	29850	29140
	200	......	......	50890	49000	47250	45620	44100	42680	41340	40090	38910	37800	36750	35750	34810	33920	33070	32270	31500
	215	......	......	54700	52670	50790	49040	47410	45880	44440	43090	41830	40630	39500	38430	37420	36460	35550	34690	33860
	230	......	......	58520	56350	54340	52460	50720	49080	47550	46100	44750	43470	42260	41110	40030	39010	38030	37110	36220

Table I.— (Continued).

TRACTIVE POWER OF LOCOMOTIVES, IN POUNDS, FOR DIFFERENT MEAN EFFECTIVE PRESSURES.

CYLINDERS DIA. STROKE	MEAN EFF. PRES.	DIAMETER OF DRIVERS 54″	56″	58″	60″	62″	64″	66″	68″	70″	72″	74″	76″	78″	80″	82″	84″
21″ x 32″	1	261.33	252.00	243.31	235.20	227.61	220.50	213.81	207.54	201.60	196.00	190.70	185.69	180.92	176.40	172.10	168.00
	65	16980	16380	15810	15290	14790	14330	13900	13490	13100	12740	12390	12070	11760	11460	11180	10920
	80	20900	20160	19460	18810	18210	17640	17100	16600	16120	15680	15250	14850	14470	14110	13760	13440
	95	24820	23940	23110	22340	21620	20950	20310	19710	19150	18620	18110	17640	17190	16760	16350	15960
	110	28750	27720	26760	25870	25040	24250	23520	22830	22170	21560	20980	20420	19900	19400	18930	18480
	125	32670	31500	30410	29400	28450	27560	26720	25940	25200	24500	23840	23210	22610	22050	21510	21000
	140	36580	35280	34060	32930	31860	30870	29930	29050	28220	27440	26700	25990	25330	24700	24090	23520
	155	40510	39060	37710	36460	35280	34180	33140	32170	31240	30380	29560	28780	28040	27340	26670	26040
	170	44420	42840	41360	39980	38690	37480	36350	35280	34270	33320	32420	31560	30750	29990	29250	28560
	185	48350	46620	45010	43510	42110	40790	39550	38390	37290	36260	35280	34350	33470	32630	31840	31080
	200	52260	50400	48600	47040	45520	44100	42760	41510	40320	39200	38140	37140	36180	35280	34420	33600
	215	56180	54180	52310	50570	48930	47410	45970	44620	43340	42140	41000	39920	38890	37920	37000	36120
	230	60110	57960	55960	54100	52350	50720	49170	47730	46370	45080	43860	42710	41610	40570	39580	38640
21″ x 34″	1	......	267.75	258.52	249.90	241.84	234.25	227.18	220.50	214.20	208.25	202.62	197.29	192.23	187.42	182.85	178.50
	65	......	17400	16800	16240	15720	15220	14760	14330	13920	13530	13170	12820	12490	12180	11880	11600
	80	......	21420	20680	19990	19340	18740	18170	17640	17130	16660	16210	15780	15380	14990	14630	14280
	95	......	25430	24560	23740	22970	22250	21580	20950	20350	19780	19250	18740	18260	17800	17370	16950
	110	......	29450	28440	27490	26600	25770	24990	24250	23560	22910	22290	21700	21140	20620	20110	19630
	125	......	33470	32310	31240	30230	29280	28390	27560	26770	26030	25330	24660	24030	23430	22850	22310
	140	......	37480	36190	34980	33860	32790	31800	30870	29980	29150	28370	27620	26910	26240	25600	24990
	155	......	41500	40070	38730	37480	36310	35210	34180	33200	32280	31400	30580	29790	29050	28340	27670
	170	......	45520	43950	42480	41110	39820	38620	37480	36410	35400	34440	33540	32680	31860	31080	30340
	185	......	49530	47830	46230	44740	43340	42020	40790	39620	38530	37480	36500	35560	34670	33830	33020
	200	......	53550	51700	49980	48370	46850	45430	44100	42840	41650	40520	39460	38440	37480	36570	35700
	215	......	57560	55580	53720	51990	50360	48840	47410	46050	44770	43560	42410	41330	40290	39310	38370
	230	......	61580	59460	57480	55620	53880	52250	50720	49260	47900	46600	45380	44210	43110	42050	41050
21″ x 36″	1	......	......	273.71	264.60	256.05	248.06	240.55	233.48	226.80	220.50	214.53	208.89	203.53	198.45	193.61	189.00
	65	......	......	17790	17200	16640	16120	15630	15170	14740	14330	13940	13580	13230	12900	12580	12280
	80	......	......	21890	21160	20480	19840	19240	18680	18140	17640	17160	16710	16280	15870	15490	15120
	95	......	......	26000	25130	24320	23560	22850	22180	21540	20950	20380	19840	19330	18850	18390	17950
	110	......	......	30110	29100	28160	27290	26460	25680	24950	24250	23600	22980	22390	21830	21300	20790
	125	......	......	34210	33070	32010	31000	30070	29180	28350	27560	26820	26110	25440	24800	24200	23620
	140	......	......	38320	37040	35850	34730	33680	32680	31750	30870	30030	29240	28490	27780	27110	26460
	155	......	......	42430	41010	39690	38450	37280	36190	35150	34180	33250	32370	31550	30760	30010	29290
	170	......	......	46530	44980	43530	42170	40890	39690	38550	37480	36470	35510	34600	33740	32910	32130
	185	......	......	50640	48950	47370	45890	44500	43190	41950	40790	39690	38640	37650	36710	35820	34960
	200	......	......	54740	52920	51210	49610	48110	46690	45360	44100	42900	41770	40700	39690	38720	37800
	215	......	......	58840	56890	55050	53330	51720	50200	48760	47410	46120	44910	43760	42670	41620	40630
	230	......	......	62960	60860	58890	57060	55330	53700	52160	50720	49340	48040	46810	45640	44530	43470

Table I.—(Continued).

TRACTIVE POWER OF LOCOMOTIVES, IN POUNDS, FOR DIFFERENT MEAN EFFECTIVE PRESSURES.

Cylinders Dia. Stroke	Mean Eff. Pres.	Diameter of Drivers 50″	52″	54″	56″	58″	60″	62″	64″	66″	68″	70″	72″	74″	76″	78″	80″	82″	84″
22″ x 28″	1	271.04	260.60	250.95	242.00	233.64	225.86	218.58	211.75	205.32	199.30	193.60	188.22	183.13	178.31	173.74	169.40	165.27	161.33
	65	17610	16940	16310	15730	15190	14680	14210	13760	13340	12950	12580	12230	11900	11590	11290	11010	10740	10480
	80	21680	20850	20070	19360	18690	18070	17480	16940	16420	15940	15490	15060	14650	14260	13900	13550	13220	12900
	95	25750	24750	23840	22990	22190	21450	20760	20110	19500	18930	18390	17880	17400	16940	16500	16090	15700	15320
	110	29810	28670	27600	26620	25700	24840	24040	23290	22590	21920	21300	20710	20150	19610	19110	18630	18180	17740
	125	33880	32570	31370	30250	29200	28230	27320	26470	25670	24910	24200	23530	22890	22290	21720	21170	20660	20170
	140	37940	36480	35130	33880	32710	31620	30600	29640	28750	27900	27100	26350	25640	24960	24320	23710	23140	22590
	155	42010	40390	38900	37510	36210	35010	33880	32820	31830	30890	30010	29180	28390	27640	26930	26260	25610	25010
	170	46070	44300	42660	41140	39720	38390	37150	36000	34900	33880	32910	32000	31130	30310	29530	28800	28090	27420
	185	50140	48210	46420	44770	43220	41780	40430	39170	37980	36870	35810	34820	33880	32990	32140	31340	30570	29850
	200	54210	52120	50190	48400	46730	45170	43710	42350	41060	39860	38720	37640	36620	35660	34750	33880	33050	32260
	215	58270	56030	53950	52030	50230	48560	46990	45520	44140	42850	41620	40470	39370	38340	37350	36420	35530	34690
	230	62340	59940	57720	55660	53740	51940	50270	48700	47220	45840	44520	43290	42120	41010	39960	38960	38010	37100
22″ x 30″	1	......	279.20	268.89	259.28	250.31	242.00	234.18	226.87	220.00	213.52	207.43	201.66	196.20	191.06	186.16	181.50	177.08	172.86
	65	......	18150	17470	16850	16270	15730	15220	14740	14300	13880	13480	13110	12750	12420	12100	11790	11510	11230
	80	......	22330	21510	20740	20020	19360	18730	18150	17600	17080	16590	16130	15690	15280	14890	14520	14160	13830
	95	......	26520	25540	24630	23780	22990	22240	21550	20900	20280	19700	19150	18640	18150	17680	17240	16820	16420
	110	......	30710	29580	28520	27530	26620	25760	24950	24200	23490	22820	22180	21580	21010	20480	19960	19480	19010
	125	......	34900	33610	32410	31290	30250	29270	28360	27500	26690	25930	25200	24520	23880	23270	22690	22130	21610
	140	......	39090	37640	36300	35040	33880	32780	31760	30800	29890	29040	28230	27470	26750	26060	25410	24790	24200
	155	......	43270	41680	40190	38800	37510	36300	35160	34100	33090	32150	31250	30410	29610	28850	28130	27440	26790
	170	......	47460	45710	44070	42550	41140	39810	38560	37400	36300	35260	34280	33350	32480	31640	30850	30100	29380
	185	......	51650	48940	47960	46310	44770	43320	41970	40700	39500	38380	37300	36300	35340	34440	33580	32760	31980
	200	......	55840	53780	51850	50060	48400	46830	45370	44000	42700	41480	40330	39240	38210	37230	36300	35410	34570
	215	......	60030	57810	55740	53820	52030	50340	48770	47300	45910	44600	43350	42180	41070	40020	39020	38070	37160
	230	......	64220	61840	59630	57570	55660	53860	52180	50600	49110	47710	46380	45120	43940	42810	41740	40730	39750
22″ x 32″	1	......	......	286.81	276.57	267.03	258.13	249.79	242.00	234.66	227.78	221.26	215.11	209.29	203.78	198.55	193.60	188.88	184.38
	65	......	......	18640	17970	17350	16780	16230	15730	15250	14800	14380	13980	13600	13240	12900	12580	12270	11980
	80	......	......	22940	22120	21360	20650	19980	19360	18770	18220	17700	17210	16740	16300	15880	15490	15110	14750
	95	......	......	27240	26270	25360	24520	23730	22990	22290	21630	21040	20430	19880	19350	18860	18390	17940	17510
	110	......	......	31550	30420	29370	28390	27470	26620	25810	25450	24340	23660	23020	22410	21840	21300	20770	20280
	125	......	......	35850	34570	33380	32270	31220	30250	29330	28470	27660	26890	26160	25470	24820	24200	23610	23050
	140	......	......	40150	38720	37380	36140	34970	33880	32850	31880	30970	30110	29300	28530	27790	27100	26440	25810
	155	......	......	44450	42870	41390	40010	38710	37510	36370	35300	34290	33340	32440	31580	30770	30010	29270	28580
	170	......	......	48750	47010	45390	43880	42460	41140	39890	38720	37610	36570	35580	34640	33750	32910	32110	31340
	185	......	......	53060	51170	49400	47750	46210	44770	43410	42140	40930	39800	38720	37700	36730	35810	34940	34110
	200	......	......	57360	55310	53400	51620	49950	48400	46930	45550	44250	43020	41860	40750	39710	38720	37770	36870
	215	......	......	61660	59460	57410	55500	53700	52030	50450	48970	47570	46250	45000	43810	42690	41620	40600	39640
	230	......	......	65960	63610	61420	59370	57450	55660	53970	52380	50890	49470	48140	46860	45670	44520	43440	42400

Table I.—(Continued).

TRACTIVE POWER OF LOCOMOTIVES, IN POUNDS, FOR DIFFERENT MEAN EFFECTIVE PRESSURES.

CYLINDERS Dia. Stroke	Mean Eff. Pres.	DIAMETER OF DRIVERS 56″	58″	60″	62″	64″	66″	68″	70″	72″	74″	76″	78″	80″	82″	84″
22″ x 34″	1	293.86	283.71	274.26	265.40	257.12	249.33	242.00	235.08	228.55	222.37	216.52	211.00	205.70	200.70	195.90
	65	19100	18440	17820	17250	16710	16200	15730	15280	14850	14450	14070	13710	13370	13040	12730
	80	23500	22690	21940	21230	20570	19940	19360	18800	18280	17790	17320	16880	16450	16050	15770
	95	27910	26950	26050	25210	24420	23680	22990	22330	21710	21120	20570	20040	19540	19060	18610
	110	32320	31210	30170	29190	28280	27430	26620	25860	25140	24460	23820	23210	22630	22070	21550
	125	36730	35460	34280	33170	32140	31170	30250	29380	28570	27790	27070	26370	25710	25090	24480
	140	41140	39720	38390	37150	36000	34910	33880	32910	32000	31130	30310	29540	28800	28100	27420
	155	45550	43970	42510	41130	39860	38650	37510	36440	35420	34470	33560	32700	31880	31110	30360
	170	49950	48230	46620	45120	43710	42390	41140	39960	38850	37800	36810	35870	34970	34120	33300
	185	54360	52490	50740	49100	47570	46130	44770	43490	42280	41140	40060	39030	38050	37130	36240
	200	58770	56740	54850	53080	51420	49860	48400	47010	45710	44470	43300	42200	41140	40140	39180
	215	63180	61000	58960	57060	55280	53610	52030	50540	49140	47810	46550	45360	44220	43150	42120
	230	67590	65260	63080	61040	59140	57350	55660	54070	52560	51140	49800	48530	47310	46160	45060
22″ x 36″	1	......	300.41	290.40	281.04	272.25	264.00	256.24	248.91	242.00	235.45	229.26	223.38	217.80	212.50	207.42
	65	......	19520	18870	18270	17690	17160	16650	16180	15730	15300	14900	14520	14150	13810	13480
	80	......	24030	23230	22480	21780	21120	20500	19910	19360	18830	18340	17870	17420	17000	16590
	95	......	28530	27580	26700	25860	25080	24340	23640	22990	22360	21780	21220	20690	20180	19700
	110	......	33040	31940	30910	29950	29040	28190	27380	26620	25900	25220	24570	23960	23370	22820
	125	......	37550	36300	35130	34030	33000	32030	31110	30250	29430	28660	27920	27220	26560	25930
	140	......	42060	40650	39350	38110	36960	35870	34850	33880	32960	32090	31270	30490	29750	29040
	155	......	46560	45010	43560	42200	40920	39720	38580	37510	36490	35530	34620	33760	32930	32150
	170	......	51070	49370	47780	46280	44880	43560	42310	41140	40020	38970	37970	37020	36120	35260
	185	......	55570	53720	51990	50360	48840	47410	46050	44770	43560	42410	41320	40290	39310	38370
	200	......	60080	58080	56210	54450	52800	51250	49780	48400	47090	45850	44670	43560	42500	41480
	215	......	64590	62440	60420	58530	56760	55090	53510	52030	50620	49290	48020	46830	45680	44600
	230	......	69100	66790	64640	62620	60720	58940	57250	55660	54150	52730	51380	50090	48870	47710
22″ x 38″	1	......	......	306.53	296.65	287.37	278.66	270.47	262.74	255.44	248.52	242.00	235.78	229.90	224.29	218.95
	65	......	......	19920	19280	18680	18110	17580	17080	16600	16150	15730	15320	14940	14580	14230
	80	......	......	24520	23730	22990	22290	21630	21020	20430	19880	19360	18860	18390	17940	17510
	95	......	......	29120	28180	27300	26470	25690	24960	24260	23610	22990	22390	21840	21300	20800
	110	......	......	33720	32630	31610	30650	29750	28900	28100	27340	26620	25930	25290	24670	24080
	125	......	......	38320	37080	35920	34830	33810	32840	31930	31060	30250	29470	28740	28030	27370
	140	......	......	42910	41530	40230	39010	37860	36780	35760	34790	33880	33010	32180	31400	30650
	155	......	......	47510	45980	44540	43190	41920	40730	39590	38520	37510	36540	35630	34760	33930
	170	......	......	52110	50430	48850	47370	45980	44660	43420	42250	41140	40080	39080	38120	37220
	185	......	......	56710	54880	53160	51550	50030	48610	47260	45980	44770	43620	42530	41490	40500
	200	......	......	61300	59330	57470	55730	54090	52550	51090	49700	48400	47150	45980	44850	43790
	215	......	......	65900	63780	61780	59910	58140	56490	54920	53430	52030	50690	49430	48220	47070
	230	......	......	70500	68230	66090	64090	62200	60430	58750	57160	55660	54230	52880	51580	50360

Table I.—(Continued).

TRACTIVE POWER OF LOCOMOTIVES, IN POUNDS, FOR DIFFERENT MEAN EFFECTIVE PRESSURES.

Cylinders Dia. × Stroke	Mean Eff. Pres.	Diameter of Drivers 52″	54″	56″	58″	60″	62″	64″	66″	68″	70″	72″	74″	76″	78″	80″	82″	84″
23″ x 28″	1	284.88	274.30	264.50	255.40	246.86	238.90	231.44	224.42	217.81	211.60	205.72	200.18	194.91	189.91	185.15	180.62	176.33
	65	18510	17830	17190	16600	16040	15530	15040	14580	14160	13750	13370	13010	12670	12340	12030	11740	11460
	80	22790	21940	21160	20430	19750	19110	18510	17950	17420	16930	16450	16010	15590	15190	14810	14450	14100
	95	27060	26060	25120	24260	23450	22690	21980	21320	20690	20100	19540	19010	18510	18040	17590	17160	16750
	110	31330	30170	29100	28090	27150	26280	25460	24680	23960	23270	22630	22020	21440	20890	20370	19870	19400
	125	35610	34290	33060	31920	30860	29860	28930	28050	27230	26450	25710	25020	24360	23740	23140	22580	22040
	140	39880	38400	37030	35760	34560	33440	32400	31420	30490	29620	28800	28020	27290	26590	25920	25290	24690
	155	44150	42520	41000	39590	38260	37030	35870	34780	33760	32800	31890	31020	30210	29430	28700	28000	27330
	170	48430	46630	44960	43420	41960	40610	39340	38150	37030	35970	34970	34030	33130	32280	31470	30700	29980
	185	52700	50750	48930	47250	45670	44190	42820	41520	40300	39140	38060	37030	36060	35130	34250	33410	32620
	200	56970	54860	52900	51080	49370	47780	46290	44880	43560	42320	41140	40030	38980	37980	37030	36120	35260
	215	61250	58980	56870	54910	53070	51360	49760	48250	46830	45490	44230	43030	41900	40830	39810	38830	37910
	230	65520	63090	60840	58740	56770	54940	53230	51620	50100	48670	47320	46040	44830	43680	42580	41540	40560
23″ x 30″	1	......	293.90	283.40	273.61	264.50	255.97	247.96	240.45	233.38	226.71	220.41	214.46	208.81	203.46	198.37	193.52	188.92
	65	......	19100	18420	17780	17190	16630	16110	15630	15170	14730	14330	13940	13570	13220	12890	12580	12280
	80	......	23510	22670	21890	21160	20470	19830	19230	18670	18130	17630	17150	16700	16270	15870	15480	15110
	95	......	27920	26920	25990	25120	24310	23550	22840	22170	21530	20940	20370	19830	19320	18840	18380	17950
	110	......	32330	31170	30100	29100	28150	27270	26450	25670	24940	24250	23590	22970	22380	21820	21290	20780
	125	......	36740	35420	34200	33060	32000	30990	30060	29170	28340	27550	26800	26100	25430	24790	24190	23610
	140	......	41150	39670	38300	37030	35830	34710	33660	32670	31740	30860	30020	29230	28480	27770	27090	26450
	155	......	45560	43930	42410	41000	39670	38430	37270	36170	35140	34160	33240	32370	31530	30740	30000	29280
	170	......	49960	48180	46510	44960	43510	42150	40870	39670	38540	37470	36450	35500	34580	33720	32900	32110
	185	......	54370	52430	50620	48930	47350	45870	44480	43170	41940	40780	39670	38630	37640	36700	35800	34950
	200	......	58780	56680	54720	52900	51190	49590	48090	46670	45340	44080	42890	41760	40690	39670	38700	37780
	215	......	63190	60930	58820	56870	55030	53310	51690	50170	48740	47390	46110	44890	43740	42650	41610	40620
	230	......	67600	65180	62930	60840	58870	57030	55300	53670	52140	50700	49330	48030	46790	45620	44510	43450
23″ x 32″	1	......	......	302.29	291.83	282.13	273.01	264.50	256.48	248.92	241.83	235.11	228.73	222.72	217.01	211.60	206.42	201.52
	65	......	......	19640	18970	18340	17740	17190	16670	16180	15720	15280	14860	14480	14100	13750	13420	13100
	80	......	......	24180	23340	22570	21840	21160	20510	19910	19340	18810	18300	17820	17360	16930	16510	16120
	95	......	......	28710	27720	26800	25930	25120	24360	23640	22970	22330	21730	21160	20610	20100	19610	19140
	110	......	......	33250	32100	31030	30030	29100	28210	27380	26600	25860	25160	24500	23870	23270	22710	22170
	125	......	......	37780	36480	35270	34130	33060	32060	31110	30230	29390	28590	27840	27130	26450	25800	25190
	140	......	......	42320	40860	39500	38220	37030	35900	34850	33860	32920	32020	31180	30380	29620	28900	28210
	155	......	......	46850	45230	43730	42320	41000	39750	38580	37480	36440	35450	34520	33640	32800	32000	31230
	170	......	......	51390	49610	47960	46410	44960	43600	42320	41110	39970	38880	37860	36890	35970	35090	34260
	185	......	......	55920	53990	52200	50510	48930	47450	46050	44740	43500	42310	41200	40150	39140	38190	37280
	200	......	......	60460	58360	56420	54600	52900	51290	49780	48360	47020	45740	44540	43400	42320	41280	40300
	215	......	......	64990	62740	60660	58700	56870	55140	53520	51990	50550	49170	47880	46660	45490	44380	43330
	230	......	......	69520	67120	64890	62790	60840	58990	57250	55620	54080	52610	51230	49910	48670	47480	46350

TABLE I.—(Continued).

TRACTIVE POWER OF LOCOMOTIVES, IN POUNDS, FOR DIFFERENT MEAN EFFECTIVE PRESSURES.

CYLINDERS DIA. STROKE	MEAN EFF. PRES.	DIAMETER OF DRIVERS 58″	60″	62″	64″	66″	68″	70″	72″	74″	76″	78″	80″	82″	84″
23″ x 34″	1	310.10	299.76	290.09	281.02	272.51	264.50	256.94	249.80	243.01	236.64	230.59	224.82	219.31	214.12
	65	20150	19480	18850	18260	17710	17190	16700	16230	15790	15380	14980	14610	14250	13920
	80	24800	23980	23200	22480	21800	21160	20550	19980	19440	18930	18440	17980	17540	17130
	95	29450	28470	27550	26690	25880	25120	24410	23730	23080	22480	21900	21360	20830	20340
	110	34110	32970	31910	30910	29980	29100	28260	27470	26730	26030	25360	24730	24120	23550
	125	38760	37470	36260	35130	34060	33060	32120	31220	30380	29580	28820	28100	27410	26770
	140	43410	41960	40610	39340	38150	37030	35970	34970	34020	33130	32280	31470	30700	29980
	155	48070	46460	44960	43560	42240	41000	39820	38710	37660	36680	35740	34850	33990	33190
	170	52720	50960	49310	47770	46330	44960	43680	42460	41310	40230	39200	38220	37280	36400
	185	57370	55450	53660	51990	50420	48930	47530	46210	44960	43780	42660	41590	40570	39610
	200	62020	59950	58020	56200	54500	52900	51390	49950	48600	47330	46110	44960	43860	42820
	215	66670	64440	62370	60420	58590	56870	55240	53700	52240	50880	49570	48340	47150	46040
	230	71320	68940	66720	64640	62670	60840	59100	57450	55890	54430	53030	51710	50440	49250
23″ x 36″	1	......	317.40	307.18	297.56	288.54	280.08	272.06	264.50	257.35	250.59	244.16	238.05	232.22	226.71
	65	......	20630	19960	19340	18750	18200	17680	17190	16720	16290	15870	15470	15090	14730
	80	......	25390	24570	23800	23080	22400	21760	21160	20580	20040	19530	19040	18580	18130
	95	......	30150	29180	28260	27410	26600	25840	25120	24450	23800	23190	22610	22060	21530
	110	......	34910	33790	32730	31740	30810	29920	29100	28310	27560	26860	26180	25550	24940
	125	......	39670	38400	37190	36070	35010	34010	33060	32170	31320	30520	29750	29030	28340
	140	......	44430	43000	41660	40400	39210	38090	37030	36030	35080	34180	33330	32510	31740
	155	......	49200	47610	46120	44720	43410	42170	41000	39890	38840	37840	36900	36000	35140
	170	......	53960	52220	50580	49050	47610	46250	44960	43750	42600	41500	40470	39480	38540
	185	......	58720	56830	55050	53380	51810	50330	48930	47610	46360	45170	44040	42960	41940
	200	......	63480	61430	59510	57710	56010	54410	52900	51470	50120	48830	47610	46440	45340
	215	......	68240	66040	63970	62040	60220	58490	56870	55330	53880	52490	51180	49930	48740
	230	......	73000	70650	68440	66370	64420	62570	60840	59190	57640	56160	54750	53410	52140
23″ x 38″	1	......	......	324.22	314.09	304.60	295.62	287.17	279.20	271.66	264.50	257.71	251.27	245.16	239.31
	65	......	......	21070	20410	19790	19210	18660	18150	17650	17190	16750	16330	15930	15550
	80	......	......	25930	25120	24360	23650	22970	22330	21730	21160	20610	20100	19610	19140
	95	......	......	30800	29830	28930	28080	27280	26520	25800	25120	24480	23870	23280	22730
	110	......	......	35660	34550	33500	32520	31590	30710	29880	29100	28350	27640	26970	26320
	125	......	......	40530	39260	38070	36950	35890	34900	33960	33060	32210	31410	30640	29910
	140	......	......	45390	43970	42640	41390	40200	39090	38030	37030	36080	35180	34320	33500
	155	......	......	50250	48680	47210	45820	44510	43270	42100	41000	39950	38950	38000	37090
	170	......	......	55120	53390	51780	50260	48810	47460	46180	44960	43810	42710	41670	40680
	185	......	......	59980	58100	56350	54690	53120	51650	50260	48930	47680	46480	45350	44270
	200	......	......	64840	62820	60920	59120	57430	55840	54330	52900	51540	50250	49030	47860
	215	......	......	69700	67530	65480	63560	61740	60030	58400	56870	55410	54020	52700	51450
	230	......	......	74570	72240	70060	67990	66050	64220	62480	60840	59270	57790	56380	55040

Table I.—(Continued).

TRACTIVE POWER OF LOCOMOTIVES, IN POUNDS, FOR DIFFERENT MEAN EFFECTIVE PRESSURES.

CYLINDERS Dia. Stroke	Mean Eff. Pres.	DIAMETER OF DRIVERS 54″	56″	58″	60″	62″	64″	66″	68″	70″	72″	74″	76″	78″	80″	82″	84″
24″ x 30″	1	320.00	308.57	297.92	288.00	278.70	270.00	261.82	254.12	246.86	240.00	233.50	227.38	221.52	216.00	210.73	205.71
	65	20800	20050	19360	18720	18110	17550	17020	16520	16040	15600	15170	14780	14400	14040	13700	13370
	80	25600	24680	23830	23040	22290	21600	20940	20330	19750	19200	18680	18190	17720	17280	16860	16450
	95	30400	29310	28300	27360	26470	25650	24870	24140	23450	22800	22180	21600	21040	20520	20020	19540
	110	35200	33940	32770	31680	30660	29700	28800	27950	27150	26400	25680	25010	24370	23760	23180	22630
	125	40000	38570	37240	36000	34840	33750	32730	31760	30860	30000	29190	28420	27690	27000	26340	25710
	140	44800	43200	41710	40320	39020	37800	36650	35580	34560	33600	32690	31830	31010	30240	29500	28800
	155	49600	47830	46180	44640	43200	41850	40580	39390	38260	37200	36190	35240	34340	33480	32660	31880
	170	54400	52460	50650	48960	47380	45900	44510	43200	41960	40800	39690	38650	37660	36720	35820	34970
	185	59200	57080	55120	53280	51560	49950	48440	47010	45670	44400	43200	42060	40980	39960	38990	38060
	200	64000	61710	59580	57600	55740	54000	52360	50820	49370	48000	46700	45470	44300	43200	42150	41140
	215	68800	66340	64050	61920	59920	58050	56290	54630	53070	51600	50200	48880	47630	46440	45310	44230
	230	73600	70970	68530	66240	64100	62100	60220	58450	56770	55200	53700	52290	50950	49680	48470	47310
24″ x 32″	1	......	329.14	317.80	307.20	297.29	288.00	279.27	271.08	263.31	256.00	249.08	242.54	236.30	230.40	224.79	219.42
	65	......	21390	20650	19960	19320	18720	18150	17620	17110	16640	16190	15760	15360	14970	14610	14260
	80	......	26330	25420	24570	23780	23040	22340	21680	21060	20480	19920	19400	18900	18430	17980	17550
	95	......	31260	30190	29180	28240	27360	26530	25750	25010	24320	23660	23040	22450	21880	21350	20840
	110	......	36210	34960	33790	32700	31680	30720	29810	28960	28160	27400	26680	25990	25340	24720	24140
	125	......	41140	39720	38400	37160	36000	34910	33880	32910	32000	31130	30320	29530	28800	28100	27430
	140	......	46080	44490	43010	41620	40320	39100	37950	36860	35840	34870	33960	33080	32250	31470	30720
	155	......	51020	49260	47610	46080	44640	43290	42010	40810	39680	38610	37590	36620	35710	34840	34010
	170	......	55950	54020	52220	50540	48960	47470	46080	44760	43520	42340	41230	40170	39170	38210	37300
	185	......	60890	58790	56830	55000	53280	51660	50150	48710	47360	46080	44870	43710	42620	41580	40590
	200	......	65830	63560	61440	59460	57600	55850	54210	52660	51200	49810	48510	47260	46080	44950	43880
	215	......	70770	68330	66040	63920	61920	60040	58280	56610	55040	53550	52150	50800	49530	48330	47180
	230	......	75710	73100	70660	68380	66240	64230	62350	60570	58880	57290	55780	54350	52990	51700	50470
24″ x 34″	1	......	......	337.67	326.40	315.85	306.00	296.73	288.00	279.77	272.00	264.63	257.70	251.06	244.80	238.81	233.14
	65	......	......	21940	21210	20530	19890	19280	18720	18180	17680	17200	16750	16320	15910	15520	15150
	80	......	......	27010	26110	25260	24480	23730	23040	22380	21760	21170	20610	20080	19580	19100	18650
	95	......	......	32070	31000	30000	29070	28180	27360	26570	25840	25140	24480	23850	23250	22680	22150
	110	......	......	37140	35900	34740	33660	32640	31680	30770	29920	29110	28350	27620	26930	26270	25650
	125	......	......	42210	40800	39480	38250	37090	36000	34970	34000	33080	32210	31380	30600	29850	29140
	140	......	......	47270	45700	44220	42840	41540	40320	39170	38080	37050	36080	35150	34270	33430	32640
	155	......	......	52340	50590	48960	47430	45990	44640	43360	42160	41020	39940	38910	37940	37020	36140
	170	......	......	57400	55490	53690	52020	50440	48960	47560	46240	44990	43810	42680	41610	40600	39630
	185	......	......	62470	60390	58430	56610	54900	53280	51760	50320	48960	47680	46440	45290	44180	43130
	200	......	......	67530	65280	63170	61200	59340	57600	55950	54400	52920	51540	50210	48960	47760	46630
	215	......	......	72590	70180	67910	65790	63800	61920	60150	58480	56900	55410	53970	52630	51340	50120
	230	......	......	77660	75070	72650	70380	68250	66240	64350	62560	60870	59270	57740	56300	54930	53620

Table I.—(Continued).

TRACTIVE POWER OF LOCOMOTIVES, IN POUNDS, FOR DIFFERENT MEAN EFFECTIVE PRESSURES.

Cylinders Dia. × Stroke	Mean Eff. Pres.	60″	62″	64″	66″	68″	70″	72″	74″	76″	78″	80″	82″	84″
		Diameter of Drivers												
24″ x 36″	1	345.60	334.42	324.00	314.18	304.94	296.23	288.00	280.19	272.83	265.80	259.20	252.87	246.86
	65	22460	21740	21060	20420	19820	19250	18720	18210	17730	17270	16850	16430	16040
	80	27640	26750	25920	25130	24390	23700	23040	22410	21820	21260	20730	20230	19740
	95	32830	31770	30780	29840	28970	28140	27360	26610	25920	25250	24620	24020	23450
	110	38020	36790	35640	34560	33540	32580	31680	30820	30010	29240	28510	27810	27150
	125	43200	41800	40500	39270	38120	37030	36000	35020	34100	33220	32400	31610	30850
	140	48380	46820	45360	43980	42690	41470	40320	39220	38200	37210	36290	35400	34560
	155	53570	51840	50220	48700	47260	45920	44640	43430	42290	41200	40170	39100	38260
	170	58750	56850	55080	53410	51840	50360	48960	47630	46380	45180	44060	42980	41960
	185	63940	61870	59940	58120	56420	54800	53280	51830	50470	49170	47950	46780	45670
	200	69120	66880	64800	62830	60990	59240	57600	56040	54560	53160	51840	50570	49370
	215	74300	71900	69660	67550	65560	63690	61920	60240	58660	57150	55730	54360	53070
	230	79490	76920	74520	72260	70140	68140	66240	64440	62750	61140	59620	58160	56780
24″ x 38″	1	.....	353.03	342.00	331.64	321.90	312.68	304.00	295.78	288.00	280.59	273.60	266.90	260.56
	65	.....	22940	22230	21550	20920	20320	19760	19220	18720	18230	17780	17350	16930
	80	.....	28240	27360	26530	25750	25010	24320	23660	23040	22440	21880	21350	20840
	95	.....	33530	32480	31500	30580	29700	28880	28090	27360	26650	25990	25350	24750
	110	.....	38830	37620	36480	35410	34390	33440	32530	31680	30860	30100	29360	28660
	125	.....	44130	42750	41450	40240	39080	38000	36970	36000	35070	34200	33360	32570
	140	.....	49420	47880	46430	45060	43770	42560	41410	40320	39280	38300	37360	36480
	155	.....	54720	53010	51400	49890	48460	47120	45840	44640	43490	42410	41370	40380
	170	.....	60020	58140	56380	54720	53150	51680	50280	48960	47700	46510	45370	44390
	185	.....	65310	63270	61360	59550	57840	56240	54720	53280	51910	50620	49370	48200
	200	.....	70610	68400	66330	64280	62530	60800	59150	57600	56120	54720	53380	52110
	215	.....	75900	73530	71300	69200	67230	65360	63600	61920	60320	58820	57380	56020
	230	.....	81200	78660	76280	74040	71920	69920	68030	66240	64530	62930	61390	59930
24″ x 40″	1	.....	.....	360.00	349.09	338.83	329.14	320.00	311.33	303.17	295.39	288.00	280.97	274.28
	65	.....	.....	23400	22690	22020	21390	20800	20230	19700	19200	18720	18260	17820
	80	.....	.....	28800	27920	27100	26330	25600	24900	24250	23630	23040	22470	21940
	95	.....	.....	34200	33160	32180	31260	30400	29570	28800	28060	27360	26690	26050
	110	.....	.....	39600	38400	37270	36210	35200	34250	33350	32490	31680	30900	30170
	125	.....	.....	45000	43640	42350	41140	40000	38920	37890	36920	36000	35120	34280
	140	.....	.....	50400	48870	47430	46080	44800	43590	42440	41350	40320	39330	38400
	155	.....	.....	55800	54110	52520	51020	49600	48260	46990	45780	44640	43550	42510
	170	.....	.....	61200	59340	57600	55950	54400	52920	51540	50210	48960	47760	46620
	185	.....	.....	66600	64580	62680	60890	59200	57600	56180	54640	53280	51980	50740
	200	.....	.....	72000	69820	67760	65830	64000	62270	60630	59080	57600	56190	54840
	215	.....	.....	77400	75060	72840	70770	68800	66940	65180	60510	61920	60410	58970
	230	.....	.....	82800	80300	77930	75710	73600	71610	69730	67940	66240	64620	63080

Table II.

NUMBER OF FEET THE PISTON TRAVELS PER ENGINE MILE.

Stroke	84″	82″	80″	78″	76″	74″	72″	70″	68″	66″	64″	62″	60″	58″	56″	54″	52″	50″	48″	46″	44″	42″	40″	38″	36″	34″	32″	30″	28″	Speed in Miles per Hour
	Diameter of Driving Wheels																													
10″																		672	700	731	764	800	840	881	934	988	1050	1120	1200	
12″																747	776	807	840	877	917	960	1008	1061	1120	1186	1260	1345	1440	
14″														811	840	871	905	941	980	1023	1069	1120	1176	1238	1307	1384	1470	1569	1680	
16″												867	896	927	960	996	1034	1075	1120	1169	1222	1280	1341	1415	1494	1582	1681	1793	1920	
18″										917	945	976	1008	1043	1080	1120	1163	1210	1260	1315	1375	1440	1512	1592	1681	1779	1891	2017	2160	
20″								960	989	1019	1050	1084	1120	1159	1200	1245	1293	1344	1400	1461	1528	1601	1680	1768	1867	1977	2101	2240		
22″					973	999	1027	1056	1087	1120	1155	1193	1232	1275	1320	1369	1422	1479	1540	1608	1681	1761	1848	1945	2054	2175				
24″	960	984	1008	1034	1061	1090	1120	1152	1186	1222	1260	1301	1344	1391	1440	1494	1551	1613	1680	1754	1833	1921	2017	2122						
26″	1040	1066	1092	1120	1150	1181	1214	1248	1285	1324	1365	1409	1456	1507	1560	1618	1680	1748	1821	1900	1986	2081	2185							
28″	1120	1148	1176	1207	1238	1272	1307	1344	1384	1426	1470	1518	1568	1623	1680	1743	1810	1882	1961	2046	2139									
30″	1200	1230	1260	1293	1327	1363	1400	1440	1483	1528	1575	1626	1680	1738	1800	1867	1939	2017	2101											
32″	1280	1312	1345	1379	1415	1454	1494	1536	1582	1630	1680	1735	1792	1851	1920	1992	2068	2151												
34″	1350	1394	1428	1465	1504	1541	1587	1633	1680	1731	1785	1843	1904	1970	2041	2116														
36″	1410	1476	1513	1551	1592	1635	1680	1729	1779	1833	1891	1952	2017	2086	2161															
38″	1520	1558	1597	1638	1681	1726	1774	1825	1878	1935	1995	2060	2128	2202																
40″	1600	1610	1681	1724	1769	1817	1867	1921	1977	2037	2100	2168																		
42″	1680	1722	1765	1810	1857	1908	1960	2017	2076	2139	2205																			
																						780	840	900	960	1020	1080	1140	1200	100
																					800	867	933	1000	1066	1133	1200	1260	1333	90
																			750	825	900	975	1050	1125	1200	1275	1350	1425	1500	80
																	771	814	857	943	1028	1114	1200	1285	1371	1457	1542	1628	1714	70
															800	850	900	950	1000	1100	1200	1300	1400	1500	1600	1700	1800	1900	2000	60
												780	840	900	960	1020	1080	1140	1200	1320	1440	1560	1680	1800	1920	2040	2160	2280	2400	50
										825	900	975	1050	1125	1200	1275	1350	1425	1500	1650	1800	1950	2100	2250	2400	2550				40
								771	857	943	1029	1114	1200	1285	1371	1457	1543	1628	1714	1886	2057	2228	2400							35
						700	800	900	1000	1100	1200	1300	1400	1500	1600	1700	1800	1900	2000	2200	2400									30
				600	720	840	960	1080	1200	1320	1440	1560	1680	1800	1920	2040	2160	2280	2400											25
		450	600	750	900	1050	1200	1350	1500	1650	1800	1950	2100	2250	2400															20
	400	600	800	1000	1200	1400	1600	1800	2000	2200	2400																			15
	600	900	1200	1500	1800	2100	2400																							10
	1200	1800	2400																											5
	100	150	200	250	300	350	400	450	500	550	600	650	700	750	800	850	900	950	1000	1100	1200	1300	1400	1500	1600	1700	1800	1900	2000	

PISTON SPEED IN FEET PER MINUTE

Table III.

MEAN AVAILABLE PRESSURES AT DIFFERENT PISTON SPEEDS AND BOILER PRESSURES.

Boiler Pressure	Piston Speed in Feet per Minute																					
	100	150	200	250	300	350	400	450	500	550	600	650	700	750	800	850	900	950	1000	1100	1200	1300	1400	1500
150	135	134	132	129	124	119	113	105	99	93	87	81	77	71	67	63	60	57	55	50	46	43	40	37
165	149	148	146	141	136	131	124	116	108	102	96	89	84	79	73	69	66	63	60	55	51	47	44	40
180	162	161	159	154	149	142	135	126	118	112	104	97	92	86	80	75	72	68	65	60	56	51	47	44
195	176	175	172	167	161	154	146	137	128	121	113	105	99	93	87	82	78	74	71	65	60	56	51	48
210	189	188	185	180	173	166	158	147	138	130	122	113	107	100	94	88	84	80	76	70	65	60	55	51
225	203	202	198	193	186	178	169	158	147	139	131	122	115	107	100	94	90	85	82	75	70	64	59	55
240	216	215	211	205	198	190	180	168	158	149	139	130	122	114	107	101	96	91	87	80	74	68	63	59
255	230	229	225	218	210	202	192	179	167	158	148	138	130	121	114	107	102	97	93	85	79	73	67	62

Table IV.

NUMBER OF REVOLUTIONS OF DRIVING WHEELS PER MILE.

Diameter of Drivers	28″	30″	32″	34″	36″	38″	40″	42″	44″	46″	48″	50″	52″	54″	56″
Revolutions per Mile	720.3	672.2	630.3	593.2	560.2	530.7	504.2	480.2	458.4	438.4	420.2	403.4	387.8	373.5	360.1
Diameter of Drivers	58″	60″	62″	64″	66″	68″	70″	72″	74″	76″	78″	80″	82″	84″	
Revolutions per Mile	347.7	336.1	325.3	315.1	305.5	296.6	288.1	280.1	272.5	265.3	258.5	252.1	245.9	240.1	....

Table V.

TRAIN RESISTANCE IN POUNDS PER TON.

	GRADE																
Per Cent.	0	.09	.19	.28	.38	.47	.57	.76	.95	1.14	1.33	1.52	1.71	1.89	2.08	2.27	2.46
Feet per Mile	0	5	10	15	20	25	30	40	50	60	70	80	90	100	110	120	130
Speed in Miles per Hour.																	
0	.	1.89	3.79	5.68	7.58	9.47	11.36	15.15	18.94	22.73	26.52	30.30	34.09	37.88	41.67	45.46	49.24
5	3.25	5.1	7.0	8.9	10.8	12.7	14.6	18.4	22.2	26.0	29.8	33.5	37.3	41.1	44.9	48.7	52.5
10	4.50	6.4	8.3	10.2	12.1	14.0	15.9	19.7	23.5	27.2	31.0	34.8	38.6	42.4	46.2	50.0	53.8
15	5.75	7.6	9.5	11.4	13.3	15.2	17.1	20.9	24.7	28.5	32.3	36.1	39.9	43.7	47.4	51.2	55.0
20	7.00	8.9	10.8	12.7	14.6	16.5	18.4	22.2	26.0	29.8	33.6	37.3	41.1	44.9	48.7	52.5	56.3
25	8.25	10.1	12.0	13.9	15.8	17.7	19.6	23.4	27.2	31.0	34.8	38.6	42.3	46.2	49.9	53.7	57.5
30	9.50	11.4	13.3	15.2	17.1	19.0	20.9	24.7	28.5	32.2	36.0	39.8	43.6	47.4	51.2	55.0	58.8
35	10.75	12.6	14.5	16.4	18.3	20.2	22.1	25.9	29.7	33.5	37.3	41.1	44.9	48.6	52.4	56.2	60.0
40	12.00	13.9	15.8	17.7	19.6	21.5	23.4	27.2	30.9	34.7	38.5	42.3	46.1	49.9	53.7	57.5	61.3
50	14.5	16.4	18.3	20.2	22.1	24.0	25.9	29.7	33.4	37.2	41.0	44.8	48.6	52.4	56.2	60.0	63.8
60	17.0	18.9	20.8	22.7	24.6	26.5	28.4	32.2	35.9	39.7	43.5	47.3	51.1	54.9	58.7	62.5	66.3
70	19.5	21.4	23.3	25.2	27.1	29.0	30.9	34.7	38.4	42.2	46.0	49.8	53.6	57.4	61.2	65.0	68.8
80	22.0	23.9	25.8	27.7	29.6	31.5	33.4	37.2	40.9	44.8	48.5	52.3	56.1	59.9	63.7	67.5	71.3
90	24.5	26.4	28.3	30.2	32.1	34.0	35.9	39.7	43.4	47.2	51.0	54.8	58.6	62.4	66.2	70.0	.....
100	27.0	28.9	30.8	32.7	34.6	36.5	38.4	42.2	45.9	49.7	53.5	57.3	61.1	64.9	.....	.....	.....
Per Cent.	2.65	2.84	3.03	3.22	3.41	3.60	3.79	3.98	4.17	4.36	4.55	4.74	4.93	5.12	5.31	5.50	5.69
Feet per Mile.	140	150	160	170	180	190	200	210	220	230	240	250	260	270	280	290	300
Speed in Miles per Hour.																	
0	53.03	56.82	60.61	64.40	68.18	71.97	75.76	79.55	83.34	87.12	90.92	94.70	98.18	102.27	106.06	109.84	113.63
5	56.3	60.1	63.9	67.7	71.4	75.2	79.0	82.8	86.6	90.4	94.2	98.0	101.8	105.5	109.3	113.1	116.9
10	57.5	61.4	65.1	68.9	72.7	76.5	80.3	84.1	87.9	91.7	95.4	99.2	103.0	106.8	110.6	114.4	118.1
15	58.8	62.6	66.4	70.2	73.9	77.7	81.5	85.3	89.1	92.9	96.7	100.5	104.2	108.0	111.8	115.6	119.4
20	60.1	63.9	67.6	71.4	75.2	79.0	82.8	86.6	90.4	94.2	97.9	101.7	105.5	109.3	113.1	116.9	120.7
25	61.3	65.1	68.9	72.7	76.4	80.2	84.0	87.8	91.6	95.4	99.2	103.0	106.7	110.5	114.3	118.1	121.9
30	62.6	66.1	70.1	73.9	77.7	81.5	85.3	89.1	92.8	96.7	100.4	101.2	108.0	.....	.....	.....	.....
35	63.8	67.6	71.4	75.1	78.9	82.7	86.5	90.3	94.1	97.9	101.7	.....	.....	.....	.....	.....	.....
40	65.1	68.9	72.6	76.4	80.2	84.0	87.8	91.6	95.3	.....	.....	.....	.....	.....	.....	.....	.....
50	67.6	71.4	75.1	78.9	82.7	86.5	90.3	.....	.....	.....	.....	.....	.....	.....	.....	.....	.....
60	70.1	73.9	77.6	81.4	85.1	.....	.....	.....	.....	.....	.....	.....	.....	.....	.....	.....	.....
70	72.6	76.4	80.1	.....	.....	.....	.....	.....	.....	.....	.....	.....	.....	.....	.....	.....	.....
80	75.1	.....	.....	.....	.....	.....	.....	.....	.....	.....	.....	.....	.....	.....	.....	.....	.....
90	.....	.....	.....	.....	.....	.....	.....	.....	.....	.....	.....	.....	.....	.....	.....	.....	.....
100	.....	.....	.....	.....	.....	.....	.....	.....	.....	.....	.....	.....	.....	.....	.....	.....	.....

Table VI.

RESISTANCE OF CURVES.

GRADE EQUIVALENTS OF CURVES

Degree of Curve.	1	2	3	4	5	6	7	8	9	10	11	12	13	14	15	16	17	18	19	20	21	22	23	24	25	26	27	28	29	30
Radius of Curve	5730	2865	1910	1433	1146	955	819	717	637	574	522	478	442	410	383	359	338	320	303	288	274	262	251	240	231	222	214	207	200	193
Equivalent Grade..	1.32	2.64	3.96	5.28	6.60	7.92	9.24	10.6	11.9	13.2	14.5	15.8	17.2	18.5	19.8	21.1	22.4	23.8	25.1	26.4	27.7	29.0	30.4	31.7	33.0	34.3	35.7	37.0	38.3	39.6

Curve Resistance=.05 pound per degree of curvature. Equivalent Grade in Feet per Mile=1.32 x degree of curve.

Table VII.

SPEED IN MILES PER HOUR.

DIAMETER OF DRIVING WHEELS

Rev. Per Min.	28″	30″	32″	34″	36″	38″	40″	42″	44″	46″	48″	50″	52″	54″	56″	58″	60″	62″	64″	66″	68″	70″	72″	74″	76″	78″	80″	82″	84″
10	.83	.89	.95	1.0	1.1	1.1	1.2	1.2	1.3	1.4	1.4	1.5	1.5	1.6	1.7	1.7	1.8	1.8	1.9	2.0	2.0	2.1	2.1	2.2	2.3	2.3	2.4	2.4	2.5
20	1.7	1.8	1.9	2.0	2.1	2.3	2.4	2.5	2.6	2.7	2.9	3.0	3.1	3.2	3.3	3.5	3.6	3.7	3.8	3.9	4.0	4.2	4.3	4.4	4.5	4.6	4.7	4.9	5.0
30	2.5	2.7	2.8	3.0	3.2	3.4	3.6	3.7	3.9	4.1	4.3	4.5	4.6	4.8	5.0	5.2	5.3	5.5	5.7	5.9	6.1	6.2	6.4	6.6	6.8	7.0	7.1	7.3	7.5
40	3.3	3.6	3.8	4.0	4.3	4.5	4.8	5.0	5.2	5.5	5.7	6.0	6.2	6.4	6.7	6.9	7.1	7.4	7.6	7.9	8.1	8.3	8.5	8.8	9.0	9.3	9.5	9.8	10.0
50	4.2	4.5	4.8	5.0	5.4	5.7	6.0	6.3	6.5	6.8	7.1	7.4	7.7	8.0	8.3	8.6	8.9	9.2	9.5	9.8	10.1	10.4	10.7	11.0	11.3	11.6	11.9	12.2	12.5
60	5.0	5.4	5.7	6.1	6.4	6.8	7.2	7.5	7.8	8.2	8.6	8.9	9.3	9.6	10.0	10.4	10.7	11.1	11.4	11.8	12.1	12.5	12.8	13.2	13.5	13.9	14.3	14.6	15.0
70	5.8	6.3	6.7	7.1	7.5	7.9	8.3	8.8	9.2	9.6	10.0	10.4	10.8	11.2	11.7	12.1	12.5	12.9	13.3	13.8	14.1	14.6	15.0	15.4	15.8	16.3	16.7	17.1	17.5
80	6.7	7.1	7.6	8.1	8.6	9.1	9.5	10.0	10.5	10.9	11.4	11.9	12.4	12.8	13.4	13.8	14.3	14.8	15.2	15.7	16.2	16.7	17.1	17.6	18.1	18.6	19.0	19.5	20.0
90	7.5	8.0	8.6	9.1	9.6	10.2	10.7	11.3	11.8	12.3	12.9	13.4	13.9	14.5	15.0	15.5	16.1	16.6	17.2	17.7	18.2	18.8	19.2	19.8	20.3	20.9	21.4	22.0	22.5
100	8.3	8.9	9.5	10.1	10.7	11.3	11.9	12.5	13.1	13.7	14.3	14.9	15.5	16.1	16.7	17.3	17.8	18.5	19.0	19.7	20.2	20.8	21.4	22.0	22.6	23.2	23.8	24.4	25.0
110	9.1	9.8	10.5	11.2	11.8	12.4	13.1	13.7	14.4	15.1	15.7	16.4	17.0	17.7	18.3	19.0	19.6	20.3	20.9	21.6	22.2	22.9	23.5	24.2	24.9	25.5	26.2	26.8	27.5
120	10.0	10.7	11.4	12.2	12.8	13.6	14.3	15.0	15.7	16.4	17.1	17.9	18.6	19.3	20.0	20.7	21.4	22.2	22.8	23.6	24.3	25.0	25.7	26.4	27.1	27.9	28.6	29.3	30.0
130	10.8	11.6	12.4	13.2	13.9	14.7	15.5	16.2	17.0	17.8	18.6	19.3	20.1	20.9	21.7	22.4	23.2	24.0	24.7	25.6	26.3	27.1	27.8	28.6	29.4	30.2	31.0	31.7	32.5
140	11.7	12.5	13.3	14.2	15.0	15.8	16.7	17.5	18.3	19.2	20.0	20.8	21.7	22.5	23.3	24.1	25.0	25.9	26.6	27.5	28.3	29.2	30.0	30.8	31.6	32.5	33.3	34.2	35.0
150	12.5	13.4	14.3	15.2	16.1	17.0	17.9	18.8	19.6	20.5	21.4	22.3	23.2	24.1	25.0	25.9	26.8	27.7	28.6	29.5	30.3	31.3	32.1	33.0	33.9	34.8	35.7	36.6	37.5
160	13.3	14.3	15.2	16.2	17.1	18.1	19.1	20.0	21.0	21.9	22.8	23.8	24.8	25.7	26.7	27.6	28.5	29.5	30.5	31.5	32.4	33.3	34.3	35.2	36.2	37.1	38.1	39.0	40.0
170	14.2	15.2	16.2	17.2	18.2	19.2	20.3	21.3	22.3	23.3	24.3	25.3	26.3	27.3	28.4	29.4	30.3	31.4	32.4	33.4	34.4	35.4	36.4	37.4	38.4	39.5	40.5	41.5	42.5
180	15.0	16.1	17.1	18.2	19.3	20.4	21.5	22.5	23.6	24.6	25.7	26.8	27.8	28.9	30.0	31.1	32.1	33.2	34.3	35.4	36.4	37.5	38.6	39.7	40.7	41.8	42.9	44.0	45.0
190	15.8	17.0	18.1	19.2	20.3	21.5	22.7	23.8	24.9	26.0	27.2	28.3	29.4	30.5	31.7	32.8	33.9	35.1	36.2	37.4	38.4	39.6	40.7	41.9	42.9	44.1	45.3	46.4	47.5
200	16.7	17.9	19.0	20.3	21.4	22.6	23.8	25.0	26.2	27.4	28.6	29.8	31.0	32.1	33.3	34.5	35.7	37.0	38.1	39.3	40.5	41.7	42.9	44.0	45.2	46.5	47.6	48.8	50.0
210	17.5	18.8	20.0	21.3	22.5	23.8	25.0	26.3	27.5	28.8	30.0	31.3	32.5	33.7	35.0	36.3	37.5	38.8	40.0	41.3	42.5	43.8	45.0	46.2	47.5	48.8	50.0	51.2	52.5
220	18.3	19.7	20.9	22.3	23.6	24.9	26.2	27.5	28.8	30.1	31.4	32.8	34.0	35.3	36.7	38.0	39.3	40.6	41.9	43.2	44.5	45.8	47.1	48.4	49.8	51.0	52.4	53.7	55.0
230	19.2	20.6	21.9	23.3	24.6	26.0	27.4	28.8	30.1	31.5	32.9	34.3	35.6	36.9	38.3	39.7	41.1	42.5	43.8	45.2	46.5	47.9	49.2	50.6	52.0	53.4	54.8	56.0	57.5
240	20.0	21.5	22.8	24.3	25.7	27.2	28.6	30.0	31.4	32.8	34.3	35.8	37.2	38.5	40.0	41.5	42.8	44.4	45.7	47.2	48.6	50.0	51.4	52.8	54.2	55.7	57.1	58.5	60.0
250	20.8	22.4	23.8	25.3	26.8	28.3	29.8	31.3	32.8	34.2	35.7	37.2	38.7	40.1	41.7	43.2	44.6	46.2	47.6	49.1	50.6	52.1	53.6	55.0	56.5	58.0	59.5	61.0	62.5
260	21.7	23.3	24.7	26.4	27.9	29.4	31.0	32.5	34.0	35.6	37.2	38.7	40.2	41.7	43.3	44.9	46.4	48.1	49.5	51.1	52.6	54.2	55.7	57.2	58.8	60.4	61.9	63.5	65.0
270	22.5	24.1	25.7	27.1	28.9	30.6	32.2	33.8	35.3	37.0	38.6	40.1	41.8	43.3	45.0	46.6	48.2	50.0	51.4	53.0	54.7	56.3	57.9	59.4	61.0	62.7	64.3	65.9	67.5
280	23.4	25.0	26.6	28.4	30.0	31.7	33.4	35.0	36.6	38.3	40.0	41.7	43.3	45.0	46.7	48.3	50.0	51.7	53.3	55.0	56.7	58.4	60.0	61.6	63.3	65.0	66.7	68.4	70.0
290	24.2	25.9	27.6	29.4	31.1	32.8	34.6	36.2	38.0	39.7	41.4	43.2	44.9	46.6	48.3	50.0	51.8	53.6	55.2	57.0	58.7	60.5	62.1	63.8	65.5	67.3	69.1	70.8	72.5
300	25.0	26.8	28.6	30.4	32.1	34.0	35.8	37.5	39.3	41.0	42.9	44.7	46.5	48.2	50.0	51.9	53.6	55.5	57.1	59.0	60.7	62.6	64.2	66.0	67.8	69.6	71.5	73.2	75.0
310	25.8	27.7	29.5	31.4	33.2	35.1	36.9	38.8	40.6	42.4	44.3	46.1	48.0	49.8	51.7	53.6	55.3	57.3	59.0	60.9	62.8	64.6	66.4	68.2	70.1	71.9	73.9	75.6	77.5
320	26.6	28.6	30.5	32.5	34.3	36.2	38.1	40.0	42.0	43.8	45.8	47.6	49.6	51.4	53.3	55.3	57.1	59.1	60.9	62.9	64.8	66.7	68.5	70.4	72.3	74.3	76.2	78.1	80.0
330	27.5	29.5	31.5	33.5	35.4	37.4	39.3	41.2	43.2	45.2	47.2	49.1	51.1	53.0	55.0	57.0	58.9	61.0	62.8	64.8	66.8	68.8	70.6	72.6	74.6	76.6	78.6	80.6	82.5
340	28.3	30.4	32.4	34.5	36.4	38.5	40.5	42.5	44.5	46.6	48.6	50.6	52.7	54.6	56.7	58.8	60.7	62.9	64.7	66.8	68.8	70.9	72.8	74.8	76.8	78.9	81.0	83.0	85.0
350	29.1	31.3	33.3	35.5	37.5	39.6	41.7	43.7	45.9	47.9	50.0	52.1	54.2	56.2	58.4	60.5	62.4	64.7	66.6	68.8	70.9	73.0	75.0	77.0	79.1	81.2	83.4	85.4	87.5
360	30.0	32.2	34.3	36.5	38.6	40.8	42.9	45.0	47.2	49.3	51.4	53.7	55.8	57.8	60.0	62.2	64.2	66.5	68.6	70.7	72.9	75.1	77.1	79.2	81.4	83.5	85.8	87.9	90.0
370	30.8	33.1	35.3	37.5	39.7	41.9	44.1	46.2	48.5	50.7	52.9	55.1	57.3	59.4	61.7	64.0	66.0	68.3	70.5	72.7	74.9	77.2	79.2	81.4	83.7	85.9	88.2	90.3	92.5
380	31.6	34.0	36.2	38.6	40.7	43.1	45.3	47.5	49.8	52.0	54.2	56.7	58.9	61.0	63.4	66.8	67.8	70.2	72.4	74.7	76.9	79.3	81.4	83.6	86.0	88.2	90.6	92.8	95.0
390	32.5	34.9	37.2	39.6	41.8	44.2	46.5	48.8	51.1	53.4	55.8	58.1	60.4	62.6	65.0	67.5	69.6	72.0	74.2	76.6	78.9	81.3	83.5	85.8	88.3	90.5	93.0	95.2	97.5
400	33.3	35.8	38.2	40.6	42.9	45.3	47.7	50.0	52.4	54.8	57.1	59.6	62.0	64.2	66.7	69.2	71.4	73.9	76.2	78.6	81.0	83.4	85.6	88.0	90.6	92.9	95.4	97.7	100.0

Table VIII.

Mean Effective Pressure.

Ratio of Mean Effective Pressure to Boiler Pressure.

.9
.8
.7
.6
.5
.4
.3
.2
.1

100 200 300 400 500 600 700 800 900 1000 1100 1200 1300 1400 1500 1600

Piston Speed in Feet per Minute.

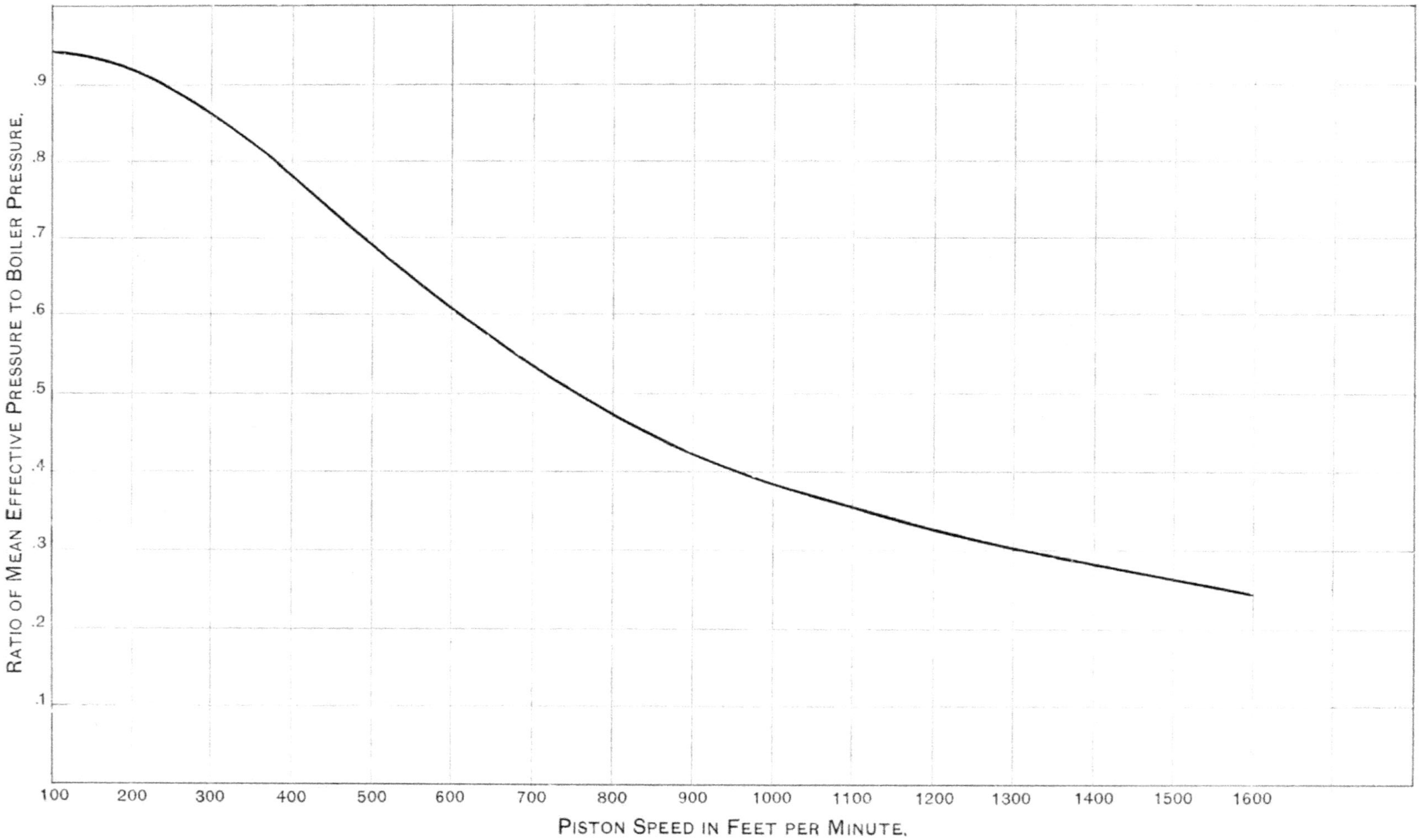

Table IX.

Mean Available Pressure.

Ratio of Mean Available Pressure to Boiler Pressure.

.9
.8
.7
.6
.5
.4
.3
.2
.1

100 200 300 400 500 600 700 800 900 1000 1100 1200 1300 1400 1500

Piston Speed in Feet per Minute.

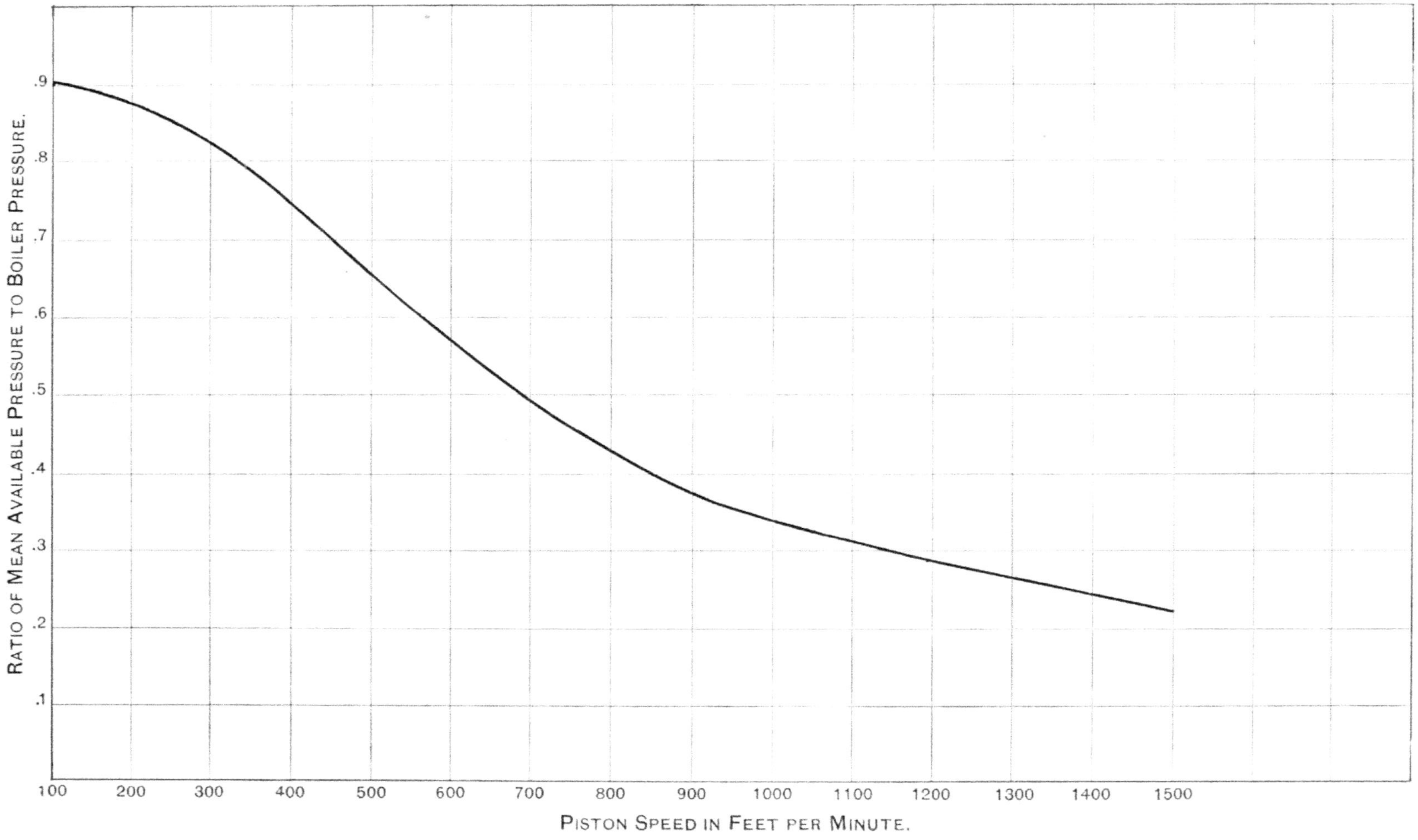

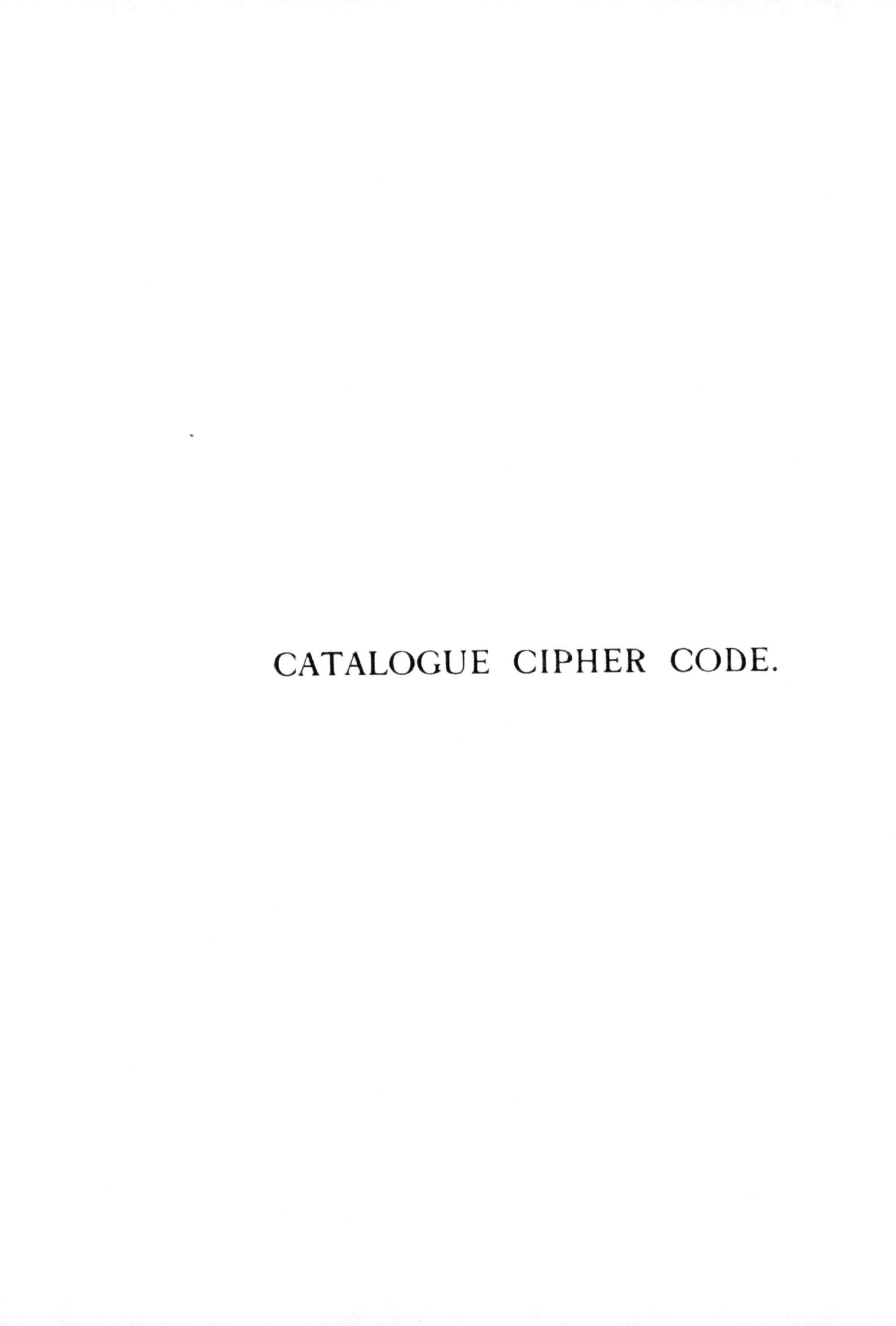

CATALOGUE CIPHER CODE.

Code Word	MESSAGE
OAKMAN..........	Wire price, earliest delivery, and mail specifications covering.........locomotives, similar in general design to that described in your 1899 Catalogue, under Code Word.............................
OAKUM............	Wire price, earliest delivery, and mail specifications covering.........locomotives, similar in general design to that described in your 1899 Catalogue, under Code Word...........................except...
OARLOCK.........	Wire price, earliest delivery, and mail specifications covering.........locomotives, duplicates of those last furnished us.
OASIS..............	Wire price, earliest delivery, and mail specifications covering.........locomotives, duplicates of those last furnished us, except..
OATH................	Wire price, earliest delivery, and mail specifications covering.........locomotives, duplicates of those furnished us...
OBACE..............	Wire price, earliest delivery, and mail specifications covering.........locomotives, duplicates of those furnished us..............................except..................................
OBACAL............	We will furnish you........ locomotives, similar in general design to that described in our 1899 Catalogue under Code Word..............................for...............dollars each, delivered at.....................................
OBDALE...........	delivered f. o. b..
OBDROME.........	delivered alongside vessel, New York Harbor.
OBDUCE............	delivered alongside vessel..
OBED................	We will furnish you...........locomotives, similar in general design to that described in our 1899 Catalogue under Code Word........................except......................... for.............................dollars each, delivered at..
OBEGO..............	delivered f. o. b..
OBEKKO...........	delivered alongside vessel, New York Harbor.
OBELISK...........	delivered alongside vessel..
OBELLUM.........	We will furnish you..............locomotives, duplicates of those we furnished you ....for........................dollars each, delivered at..............................
OBELUS............	delivered f. o. b..
OBERON...........	delivered alongside vessel, New York Harbor.
OBERUS............	delivered alongside vessel..
OBESE.............	We will furnish you..............locomotives, duplicates of those we furnished you ....except.................................for.............................. dollars each, delivered at..
OBEY...............	delivered f. o. b..
OBIME..............	delivered alongside vessel New York Harbor.
OBIT.................	delivered alongside vessel..
OBITER...........	We will furnish you...........locomotives, duplicates of those we last furnished you, for...............................dollars each, delivered at...................................
OBJOIN............	delivered f. o. b..
OBKALE...........	delivered alongside vessel New York Harbor.
OBLATE...........	delivered alongside vessel..
OBLATION.......	We will furnish you...........locomotives, duplicates of those we last furnished you, except...................for.................dollars each, delivered at................................
OBLAW............	delivered f. o. b..
OBLESE...........	delivered alongside vessel, New York Harbor.
OBLETTO.........	delivered alongside vessel..
OBLEVOR.........	Quotation is for plain engine only. By a plain engine is meant one having steel fire-box, charcoal iron tubes, steel tyred driving wheels and cast iron engine truck (bogie) and tender truck wheels. It does not include brakes, copper fire box, brass tubes, headlights or other extras as coded on pages 326 and 327 of this catalogue.
OBLICEE..........	Are you prepared to tender for...........locomotives, similar in general design to that described in your 1899 Catalogue, under Code Word..........................for delivery not later than.............................?
OBLINK...........	We will submit tender by first outgoing mail, covering...........locomotives, similar in general design to that described in our 1899 Catalogue, under Code Word............. delivery..............................
OBLIQUE..........	Are you prepared to tender for...........locomotives, similar in general design to that described in your 1899 Catalogue, under Code Word.......................except............ for delivery not later than.............................?
OBLONG..........	We will submit tenders by first outgoing mail covering...........locomotives, similar in general design to that described in your 1899 Catalogue under Code Word ....except..............................delivery................................
OBLUS.............	We are unable to tender. Have written.
OBOE..............	Enter our order for...........locomotives, as described under Code Word..................

Code Word	MESSAGE
OBOLO	Enter our order for...........locomotives, as described under Code Word.................... except..............................
OBSCURE	Enter our order for...........locomotives, duplicates of those last furnished us.
OBSEQUY	Enter our order for..............locomotives, duplicates of those last furnished us, except..............................
OBSERT............	Enter our order for...........locomotives, duplicates of those furnished us.................
OBSESS............	Enter our order for...........locomotives, duplicates of those furnished us................. except..............................
OBSIGN............	Enter our order for...........locomotives, as per { our / my } message of.......................... and your answer of..............................
OBSOLETE..........	Enter our order. Have written.
OBSOLTE	Have entered order, will confirm by mail.
OBSTAB............	If specifications can be modified to read..............................our price will be ....dollars.
OBSTACLE..........	If specifications can be modified to read..............................we will tender.
OBSTADIO	You may modify specifications to read..............................
OBSTADIX..........	Specifications cannot be modified.
OBSTELT	Omit from the construction..............................
OBSTINATE	Omit from the construction..............................and include..............................
OBSTINT	Tenders will be opened..............................
OBSTIPO...........	Your tender must be here not later than..............................
OBSTIQUE..........	We will cable proposal..............................
OBSTUDO...........	We will mail proposal..............................
OBSTUM	Our proposal mailed..............................
OBTATE............	We desire shipment via steamer..............................which will receive freight on or about..............................
OBTAX	We will arrange to make shipment via steamer..............................as desired.
OBTEGO	We will make shipment via steamer..............................if possible.
OBTEMMO	Impossible to make shipment via steamer..............................
OBTEND	Cannot make shipment in time for steamer..............................will ship by next boat.
OBTENGO.....	Shipment of...........locomotives made to-day.
OBTEPPO	Will make shipment of...........locomotives..............................
OBTERT	Locomotives will go forward on steamer..............................
OBTEST............	Have locomotives arrived at..............................?
OBTEVAL	Will locomotives be completed within the specified time?
OBTEW	The locomotives will be completed within the specified time.
OBTRAND	We can complete the locomotives within the time specified, if complete details are furnished at once.
OBTRAP............	Impossible to complete engines within the time specified. Have written.
OBTRAPSIT	...........locomotives now completed.
OBTRARRO..........	...........locomotives completed to-day.
OBTRARTAL	Can you make delivery of...........locomotives within...........months?
OBTRASCO	Name earliest delivery..............................
OBTRASCUM	Name earliest delivery alongside New York.
OBTRAST...........	Name earliest delivery alongside..............................
OBTRATOR	Earliest delivery alongside New York..............................
OBTRESTO..........	Earliest delivery alongside..............................
OBTRELT	Earliest delivery ....
OBTRISM	Delivery not later than..............................
OBTRITIO	Delivery not earlier than..............................
OBTRIVO	Delivery about..............................

CONSTRUCTION.

Code Word	MESSAGE
OBTRUDE...........	Locomotives to have cylinders one-half inch larger diameter.
OBTRUFF	Locomotives to have cylinders one inch larger diameter.
OBTRUGAL..........	Locomotives to have cylinders...........inches larger diameter.
OBTRUGAM..........	Locomotives to have cylinders one-half inch smaller diameter.
OBTRUGIO..........	Locomotives to have cylinders one inch smaller diameter.
OBTRUNK	Locomotives to have cylinders...........inches smaller diameter.
OBTRUST...........	Locomotives to have stroke of piston...........inches longer.

Code Word	MESSAGE
Obtrux	Locomotives to have stroke of piston...........inches shorter.
Obtuse............	Locomotives to have diameter of cylinders and stroke of piston of same dimensions as engine described in {your / our} 1899 Catalogue under Code Word........................
Obtuto............	Locomotives to be equipped with Brooks Improved Piston Valves.
Obvano	Locomotives to have driving wheels...........inches diameter.
Obvampo	Locomotives to have engine truck (bogie) wheels...........inches diameter.
Obverse	Locomotives to have Player Patent Improved Belpaire Boilers.
Obvert	Locomotives to have Radial Stay Wagon Top Boilers.
Obvesco	Locomotives to have Straight Top Boilers.
Obvestit	Gauge of track...........inches.
Obvetok	Gauge of track...........millimeters.
Obvetum..........	Driving wheel base must not exceed...........inches.
Obvexor...........	Driving wheel base must not exceed...........millimeters.
Obvibor	Rigid wheel base must not exceed...........inches.
Obvica	Rigid wheel base must not exceed...........millimeters.
Obvidia	Total wheel base of engine must not exceed...........inches.
Obvidore..........	Total wheel base of engine must not exceed...........millimeters.
Obvidunt	Total wheel base of engine and tender must not exceed...........inches.
Obvidus...........	Total wheel base of engine and tender must not exceed ....millimeters.
Obviduto.........	Total weight of engine must not exceed ....pounds in working order.
Obvigant	Total weight of engine must not exceed...........kilogrammes in working order.
Obvigo	Total weight on drivers...........pounds in working order.
Obvigust..........	Total weight on drivers...........kilogrammes in working order.
Obvimal	Total weight of tender, loaded...........pounds.
Obvimet...........	Total weight of tender, loaded...........kilogrammes.
Obvimus...........	Height of engine from top of rail must not exceed...........inches.
Obvito	Height of engine from top of rail must not exceed ....millimeters.
Obvitule..........	Must have tank capacity of...........U. S. gallons.
Obvitum	Must have tank capacity of...........imperial gallons.
Obvunt............	Must have tank capacity...........cubic inches.
Obvuto............	Must have tank capacity...........liters.
Obvutus...........	Fuel, bituminous coal.
Obvuvum..........	Fuel, anthracite coal.
Ocadia	Fuel, wood or coal.
Ocador	Fuel, wood.
Ocadus............	What is the estimated cubical measurement of each engine knocked down and packed for sea shipment?
Ocafad	The estimated cubical measurement of each engine knocked down and packed for sea shipment is.............................cubic feet.
Ocafale	is.............................cubic decimeters.
Ocafamo..........	What is the estimated weight of each engine knocked down and packed for sea shipment?
Ocafarn..........	The estimated weight of each engine knocked down and packed for sea shipment is.............................pounds.
Ocafarod.........	is.............................kilogrammes.
Ocagon............	What is the weight of heaviest piece?
Ocagunt	The weight of heaviest piece is...........pounds.
Ocala.............	is...........kilogrammes.
Ocalot............	What is measurement of bulkiest piece?
Ocalux	The measurement of bulkiest piece is...........
Ocamon	What is the weight per yard of rail on which engines are to run?
Ocamus	Weight of rail per yard is...........pounds.
Ocator............	is...........kilogrammes.
Ocbanal..........	What is heaviest grade?
Ocbaral	Heaviest grade does not exceed...........feet in 100 feet.
Ocbarro	Heaviest grade does not exceed...........feet per mile.
Occasion	What is length of heaviest grade?
Occatrum	Length of heaviest grade does not exceed...........feet.
Occavus..........	What is radius of sharpest curve?
Occident.........	Radius of sharpest curve does not exceed...........feet.
Occido............	...........millimeters.

Code Word	MESSAGE
OCCIPITAL	What is length of turntable?
OCCIPUT	Length of turntable is...........feet.
OCCITUM	...........millimeters.
OCCITUS	Send dimensions of smallest tunnel.
OCCLUDE	Send profile of road.
OCCULT	Wire at once lettering and numbering for locomotives.
OCCULUS	Letter locomotives as follows: ....
OCCUMAS	Number locomotives as follows: ....
OCCUMOID	Cost of freight and insurance from New York is...........................dollars.
OCCUMOLO	Cost of freight and insurance from...........................is...........................dollars.

EXTRA EQUIPMENT.

Code Word	MESSAGE
OCCUPANT	Include the following extra equipment in your tender;
OCCUPATE	Quote price at which you will furnish the following extra equipment, per engine.
OCCUPEDE	Quotation includes the following extra equipment................................
OCCUPULT	Extra equipment for each engine will cost as follows:...............................
OCCUPY	You may furnish and apply to each of the engines you have under construction for us, the following extra equipment, at the price you have quoted for same.
OCCUPYOR	To price quoted add for extra equipment for each engine as follows.

BRAKES.

Code Word	MESSAGE
OCCUR	Hand brakes on drivers.
OCEAN	Steam brakes on drivers.
OCEANIC	Hand and steam driver brakes.
OCELLUS	American steam driver brake.
OCELOT	American steam engine truck brake.
OCHRE	Westinghouse tender brake.
OCHRY	Westinghouse train brake.
OCREA	Westinghouse tender and train brake, 8-inch pump.
OCREATE	Westinghouse tender and tender brake, 9½-inch pump.
OCTAD	American-Westinghouse driver, tender and train brake, 8-inch pump.
OCTAGON	American-Westinghouse driver, tender and train brake, 9½-inch pump.
OCTANDER	New York air brake on drivers.
OCTANE	New York air brake on tender.
OCTANT	New York air brake on train.
OCTASTYLE	New York air brake on tender and train.
OCTAVE	New York air brake on drivers, tender and train.
OCTENE	Eames vacuum brake on drivers.
OCTET	Eames vacuum brake on tender.
OCTIC	Eames vacuum brake on train.
OCTILE	Eames vacuum brake on tender and train.
OCTILLION	Eames vacuum brake on drivers, tender and train.
OCTOATE	Smith automatic brake on drivers.
OCTODONT	Smith automatic brake on tender.
OCTOFID	Smith automatic brake on train.
OCTOIC	Smith automatic brake on tender and train.
OCTONARY	Smith automatic brake on drivers, tender and train.
OCTOPUS	American practice.
OCTOROON	Railway Co.'s practice.

BOILER COVERING.

Code Word	MESSAGE
OCTOYL	Asbestos board.
OCTUPLE	Asbestos cement.
OCULAR	Sectional asbestos.
OCULATE	Sectional magnesia.
OCULIST	John's fire felt.

Code Word	MESSAGE
Oculus	BELL RINGER—Gollmar.
Ocusier	—Heginbottom.
Ocutor	—Sansom.
	COUPLERS.
Odalisque	American automatic M. C. B. standard.
Odalix	Screw—English practice.
	FIRE-BOX.
Odapax	Copper fire-box, brass tubes.
Odax	Copper fire-box, iron tubes.
	HEADLIGHTS.
Oddity	Ordinary American pattern, square case, 18-inch reflector.
Odds	Ordinary American pattern, round case, 18-inch reflector.
Ode	Ordinary American pattern, square case, 23-inch reflector.
Odeon	Ordinary American pattern, round case, 23-inch reflector.
Odic	Special pattern.
Odin	Electric (National).
Odinic	Electric (Pyle National).
Odious	Three head lamps (Japanese style).
	JACKS, TRAVERSING.
Odist	Ten tons capacity.
Odiumal	Twelve tons capacity.
Odize	Fifteen tons capacity.
	SANDING DEVICE.
Odmyl	Leach sander, single pipe.
Odonto	Leach sander, double pipe.
Odontoax	Houston sander.
Odontoid	SYPHON, with...........feet of hose.
	TIRES.
Odopare	Krupp, crucible.
Odopass	Krupp, open hearth.
Odor	TRACINGS, one set.
Odorant	two sets.
Odorine	three sets.
Odorous	TRAIN SIGNAL, Westinghouse.
Odylic	WRECKING FROGS, one.
Odyline	one pair.

CALENDAR CODE.

	JANUARY	FEBRUARY	MARCH	APRIL	MAY	JUNE
1	Nab.	Napus.	Natch.	Navew.	Needle.	Neocene.
2	Nabit.	Narcosis.	Nates.	Navicular.	Needy.	Neocracy.
3	Nabob.	Narcotic.	Nath.	Navigable.	Neese.	Neogen.
4	Nacre.	Narcotine.	Nathmore.	Navigate.	Nefand.	Neology.
5	Nadir.	Narcotism.	Natica.	Navy.	Nefast.	Neomorph.
6	Nagor.	Nard.	Naticord.	Nawab.	Negation.	Neonism.
7	Naid.	Nardine.	Nation.	Nawl.	Negative.	Neophyte.
8	Naik.	Nardoo.	National.	Nayt.	Neginoth.	Neoplasm.
9	Nail.	Nares.	Native.	Nazarene.	Neglect.	Neorama.
10	Nainsook.	Nargile.	Nativity.	Nazarite.	Negligee.	Neoteric.
11	Nais.	Narica.	Natka.	Naze.	Negoce.	Neozoic.
12	Naive.	Nariform.	Natrium.	Neal.	Negress.	Nepa.
13	Naked.	Narine.	Natralite.	Neap.	Negritta.	Nepenthe.
14	Naker.	Narrate.	Natron.	Nearctic.	Negritic.	Nephew.
15	Nakoo.	Narrative.	Natter.	Neat.	Negro.	Nephrite.
16	Nale.	Narrator.	Natty.	Nebalia.	Negroid.	Nepotic.
17	Namby.	Narthex.	Natural.	Nebular.	Negus.	Nepotism.
18	Namo.	Narwal.	Nature.	Nebule.	Neif.	Neptune.
19	Nandine.	Nasal.	Naufrage.	Nebulose.	Neigh.	Nereid.
20	Nandu.	Nascal.	Naught.	Neck.	Neighbor.	Nerita.
21	Nankeen.	Nascent.	Naughty.	Neckband.	Nelumbo.	Nero.
22	Nanny.	Nash.	Nausea.	Necking.	Nemaline.	Nervate.
23	Nanpie.	Nasiform.	Nauseate.	Necklet.	Nemato.	Nerve.
24	Naos.	Nasion.	Nautch.	Necktie.	Nematoid.	Nervine.
25	Nape.	Nassa.	Nautic.	Necrolite.	Nemean.	Nervous.
26	Naphtha.	Nasute.	Nautical.	Necrose.	Nemertid.	Nescience.
27	Napthol.	Natal.	Nautiform.	Necrotic.	Nemesis.	Nesh.
28	Napkin.	Natalin.	Nautilus.	Nectar.	Nemoral.	Nest.
29	Napless.	Natant.	Naval.	Nectarine.	Nempne.	Nestle.
30	Nappe.	....	Navarch.	Nedder.	Nenia.	Nestor.
31	Napping.	....	Nave.	....	Nentor.	....

	JULY	AUGUST	SEPTEMBER	OCTOBER	NOVEMBER	DECEMBER
1	Netfish.	Nickar.	Nimmer.	Nocive.	Nomadic.	Noontide.
2	Nether.	Nickel.	Ninefold.	Nock.	Nomarch.	Noose.
3	Netify.	Nicking.	Ninny.	Noctam.	Nombril.	Nopal.
4	Netting.	Nickname.	Niobate.	Noctuid.	Nome.	Norian.
5	Nettle.	Nicotic.	Niobe.	Noctule.	Nomen.	Norite.
6	Netty.	Nicotine.	Niobium.	Nocturne.	Nomial.	Norma.
7	Network.	Nictate.	Nipper.	Nocturnal.	Nomic.	Normal.
8	Neural.	Nidary.	Nipping.	Nocuous.	Nominal.	Norse.
9	Neuralgia.	Nide.	Nipple.	Nod.	Nominate.	Nosel.
10	Neuraxis.	Nidget.	Nirvana.	Nodal.	Nominee.	Nostril.
11	Neurine.	Niding.	Nisan.	Nodation.	Nonage.	Nostrum
12	Neuro.	Nidor.	Niste.	Nodder.	Nonagon.	Notable.
13	Neuroma.	Nidulate.	Nisus.	Noddle.	Nonane.	Notary.
14	Neuron.	Nidus.	Niter.	Noddy.	Nonce.	Notarial.
15	Neurosis.	Niece.	Nitrate.	Node.	Nonda.	Notate.
16	Neurotic.	Nief.	Nitride.	Nodical.	Nonego.	Notch.
17	Neuter.	Niello.	Nitrify.	Nodular.	Nones.	Notion.
18	Neutral.	Niggard.	Nitrile.	Nodule.	Nonetto.	Notist.
19	Newel.	Niggle.	Nitroform.	Noel.	Nonius.	Notum.
20	Newsboy.	Nigh.	Nitrol.	Noemic.	Nonoic.	Nouch.
21	Newt.	Night.	Nitrum.	Noetic.	Nonpareil.	Nougat.
22	Newton.	Nightfall.	Nivose.	Nog.	Nonplus.	Nounal.
23	Nexible.	Nightmare.	Nixie.	Noggin.	Nonsane.	Nourish.
24	Nexus.	Nightshade.	Noah.	Noils.	Nonsense.	Noursel.
25	Nias.	Nigrine.	Nobby.	Noise.	Nonsuit.	Novation.
26	Nibble.	Nihil.	Noble.	Noisette.	Nonylic.	Novel.
27	Nicolite.	Nilotic.	Nobility.	Noisome.	Noodle.	Novelist.
28	Nicene.	Nilt.	Noblesse.	Nolde.	Nook.	Novice.
29	Nicety.	Nimble.	Nobley.	Nole.	Noon.	Novitiate.
30	Niche.	Nimbose.	Nocent.	Nolition.	Noonday.	Noxious.
31	Nick.	Nimbus.	....	Nomad.	....	Noyance.

$\frac{1}{16}$ Sabal.
$\frac{1}{8}$ Sabaoth.
$\frac{3}{16}$ Sabbat.
$\frac{1}{4}$ Sabean.
$\frac{5}{16}$ Sabella.
$\frac{3}{8}$ Sabre.
$\frac{7}{16}$ Sabian.
$\frac{1}{2}$ Sabine.
$\frac{9}{16}$ Sable.
$\frac{5}{8}$ Sabot.
$\frac{11}{16}$ Sabulose.
$\frac{3}{4}$ Sac.
$\frac{13}{16}$ Sacalait.
$\frac{7}{8}$ Sacar.
$\frac{15}{16}$ Saccate.
1 Saccharin.
2 Saccharoid.
3 Saccharum.
4 Sacchalic.
5 Sacchulmic.
6 Sacciform.
7 Saccule.
8 Sacculus.
9 Saccus.
10 Sacellum.
11 Sacerdos.
12 Sachem.
13 Sachet.
14 Sack.
15 Sackbut.
16 Sackcloth.
17 Sacking.
18 Sacque.
19 Sacral.
20 Sacrament.
21 Sacrate.
22 Sacre.
23 Sacred.
24 Sacrifice.
25 Sacrilege.
26 Sacrist.
27 Sacristan.
28 Sacrum.
29 Sadden.
30 Saddle.
31 Saddlery.
32 Sadducee.
33 Sadiron.
34 Safeguard.
35 Safety.
36 Saffron.
37 Safranin.
38 Saga.
39 Sagacity.
40 Sagamore.
41 Sagapen.
42 Sage.
43 Sagene.
44 Sagenite.
45 Sagger.
46 Saginate.
47 Sagitta.
48 Sago.
49 Sagum.
50 Sahib.
51 Sahidic.
52 Saic.
53 Saikyr.
54 Sailor.
55 Saimir.
56 Sainfoin.
57 Saint.
58 Saintlike.
59 Saithe.
60 Saiva.
61 Sajene.
62 Saker.
63 Saki.
64 Salaam.
65 Salad.
66 Salagane.
67 Salary.
68 Salebrous.
69 Salep.
70 Salic.
71 Salicin.
72 Salicyl.
73 Salient.
74 Saliferous.
75 Salify.
76 Saligat.
77 Salina.
78 Salique.
79 Salite.
80 Saliva.
81 Salivant.
82 Salivate.
83 Salix.
84 Sallet.
85 Sallow.
86 Sally.
87 Salmi.
88 Salmiac.
89 Salmon.
90 Salmonet.
91 Salogen.
92 Salol.
93 Saloon.
94 Salpa.
95 Salpicon.
96 Salpinx.
97 Salse.
98 Salsify.
99 Salsoda.
100 Salt.
101 Saltant.
102 Saltation.
103 Saltatory.
104 Saltern.
105 Saltpetre.
106 Salubrity.
107 Salutary.
108 Salute.
109 Salvable.
110 Salvage.
111 Salvation.
112 Salvatory.
113 Salver.
114 Salvitic.
115 Salvo.
116 Samara.
117 Samaroid.
118 Samaritan.
119 Sambo.
120 Sambuke.
121 Sambur.
122 Samian.
123 Samiel.
124 Samite.
125 Samlet.
126 Samoan.
127 Samovar.
128 Samp.
129 Sampan.
130 Samphire.
131 Sample.
132 Samshoo.
133 Samson.
134 Sanative.
135 Sanatory.
136 Sanctify.
137 Sanction.
138 Sanctity.
139 Sanctum.
140 Sand.
141 Sandal.
142 Sandarac.
143 Sandix.
144 Sandman.
145 Sandre.
146 Sandwich.
147 Sandwort.
148 Sandyx.
149 Sane.
150 Sanga.
151 Sangaree.
152 Sangiac.
153 Sanguine.
154 Sanhita.
155 Sanicle.
156 Sanidine.
157 Sanious.
158 Sanitary.
159 Sanity.
160 Sanjak.
161 Sankha.
162 Sannup.
163 Sanscrit.
164 Santal.
165 Santalic.
166 Santees.
167 Santon.
168 Santonic.
169 Sap.
170 Sapan.
171 Sapful.
172 Sapid.
173 Sapient.
174 Sapless.
175 Sapling.
176 Saponify.
177 Saponite.
178 Sapor.
179 Saporific.
180 Sapota.
181 Sapper.
182 Sapphic.
183 Sapphire.
184 Sappho.
185 Sappy.
186 Sapsago.
187 Saraband.
188 Saracen.
189 Sarcasm.
190 Sarcastic.
191 Sarcel.
192 Sarcenet.
193 Sarcin.
194 Sarcina.
195 Sarcle.
196 Sarcoblast.
197 Sarcode.
198 Sarcoderm.
199 Sarcoma.
200 Sarcosis.
201 Sarcotic.
202 Sarcous.
203 Sard.
204 Sardel.
205 Sardine.
206 Sardins.
207 Sardonic.
208 Sardonyx.
209 Sargasso.
210 Sargo.
211 Sark.
212 Sarkin.
213 Sarlac.
214 Sarmatic.
215 Sarment.
216 Sarong.
217 Saros.
218 Sarplar.
219 Sarsa.
220 Sarsen.
221 Sart.
222 Sash.
223 Sasin.
224 Sassafras.
225 Sassolin.
226 Sastra.
227 Satan.
228 Satanic.
229 Satchel.
230 Sate.
231 Satellite.
232 Satiate.
233 Satiety.
234 Satinet.
235 Satin.
236 Sation.
237 Satire.
238 Satirist.
239 Satisfy.
240 Sative.
241 Satrap.
242 Saturate.
243 Saturn.
244 Saturnian.
245 Saturnine.
246 Satyr.
247 Satyric.
248 Sauce.
249 Saucisse.
250 Saucy.
251 Sauger.
252 Saul.
253 Saunter.
254 Saurel.
255 Saurian.
256 Sauroid.
257 Saury.
258 Sausage.
259 Sauterne.
260 Savage.
261 Savagism.
262 Savant.
263 Savement.
264 Savor.
265 Savory.
266 Savoy.
267 Sawbill.
268 Sawbuck.
269 Sawder.
270 Sawdust.
271 Sawfly.
272 Sawmill.
273 Sawset.
274 Sawyer.
275 Saxatile.
276 Saxhorn.
277 Saxifrage.
278 Saxon.
279 Saxonic.
280 Sayette.
281 Scab.
282 Scabby.
283 Scabbard.
284 Scabling.
285 Scad.
286 Scaffold.
287 Scaglia.
288 Scalar.
289 Scald.
290 Scaldic.
291 Scale.
292 Scalene.
293 Scaling.
294 Scalled.
295 Scallion.
296 Scallop.
297 Scalp.
298 Scalpel.
299 Scalper.
300 Scaly.
301 Scamble.
302 Scamillus.
303 Scamp.
304 Scamper.
305 Scan.
306 Scandal.
307 Scandent.
308 Scandia.
309 Scandic.
310 Scansion.
311 Scant.
312 Scantily.
313 Scantle.
314 Scantling.
315 Scape.
316 Scaphite.
317 Scaphoid.
318 Scapple.
319 Scapula.
320 Scapulet.
321 Scar.
322 Scarab.
323 Scarce.
324 Scarcity.
325 Scard.
326 Scarf.
327 Scarify.
328 Scarlet.
329 Scarmage.
330 Scarp.
331 Scarry.
332 Scarus.
333 Scatch.
334 Scathe.
335 Scatter.
336 Scaup.
337 Scavenger.
338 Scelet.
339 Scene.
340 Scenery.
341 Scenic.
342 Scent.
343 Scentless.
344 Scepter.
345 Schedule.
346 Scheme.
347 Schemer.
348 Schism.
349 Scholar.
350 Scholium.
351 School.
352 Schooner.
353 Sciatic.
354 Science.
355 Scientist.
356 Scimiter.
357 Scintilla.
358 Sciolist.
359 Scion.
360 Scioptic.
361 Scissel.
362 Scissors.
363 Sclerite.
364 Scoff.
365 Scold.
366 Scolex.
367 Scomber.
368 Sconce.
369 Scoop.
370 Scoot.
371 Scope.
372 Scoppet.
373 Scorbute.
374 Scorch.
375 Score.
376 Scoria.
377 Scorify.
378 Scorn.
379 Scornful.
380 Scorpene.
381 Scorpio.
382 Scorpion.
383 Scorse.
384 Scotch.
385 Scoter.
386 Scotist.
387 Scotomy.
388 Scotsman.
389 Scottish.
390 Scoundrel.
391 Scour.
392 Scourge.
393 Scout.
394 Scowl.
395 Scrabble.

396 Scrag.
397 Scraggy.
398 Scramble.
399 Scrape.
400 Scrappy.
401 Scratch.
402 Scrawl.
403 Scrawny.
404 Scream.
405 Screech.
406 Screed.
407 Screen.
408 Screw.
409 Scribble.
410 Scribbling.
411 Scribe.
412 Scrim.
413 Scrimmage.
414 Scrimp.
415 Script.
416 Scriptory.
417 Scripture.
418 Scrofula.
419 Scroggy.
420 Scroll.
421 Scrub.
422 Scruple.
423 Scrutator.
424 Scrutiny.
425 Scuddle.
426 Scuff.
427 Scuffle.
428 Sculler.
429 Scullion.
430 Sculpin.
431 Sculptor.
432 Sculpture.
433 Scum
434 Scupper.
435 Scurf.
436 Scurry.
437 Scurvy.
438 Scutal.
439 Scutcheon.
440 Scutella.
441 Scuttle.
442 Scutum.
443 Scylla.
444 Scythe.
445 Seacoal.
446 Seagirt.
447 Seal.
448 Seam.
449 Seaman.
450 Seamless.
451 Seamster.
452 Seance.
453 Sear.
454 Search.
455 Seasick.
456 Season.
457 Seat.
458 Sebate.
459 Sebic.
460 Secant.
461 Secede.
462 Secession.
463 Seckel.
464 Seclude.
465 Seclusion.
466 Secrecy.
467 Secret.
468 Secretary.
469 Secretion.
470 Sect.
471 Sectarian.
472 Sectary.
473 Sectile.
474 Section.
475 Sector.
476 Secular.
477 Secund.
478 Secure.
479 Sedate.
480 Sedative.
481 Sedge.
482 Sediment.
483 Sedition.
484 Sedum.
485 Seedless.
486 Seedtime.
487 Seeker.
488 Seeming.
489 Seemly.
490 Seer.
491 Seesaw.
492 Seethe.
493 Segment.
494 Segregate.
495 Seignor.
496 Seismic.
497 Seismal.
498 Seizure.
499 Sekos.
500 Selah.
501 Seldom.
502 Select.
503 Selection.
504 Selenic.
505 Selenite.
506 Selfish.
507 Selfsame.
508 Selfwill.
509 Selvage.
510 Semaphore.
511 Sematrope.
512 Semblance.
513 Semester.
514 Semitic.
515 Semitone.
516 Senate.
517 Senegal.
518 Senile.
519 Senior.
520 Senna.
521 Sennet.
522 Senora.
523 Sensate.
524 Sensation.
525 Sense.
526 Senseless.
527 Sensitive.
528 Sensor.
529 Sensorium.
530 Sensory.
531 Sensuous.
532 Sentence.
533 Sentient.
534 Sentiment.
535 Sentinel.
536 Sentry.
537 Sepal.
538 Sepaline.
539 Separator.
540 Separatrix.
541 Sepia.
542 Sepose.
543 Sepoy.
544 Sepsin.
545 Sepsis.
546 Septate.
547 Septette.
548 Septic.
549 Septiform.
550 Septoic.
551 Septulate.
552 Septulum.
553 Septum.
554 Sepulcher.
555 Sequel.
556 Sequence.
557 Sequester.
558 Sequin.
559 Seraglio.
560 Serang.
561 Serape.
562 Seraph.
563 Seraphic.
564 Seraphim.
565 Serapis.
566 Serenade.
567 Serene.
568 Serenity.
569 Serge.
570 Sergeant.
571 Serial.
572 Seriation.
573 Sericite.
574 Sermon.
575 Sermonic.
576 Serosity.
577 Serous
578 Serpent.
579 Serrate.
580 Serrator.
581 Serried.
582 Serum.
583 Servage.
584 Serval.
585 Servant.
586 Servile.
587 Servitude.
588 Sesame.
589 Sesamoid.
590 Sesban.
591 Sessile.
592 Session.
593 Sesterce.
594 Sethia.
595 Seton.
596 Settee.
597 Setter.
598 Setula.
599 Sever.
600 Severe.
601 Sewage.
602 Sewer.
603 Sextain.
604 Sextant.
605 Sextette.
606 Sextile.
607 Sexton.
608 Shabby.
609 Shack
610 Shackle.
611 Shad.
612 Shadow.
613 Shady.
614 Shaffle.
615 Shag.
616 Shaggy.
617 Shagreen.
618 Shaken.
619 Shaker.
620 Shako.
621 Shale.
622 Shallop.
623 Shallow.
624 Sham.
625 Shaman.
626 Shamble.
627 Shame.
628 Shameful.
629 Shammer.
630 Shamois.
631 Shampoo.
632 Shamrock.
633 Shank.
634 Shanty.
635 Shapely.
636 Shard.
637 Shark.
638 Sharock.
639 Sharper.
640 Sharpling.
641 Shaster.
642 Shatter.
643 Shave.
644 Shaveling.
645 Shaving.
646 Shawl.
647 Shawnee.
648 Sheaf.
649 Shealing.
650 Shearer.
651 Shears.
652 Sheath.
653 Shedder.
654 Sheen.
655 Sheepcot.
656 Sheepfold.
657 Sheepish.
658 Sheepskin.
659 Sheik.
660 Shekel.
661 Shekinah.
662 Sheller.
663 Shellfish.
664 Shelter.
665 Shelve.
666 Sheol.
667 Shepherd.
668 Sherbet.
669 Sheriff.
670 Sherry.
671 Shield.
672 Shifter.
673 Shiftless.
674 Shiloh.
675 Shimmer.
676 Shindy.
677 Shine.
678 Shiner.
679 Shingle.
680 Shinto.
681 Shirk.
682 Shirting.
683 Shiver.
684 Shoal.
685 Shoat.
686 Shoddy.
687 Shogun.
688 Shola.
689 Shoot.
690 Shopman.
691 Shopworn.
692 Shortage.
693 Shorthand.
694 Shotted.
695 Shoulder.
696 Shout.
697 Shove.
698 Shovel.
699 Shower.
700 Showman.
701 Shrapnel.
702 Shrew.
703 Shrewish.
704 Shriek.
705 Shrieve.
706 Shrift.
707 Shrill.
708 Shrimp.
709 Shrine.
710 Shrivel.
711 Shroud.
712 Shrub.
713 Shrug.
714 Shuck.
715 Shudder.
716 Shuffle.
717 Shumac.
718 Shutter.
719 Shuttle.
720 Shyster.
721 Sibilant.
722 Sibyl.
723 Sibylline.
724 Siccate.
725 Sickish.
726 Sickle.
727 Sickly.
728 Sideral.
729 Siderite.
730 Sidewise.
731 Siege.
732 Sienna.
733 Sierra.
734 Siesta.
735 Sieve.
736 Sifter.
737 Sigh.
738 Sightless.
739 Sigil.
740 Sigma.
741 Sigmoid.
742 Signate.
743 Signet.
744 Silence.
745 Silent.
746 Silenus.
747 Silex.
748 Silken.
749 Sillock.
750 Silo.
751 Silurian.
752 Silvan.
753 Silvate.
754 Simian.
755 Simile.
756 Simmer.
757 Simony.
758 Simoom.
759 Simper.
760 Simplist.
761 Simulate.
762 Sinapine.
763 Sincere.
764 Sinch.
765 Sindon.
766 Sinecure.
767 Sinew.
768 Sinful.
769 Singer.
770 Singleton.
771 Sinister.
772 Sinker.
773 Sinner.
774 Sinless.
775 Sinoper.
776 Sinque.
777 Sinuate.
778 Sinus.
779 Siphoid.
780 Sipid.
781 Sipple.
782 Sircar.
783 Siren.
784 Sirius.
785 Sirloin.
786 Sirocco.
787 Sirrah.
788 Sisal.
789 Siskin.
790 Sister.
791 Sistine.
792 Sistrum.
793 Situate.
794 Situs.
795 Sivan.
796 Sizar.
797 Sizzle.
798 Skag.
799 Skaldic.
800 Skate.
801 Skean.
802 Skeel.
803 Skelder.
804 Skelly.
805 Skelter.

No.	Word
806	Skeptic.
807	Skewer.
808	Skiff.
809	Skillet.
810	Skim.
811	Skimmer.
812	Skimp.
813	Skinny.
814	Skipper.
815	Skirl
816	Skirmish.
817	Skirt.
818	Skittles.
819	Skiver.
820	Skulk.
821	Skull.
822	Slabber.
823	Slacken.
824	Slag.
825	Slake.
826	Slam.
827	Slander.
828	Slang.
829	Slant.
830	Slapjack.
831	Slashed.
832	Slater.
833	Slattern.
834	Slave.
835	Slavic.
836	Slayer.
837	Sledge.
838	Sleeky.
839	Sleeper.
840	Sleet.
841	Sleigh.
842	Slender.
843	Sleuth.
844	Slibber.
845	Slicer.
846	Slicken.
847	Sling.
848	Slipknot.
849	Slipper.
850	Sliver.
851	Sloam.
852	Slogan.
853	Sloop.
854	Sloping.
855	Slothful.
856	Slouch.
857	Slough.
858	Sloven.
859	Sluggard.
860	Sluggish.
861	Sluice.
862	Slumber.
863	Smack.
864	Smartly.
865	Smatter.
866	Smear.
867	Smectite.
868	Smelt.
869	Smerlin.
870	Smilax.
871	Smirch.
872	Smirk.
873	Smite.
874	Smithy.
875	Smitten.
876	Smock.
877	Smoky.
878	Smoulder.
879	Smother.
880	Smudge.
881	Smuggle.
882	Smutch.
883	Snack.
884	Snaffle.
885	Snaggy.
886	Snail.
887	Snake.
888	Snare.
889	Snarl.
890	Snatch.
891	Snattock.
892	Sneaking.
893	Sneer.
894	Sneeze.
895	Snicker.
896	Snipe.
897	Snivel.
898	Snobbish.
899	Snood.
900	Snowy.
901	Snub.
902	Snuff.
903	Snuggle.
904	Soaker.
905	Sobbing.
906	Sober.
907	Social.
908	Socle.
909	Socratic.
910	Soda.
911	Sodden.
912	Sofa.
913	Soften.
914	Soggy.
915	Sojourn.
916	Solace.
917	Solar.
918	Soldier.
919	Solemn.
920	Solert.
921	Solidate.
922	Solitude.
923	Soloist.
924	Solstice.
925	Soluble.
926	Solution.
927	Solvent.
928	Somal.
929	Somatic.
930	Sombre.
931	Sombrous.
932	Somnial.
933	Sonance.
934	Songster.
935	Sonnet.
936	Sontag.
937	Soothe.
938	Sooty.
939	Sophic.
940	Sophism.
941	Sopite.
942	Soprano.
943	Sorbate.
944	Sorbet.
945	Sorcery.
946	Sordid.
947	Sordint.
948	Sorel.
949	Sorex.
950	Sorghum.
951	Sorgo.
952	Sorrage
953	Sorrow.
954	Sortie.
955	Sorter.
956	Sortition.
957	Sorus.
958	Sotadic.
959	Sothic.
960	Sotted.
961	Sotto.
962	Soubrette.
963	Souffle.
964	Sough.
965	Soughing.
966	Soul.
967	Sounder.
968	Soundly.
969	Soup.
970	Sour.
971	Source.
972	Sourness.
973	Souse.
974	Soutane.
975	Souter
976	Souvenir.
977	Sozzle.
978	Spacious.
979	Spaddle.
980	Spade.
981	Spadille.
982	Spadix.
983	Spadroon.
984	Spale.
985	Spalt.
986	Spancel
987	Spandrel.
988	Spang.
989	Spangle.
990	Spaniel.
991	Spanker.
992	Spanner.
993	Spar.
994	Sparge.
995	Spark.
996	Sparkle.
997	Sparling.
998	Sparoid.
999	Sparrow.
1000	Spartan.
2000	Sparth.
3000	Sparve.
4000	Spasm.
5000	Spastic.
6000	Spate.
7000	Spathal.
8000	Spathic.
9000	Spatial.
10000	Spatter.
11000	Spatula.
12000	Spavin.
13000	Spawl.
14000	Spear.
15000	Specious.
16000	Speckle.
17000	Spectacle.
18000	Spectator.
19000	Spectatrix.
20000	Spectral.
21000	Specular.
22000	Spelding.
23000	Spelkin.
24000	Spelter.
25000	Spelunc.
26000	Spender.
27000	Sperge.
28000	Sperling.
29000	Spicate.
30000	Spicy.
31000	Spicknel.
32000	Spicula.
33000	Spider.
34000	Spight.
35000	Spignet.
36000	Spigot.
37000	Spiked.
38000	Spikelet.
39000	Spikenard.
40000	Spile.
41000	Spinach.
42000	Spindle.
43000	Spinal.
44000	Spinet.
45000	Spinner.
46000	Spinous.
47000	Spiral.
48000	Spirit.
49000	Spirtle.
50000	Spiteful.
51000	Spleen.
52000	Splendor.
53000	Splenic.
54000	Splinter.
55000	Splurge.
56000	Splutter.
57000	Spoiler.
58000	Spondee.
59000	Sponge.
60000	Sponsor.
61000	Spooler.
62000	Sporadic.
63000	Sportful.
64000	Spotless.
65000	Spousal.
66000	Spouter.
67000	Sprain.
68000	Sprawl.
69000	Spray.
70000	Sprightly.
71000	Sprinkle.
72000	Sprinter.
73000	Sprite.
74000	Sprout.
75000	Spruce.
76000	Sprunt.
77000	Spume.
78000	Spunky.
79000	Spurious.
80000	Spurling.
81000	Spurn.
82000	Spurred.
83000	Spurtle.
84000	Sputter.
85000	Squab.
86000	Squabble.
87000	Squadron.
88000	Squail.
89000	Squally.
90000	Squalor.
91000	Squamate.
92000	Squamoid.
93000	Squander.
94000	Squash.
95000	Squatter.
96000	Squaw.
97000	Squeak.
98000	Squeamish.
99000	Squeeze.
100000	Squelch.
101000	Squib.
102000	Squiggle.
103000	Squilla.
104000	Squinch.
105000	Squint.
106000	Squire.
107000	Squirm.
108000	Squirrel.
109000	Squirt.
110000	Stabat.
111000	Stabber.
112000	Stabling.
113000	Staccato.
114000	Staddle.
115000	Stadium.
116000	Staging.
117000	Stagger.
118000	Stagnant.
119000	Staidly.
120000	Stainless.
121000	Stairway.
122000	Stale.
123000	Stalder.
124000	Stalk.
125000	Stalled.
126000	Stallion.
127000	Stalwart.
128000	Stamen.
129000	Stamina.
130000	Stammel.
131000	Stammer.
132000	Stampede.
133000	Stanchion.
134000	Standish.

Number	Word
135000	Stanhope.
136000	Stannel.
137000	Stannite.
138000	Stanza.
139000	Starry.
140000	Starchy.
141000	Stark.
142000	Starling.
143000	Starlit.
144000	Startle.
145000	Starve.
146000	Statal.
147000	Statant.
148000	Stately.
149000	Static.
150000	Statuary.
151000	Statue.
152000	Stature.
153000	Staunch.
154000	Stave.
155000	Steak.
156000	Steal.
157000	Stealthy.
158000	Steeple.
159000	Steering.
160000	Stellar.
161000	Stellate.
162000	Stellify.
163000	Stemple.
164000	Stencil.
165000	Stentor.
166000	Steppe.
167000	Sterile.
168000	Sterlet.
169000	Sternite.
170000	Steward.
171000	Sticker.
172000	Stickle.
173000	Stifle.
174000	Stigma.
175000	Stiletto.
176000	Stillage.
177000	Stilted.
178000	Stimulus.
179000	Stinger.
180000	Stingy.
181000	Stipend.
182000	Stipple.
183000	Stipular.
184000	Stirrup.
185000	Stitch.
186000	Stiver.
187000	Stoat.
188000	Stockade.
189000	Stocking.
190000	Stoic.
191000	Stoicism.
192000	Stoker.
193000	Stolid.
194000	Stolon.
195000	Stomatic.
196000	Storax.
197000	Stork.
198000	Straddle.
199000	Straggle.
200000	Strainer.
201000	Strand.
202000	Stranger.
203000	Strangle.
204000	Strapper.
205000	Strapple.
206000	Strass.
207000	Stratagem.
208000	Strategy.
209000	Stratify.
210000	Stratum.
211000	Straught.
212000	Streaky.
213000	Streamlet.
214000	Strengest.
215000	Strepent.
216000	Stretcher.
217000	Striate.
218000	Strickle.
219000	Stricture.
220000	Stride.
221000	Strident.
222000	Strigate.
223000	Striker.
224000	Stringy.
225000	Stripling.
226000	Stroam.
227000	Strobile.
228000	Strockle.
229000	Stroller.
230000	Stroma.
231000	Strombus.
232000	Strontia.
233000	Strontic.
234000	Strophe.
235000	Struggle.
236000	Struntain.
237000	Strychnose.
238000	Stubble.
239000	Stubborn.
240000	Stucco.
241000	Studding.
242000	Student.
243000	Studio.
244000	Stumble.
245000	Stumpage.
246000	Stunner.
247000	Stupefy.
248000	Stupid.
249000	Stupor.
250000	Sturdy.
251000	Sturgeon.
252000	Stutter.
253000	Stygian.
254000	Stylish.
255000	Stylite.
256000	Stylus.
257000	Styptic.
258000	Styrax.
259000	Suasive.
260000	Subdue.
261000	Sublate.
262000	Sublime.
263000	Suborn.
264000	Subsist.
265000	Subsoil.
266000	Subtile.
267000	Suburb.
268000	Subvene.
269000	Subvert.
270000	Succinct.
271000	Succor.
272000	Succumb.
273000	Sucker.
274000	Sudary.
275000	Suet.
276000	Suffer.
277000	Suffix.
278000	Suffrage.
279000	Suffuse.
280000	Sugar.
281000	Suicism.
282000	Sulky.
283000	Sully.
284000	Sultan.
285000	Sultanic.
286000	Sumac.
287000	Sumbul.
288000	Summit.
289000	Summon.
290000	Sumpter.
291000	Sunder.
292000	Sunken.
293000	Sunny.
294000	Sunshine.
295000	Superb.
296000	Supine.
297000	Suppage.
298000	Supper.
299000	Supplant.
300000	Supple.
301000	Suppliant.
302000	Supreme.
303000	Surbate.
304000	Surcease.
305000	Surcoat.
306000	Surdal.
307000	Surfeit.
308000	Surfy.
309000	Surgent.
310000	Surgical.
315000	Surmise.
320000	Surmount.
325000	Surname.
350000	Surplice.
375000	Surrey.
400000	Surtout.
500000	Survey.
600000	Survive.
700000	Suspire.
800000	Sutler.
900000	Suture.
1000000	Swaddle.

INDEX.

GENERAL INFORMATION.

CLASSES OF LOCOMOTIVES, Illustrated and Described.

UNITED STATES.

FOREIGN.

RAILROADS REPRESENTED.

UNITED STATES.

* Indicates narrow gauge.

UNITED STATES.—(Continued.)

* Indicates narrow gauge.

* Indicates narrow gauge.

FOREIGN.

Note. — Foreign engines are various gauges. See description.

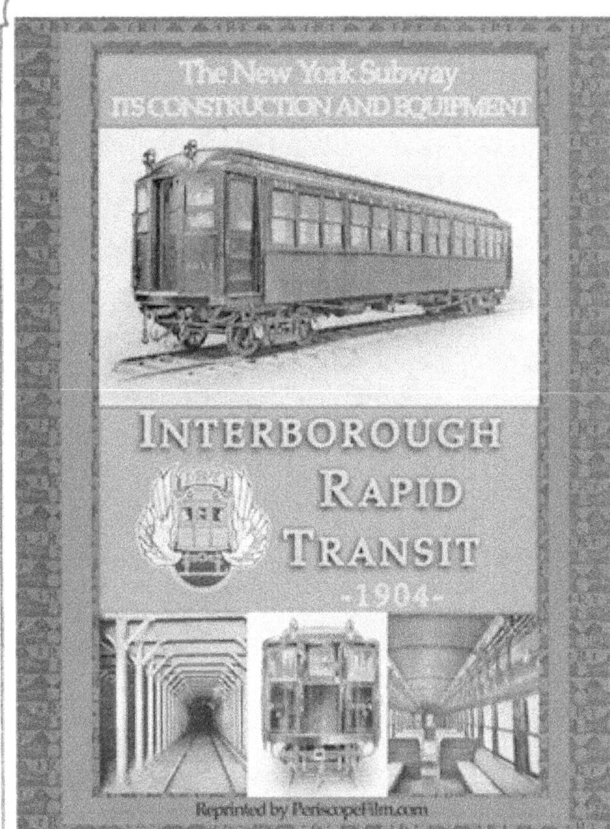

On October 27, 1904, the Interborough Rapid Transit Company opened the first subway in New York City. Running between City Hall and 145th Street at Broadway, the line was greeted with enthusiasm and, in some circles, trepidation. Created under the supervision of Chief Engineer S.L.F. Deyo, the arrival of the IRT foreshadowed the end of the "elevated" transit era on the island of Manhattan. The subway proved such a success that the IRT Co. soon achieved a monopoly on New York public transit. In 1940 the IRT and its rival the BMT were taken over by the City of New York. Today, the IRT subway lines still exist, primarily in Manhattan where they are operated as the "A Division" of the subway. Reprinted here is a special book created by the IRT, recounting the design and construction of the fledgling subway system. Originally created in 1904, it presents the IRT story with a flourish, and with numerous fascinating illustrations and rare photographs.

Originally written in the late 1900's and then periodically revised, A History of the Baldwin Locomotive Works chronicles the origins and growth of one of America's greatest industrial-era corporations. Founded in the early 1830's by Philadelphia jeweler Matthais Baldwin, the company built a huge number of steam locomotives before ceasing production in 1949. These included the 4-4-0 American type, 2-8-2 Mikado and 2-8-0 Consolidation. Hit hard by the loss of the steam engine market, Baldwin soldiered on for a brief while, producing electric and diesel engines. General Electric's dominance of the market proved too much, and Baldwin finally closed its doors in 1956. By that time over 70,500 Baldwin locomotives had been produced. This high quality reprint of the official company history dates from 1920. The book has been slightly reformatted, but care has been taken to preserve the integrity of the text.

NOW AVAILABLE AT
WWW.PERISCOPEFILM.COM

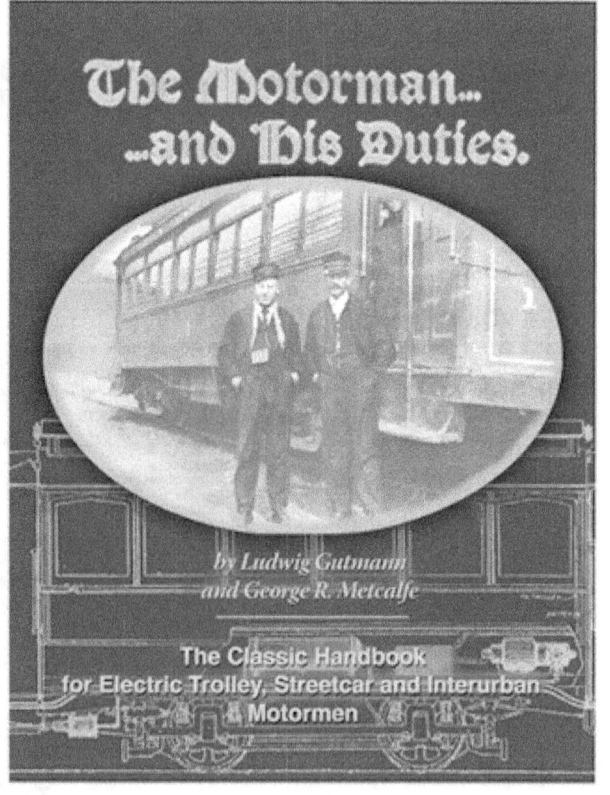

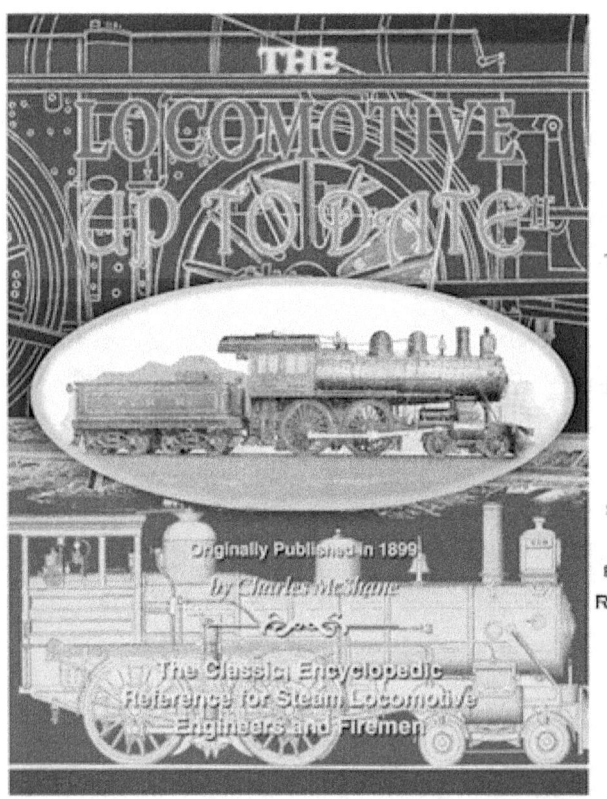

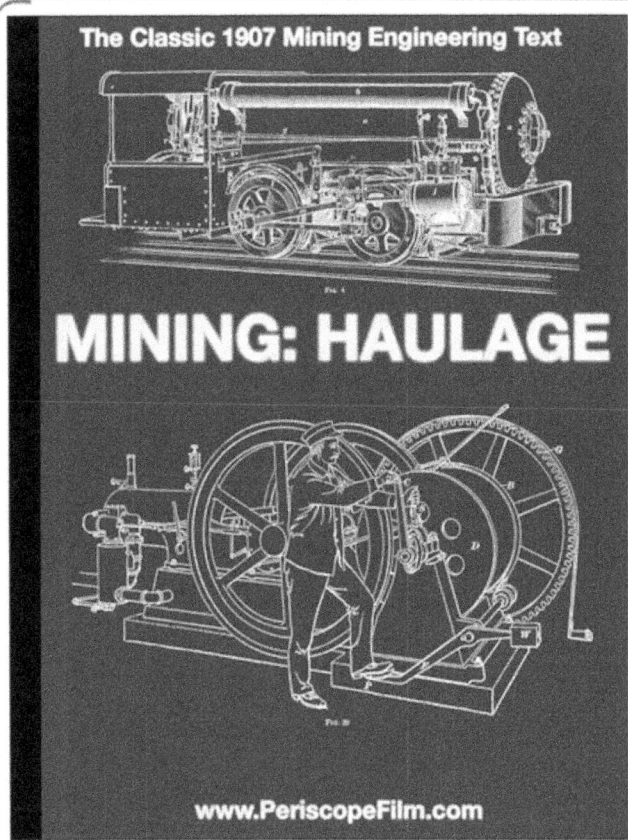

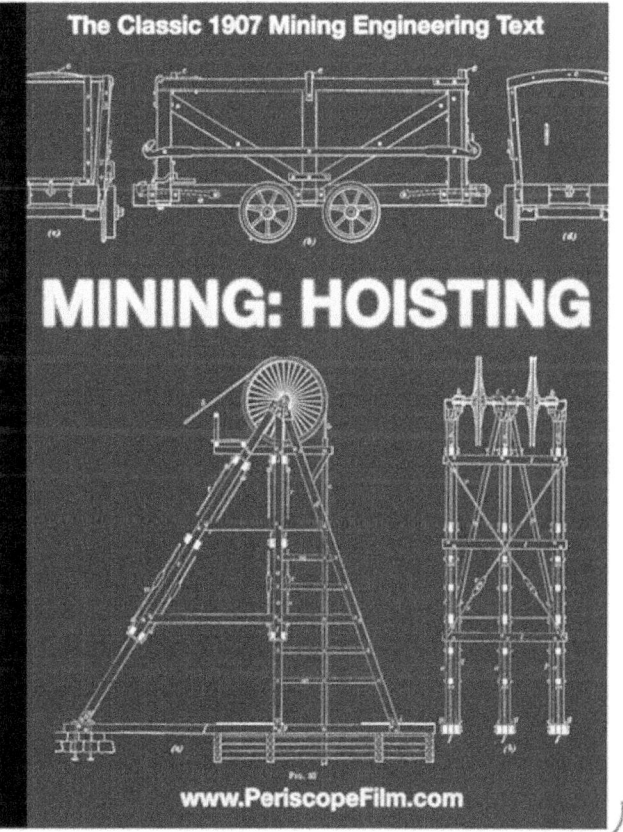

ISBN #978-1-935700-14-2
www.PeriscopeFilm.com

www.ingramcontent.com/pod-product-compliance
Lightning Source LLC
Chambersburg PA
CBHW082034230426
43670CB00016B/2655

* 9 7 8 1 9 3 5 7 0 0 1 4 2 *